Managerial Strategies and Industrial Relations

Managerial Strategies and Industrial Relations

An Historical and Comparative Study

edited by
Howard F. Gospel and Craig R. Littler

Heinemann Educational Books

Contributors

Howard F. Gospel, Lecturer in Industrial Relations, University of Kent at Canterbury, and Visiting Fellow, Business History Unit, London School of Economics.

Heidrun Homburg, Lecturer in Economic History, University of Bielefeld, W. Germany.

William H. Lazonick, Assistant Professor, Department of Economics, Harvard University, USA.

Wayne Lewchuk, Assistant Professor, Department of Economics, McMaster University, Canada.

Craig R. Littler, Research Officer, Imperial College, London.

Joe Melling, Research Fellow, Department of Social and Economic Research, Glasgow University.

Reiko Okayama, Professor, Institute of Social Sciences, Meiji University, Japan.

Jonathan Zeitlin, Research Fellow, King's College, Cambridge.

Heinemann Educational Books
22 Bedford Square, London WC1B 3HH
LONDON EDINBURGH MELBOURNE AUCKLAND HONG KONG
SINGAPORE KUALA LUMPUR NEW DELHI IBADAN NAIROBI
JOHANNESBURG EXETER (NH) KINGSTON PORT OF SPAIN

ISBN 0 435 32365 2

Typeset by Colset Pte Ltd, Singapore.
Printed by Biddles Ltd, Guildford, Surrey.

Contents

Preface

The present volume had its origins in a conference of business and labour historians, economists, sociologists, and academics from industrial relations and management science held in London in March 1981. The conference was organised by Howard Gospel and supported by the Social Science Resarch Council and the Business History Unit at London School of Economics. The idea for the conference had grown out of the belief that the development of management policies in labour and industrial relations had been neglected. The conference was therefore seen as playing a part in filling this gap by bringing together scholars researching in the field from both Britain and overseas.

Later, Craig Littler, who gave a paper at the conference, was invited to be co-editor of this volume. We would both like to thank those who made the conference and the volume possible. The Social Science Research Council provided a grant towards conference travel and organisation. Les Hannah of the Business History Unit provided encouragement and made available the secretarial facilities of the Unit. Donald Coleman and Eric Hobsbawm acted as chairmen on the day of the conference. Patrick Joyce, Hans de Geer and Arthur McIvor also gave papers and helped our discussions. Our own and the contributors' thanks must also go to all the participants, many of whose suggestions have been taken into account in the revised papers.

Howard F. Gospel

1 Managerial Structure and Strategies: An Introduction
Howard Gospel

This book is about employers, managers, and their labour relations strategies. It presents new theoretical and empirical material, aiming to fill a gap in what has until recently been a largely neglected area of study. The first part of the book deals mainly with the structure and strategies of employers in the United Kingdom in the formative decades of the late nineteenth and early twentieth centuries, though it traces some developments through into the post-Second World War period. The second half of the book deals comparatively with similar aspects of employer labour policies in the USA, Germany, and Japan, as the other leading capitalist economies. The introductory and concluding chapters present a general overview at an empirical and theoretical level: the former dealing mainly with the United Kingdom, the latter linking the four countries covered in the volume.

The study of employers' labour policies has on the whole been neglected in the two most likely historical fields. On the one hand, in business history there is no really good study of a particular firm or group of firms in terms of industrial relations. With a few notable exceptions most business histories which touch on the labour activities of the firm do so only briefly and almost as an aside.[1] On the other hand, in labour history, studies of the development of the British system of industrial relations tend to be from the perspective of the trade union and the role of the employer is often overlooked.[2] Yet it could be argued that it is the employer who plays a predominant role in shaping work relations and the industrial relations system and that workers and their trade unions have in large part reacted to initiative on the employers' side.[3]

Various reasons might be suggested for the relative neglect in historical writings of the employer–manager side of the industrial relations systems. First, the majority of students of labour history have been sympathetic towards, and have preferred to study, trade unions. Business historians have, for the most part, been ideologically committed to the business enterprise, have concentrated on its higher level entrepreneurial, commercial, and administrative features, and have neglected the labour and industrial relations aspects of business development. Second, there has been a problem of evidence. In so far as many British employers lacked formal industrial relations policies and handed labour matters over to employers' organisations or delegated them to lower line management, historical records at company level are often sparse. Firms and business organisations have also tended in the past to be more secretive than workers' organisations and less willing to allow access to their records on labour matters. Third, there are problems of conceptualisation. Though there are various theories of management behaviour (as will be discussed below), these have not been readily transferred nor easily operationalised in the labour field. As Asa Briggs has pointed out, 'entrepreneurial theory has never provided the kind of unifying concepts which "labour movement" theory or theories have provided.'[4]

There have, however, been developments in recent historical work which offer hope of filling this gap. In labour history the movement away from a narrow focus on trade unions has been under way for some time. The new focus is not only on wider social and cultural aspects of working-class lives, but also more recently on work processes and work-place relations. This latter development has inevitably more directly introduced the role of management.[5] In business history there have been two relevant developments. First, there has been a movement away from the empirical tradition of individual company histories to a broader more theoretical approach. The work of Chandler in the United States is particularly notable in this respect and is referred to more fully below. Second, there has been the beginnings of a concentration on 'lower' level aspects of the firm, viz. personnel management, the role of the foreman, and the factory context of labour relations.[6] These historiographical developments have taken place in both Britain and the United States, as well as in continental Europe and in Japan.[7]

The neglect of the employer–manager side of labour relations has not been confined to historians. In the industrial relations literature Bain and Clegg have hypothesised the fundamental importance of 'organisation among employers and control systems within the firm' as the major explanatory variable in labour relations, but have noted the absence of work and have called for new research efforts in this area.[8] For the United States, Lester had earlier concluded that, 'A systematic theory of the industrial relations activities of business management has still to be developed.'[9] The same applies, in the main, to the literature in classical and neo-classical economics. Though the 'theory of the firm' holds a central place in economics, it is in large part a featureless abstraction of the real firm and offers little in the way of insights to those interested in firms as actual employers of labour. Neo-classical economics reduces the firm to the status of a passive reactive mechanism which in the long term can pursue only the one single objective of profit maximisation.

Yet the various social science disciplines do offer some useful insights into management which may be developed in historical perspective. In economics, it is not the neo-classical paradigm, but the institutional tradition and more recently behavioural economics which offers useful concepts. In the institutionalist tradition (where there was always an overlap with industrial relations and labour history) one must mention in particular the work of Commons. In his famous article on the history of American shoemakers he demonstrated the crucial importance of employers in shaping the historical development of the American industrial relations system.[10] In particular he emphasised the various forms of ownership and production and stressed the 'extension of the market' and the 'competitive menace' as key environmental factors. Herein lay considerable insights, which, perhaps because they were not developed into a more general theory of management in industrial relations, were largely forgotten. The importance of the market is taken up again in this introduction and in a number of the subsequent chapters in this collection. In particular, in line with Commons, emphasis is placed on the structure of the market in terms of boundaries and on the level of demand and competition.

In the behavioural economics literature, more recent theories have moved away from neo-classical analysis, have postulated various objectives other than simple profit maximisation, and have examined the firm's decision making processes. Notable among these in recent years has been Williamson's development of the transaction cost approach.[11] This, put baldly, takes economic transactions, rather than commodities, as the basic unit of economic analysis. It argues that firms seek to economise on transaction costs (such as the cost of gaining information or making and enforcing contracts). Firms pursue strategies which aid this, and relative transaction costs and efficiency properties in large part determine the organisational forms which firms have developed. Williamson and other economists have explicitly used this to examine labour management and employment relations.[12] More recently a number of business historians have utilised parts of the framework to examine the rise of the modern industrial enterprise.[13] The hypotheses which this approach contains are certainly challenging for those concerned with the history of labour management, but as yet its application and testing is still in its early days.

In the area of management theory and organisational sociology there are some frameworks suggestive for development historically. Woodward and Reeves, in probably the best known example, developed a typology of control which might be applied to different historical situations.[14] They identified three main types of managerial control: 'personal' control through direct supervision and the development of managerial hierarchies; 'mechanical' control embedded in machinery and production processes; and 'administrative' control based on more impersonal rules specifying required behaviour. From a historical point of view one of the main weaknesses of much of this literature is that it has often contained a strong normative element. Much of the early work was concerned to develop 'principles', and the later work has been concerned to find the most appropriate 'fit' between the organisation and its environment. A potentially more promising approach, however, has developed with the idea of 'strategic choice'.[15] In part drawing its empirical basis from business histories, this approach suggests that, within constraints, management has a choice as to the course of action it follows and the structural arrangements it adopts. The choice is made by a 'dominant coalition' of managers, but is subject to negotiation and accommodation with other groups, for example, workers and their organisations. The outcome of choice is not only the establishment of structural forms but also the moulding of the environment within which the firm operates. This idea of a range of alternative strategies, experimentation, and constrained choice is one underlying much of this volume.

Marxists, with a historical orientation, but working outside the fields of labour and business history, have recently made some important contributions to the study of employers and employment relations. In his major work, *Labor and Monopoly Capital*, Braverman argued that under capitalism there is a tendency over time to the deskilling of work as employers rationalise the production process and subdivide jobs.[16] Braverman's book has directed historians' attention to Taylorism and the Scientific Management movement, seen by him at one and the same time as historically crucial while still informing the underlying dynamic of work organisation. Around this has developed a growing body of literature. At both a theoretical and empirical level this collection adds significantly to this literature by questioning the overall deskilling thesis and in particular Braverman's implication that deskilling constituted the one main employer strategy.

Marxist economists have also recently produced some historically based work which has started to influence mainstream historical writings. In an influential article Marglin re-examined the origins of the factory system and argued that this developed as a form of labour management, not for efficiency or technological reasons, but because it provided employers with a superior means of control and discipline over workers.[17] This stands in stark contrast to the Williamson transaction cost and efficiency approach outlined above. Around this has developed a debate drawing heavily on historical evidence.[18] In another study, Edwards, in tracing the growth of labour management in America from the late nineteenth century onwards, has identified the gradual development of employer strategies through a number of stages: from 'simple' control by foremen and relatively unsophisticated piece-work systems, through 'technical' control via machines and methods of work organisation, to a 'bureaucratic' stage where employers seek to develop elaborate systems of rules and procedures to control workers.[19] As a typology there are some obvious parallels with the work of Woodward and Reeves referred to above. On somewhat similar lines again, Friedman, examining the history of the British hosiery and motor car industries, has written about strategies of 'direct control' by coercion and close supervision and 'responsible autonomy' where workers are given more say and treated in a more co-optive manner.[20] Friedman's is not a stage theory, but allows for some backward and forward movement between types. Like Edwards, however, he seeks to place strategies in the context of different product and labour markets and different competitive and demand situations.

Finally, in this survey of the literature we turn to the insights offered in Chandler's two major works, *Strategy and Structure* and *The Visible Hand*.[21] In tracing the development of the modern American business enterprise, Chandler has shown how the rapid expansion of the market and changing technologies led firms over time to pursue strategies of geographical and product differentation. These strategies in turn induced new organisational structures to deal with the problems which growth created; in particular firms developed centralised and divisionalised forms of organisation. In this way bureaucratic hierarchies developed to replace Adam Smith's 'invisible hand' in co-ordinating economic activities, though Chandler still allows for markets to guide management decisions. These developments, he argues, occurred in the early decades of the century in the United States, at about the same time in Germany, and in the post-Second World War period in the United Kingdom and other European economies.[22]

In Chandler's work there is possibly something of a bridge between business historians, labour historians, and other social scientists. His approach, historically based, offers a useful set of organising concepts which relate together in a dynamic model. It provides a framework used in the remainder of this chapter and which re-emerges in the subsequent chapters. However, from the beginning, a number of caveats need to be stated. Firstly, it cannot be transplanted wholesale into the labour management sphere. Chandler is working at a higher level of the organisation and for him 'strategy' and 'structure' have special meanings. The former relates to diversification, the latter to functional or multi-divisional forms of overall company organisation. The terms 'strategy' and 'structure' need to be redefined for industrial relations purposes. Equally, the Chandler model cannot be transplanted wholesale from the United States to other countries (some of the problems of comparative analysis are taken up by Littler in the final chapter in this collection). Finally, it is not suggested here that the Chandler framework is fully reconcilable with all the various approaches which are referred to above and used in these essays. To imply this would be an injustice to all concerned. In particular it may not be reconcilable with elements of the Marxist analysis. Yet there are obvious similarities in their emphasis on productive forces and market competition, and Marxist historians have started to draw on the framework.[23]

The structure of labour management

Structure is here taken to mean the various organisational forms and personnel which entrepreneurs have used to recruit and maintain a labour force; to monitor, discipline, and reward workers; and to deal with trade unions as they have emerged. In order to locate the subsequent discussion in a historically specific context, the remainder of this chapter focuses primarily on Britain, leaving the comparative dimension to the second half of the book.

One of the earliest forms of labour management in Britain was the putting-out system, under which production was put out to geographically dispersed workers by a central merchant-manufacturer. It is often assumed that this died out in the early nineteenth century and, with the emergence of the factory, was replaced by systems of direct employment and management.[24] It is now realised that this was not the case because putting-out had a number of continuing advantages for entrepreneurs. Not least from the point of view of labour management, it economised on the costs of recruiting, maintaining and disciplining workers and allowed the entrepreneur to adjust his labour force to market fluctuations. A number of further points should be made here. First, putting-out systems not only survived the emergence of factory industry, but for a time in the early years of industrialisation probably grew simultaneously with the factory system. Moreover, putting-out continued in various forms well into the nineteenth century in industries such as textiles and clothing. Indeed in some sectors of these industries it continues to the present day in the form of homeworking. Second, it declined for a number of complex reasons. It is probably wrong to contrast efficiency and control explanations as do Williamson and Marglin. Given the advantages and problems of both putting-out and factory organisation, elements of both efficiency and control must complement one another. Finally, putting-out was not in many instances replaced by direct management by the entrepreneur and his agents but by various other types of indirect management, often in the form of internal subcontracting systems.

Subcontracting involved the entrepreneur making a production agreement with a contractor, gang master, butty man, or a leading hand for the production – usually at a fixed price – of so many tons of coal, iron or steel, or any other good or service. The subcontractor would then supply or take on a labour force, train and set them to work, monitor and discipline them, and pay them out of the price he had agreed with the entrepreneur. From the latter's point of view this had the advantage of delegating labour management to others who might also better understand the technical aspects of the work and who might in addition provide small amounts of working capital.

Various forms of subcontracting were widespread in nineteenth-century Britain.[25] It could take the form of gang work under a gang boss, as in building, coal mining, or on the docks. In craft industries, such as engineering, shipbuilding, or iron and steel, it was usually a craftsman who acted as subcontractor. In other industries, such as cotton textiles, it existed in the form of a 'helper' system where a skilled principal employed a smaller number of helpers, often family members, to assist with routine tasks. One well-informed late nineteenth-century commentator observed, 'sub-contract in fact is practically ubiquitous'.[26] However, this is not to say that it existed in all industries. It was not much used in process industries of a chemical nature nor in food processing industries such as brewing or milling. It was not used on the railways where problems of planning and co-ordination required more hierarchical and bureaucratic forms of organisation from an early date. Nor was it used in situations where putting-out methods were employed. It was also the case that subcontracting often existed alongside more direct systems of management. In building, for example, some of the big contractors employed part of their labour direct and in engineering, though component manufacture and certain operations might be controlled by inside subcontractors, very often final assembly was done by non-contract employees under the supervision of company foremen.

Parallel situations of subcontracting and direct employment probably increased in the late nineteenth century. Certainly in the final decades of the century subcontracting came under increased strain. As markets expanded the international competition intensified, so pressure was put on entrepreneurs more directly to control costs. Subcontractors could be an obstacle to this and to the introduction and efficient utilisation of new techniques. In addition entrepreneurs often feared that these middlemen might also be accruing an excessive share of the value added in production. As entrepreneurs tightened up on their subcontractors, so these in turn pressed more heavily on their workers, whose unions came to agitate for the ending of the system. However, many skilled unions were ambivalent because their members often acted as subcontractors or at least aspired to become such. Thus, the emphasis for the decline of subcontracting is here placed on product market pressures which forced entrepreneurs to control and rationalise the production process.

As with putting-out as a form of labour management, so with subcontracting, it did not entirely die out in the late nineteenth and early twentieth centuries. Modified versions continued in the form of gang or team systems in industries such as coal mining, iron and steel, and dock work. Moreover it emerged in new industries, for example, during and after the Second World War it developed in parts of the vehicle and aircraft industries to deal with situations of high product demand. It continues, of course, to the present day as a central form of labour management in the building industry.

In order to control his agents, and through them production, the entrepreneur replaced subcontractors with wage-earning foremen and others in his direct employment. The number of foremen employed in British industry increased in the late nineteenth and early twentieth centuries.[27] However, in many ways the foremen at the time had powers similar to those of the subcontractor. He could hire and fire, he played a large part in planning and allocating work, and had some discretion over the method as well as the level of wages in the shop. One engineering employer described the foreman this way:

> In most works . . . the whole industrial life of a workman is in the hands of his foreman. The foreman chooses him from among the applicants at the works gate; often he settles what wages he shall get; no advance of wage or promotion is possible except on his initiative; he often sets the piece-price and has power to cut it when he wishes; and, lastly, he almost always has unrestricted power of discharge.[28]

Delegation to foremen had advantages, but their independence and power were in themselves problems for the entrepreneur and senior managers. Almost simultaneously with the development of the foreman's power, therefore, his position began to be undermined with the introduction of new specialist personnel and new techniques. In the 1890s specialist supervisors were introduced into some large engineering factories who came to be known as 'feed and speed' men, their duty being to check that the required angles and speeds of machines were being used.[29] Where incentive bonus systems were introduced, specialist rate fixers often came to set output norms and piece prices based on primitive methods of work measurement. Cost and management accounting was also developing in Britain in the late nineteenth century, though its actual introduction in the factory was probably slower than in the United States.[30] Yet as one British accountant noted before the First World War many large factories had their own cost accounting departments, which produced reports on production and provided management with cost information.[31] At about the same time a number of firms started to employ a new class of welfare superintendents internally within the firm. These were usually females, employed by firms in light consumer industries, and initially their responsibilities were for female employees. However, their jobs often included recruitment and training, supervision of the firm's recreational and welfare facilities, and sometimes the administration of wage systems and the monitoring of output standards. Their numbers increased slowly before the First World War, but it was really during the war that there was a considerable expansion and extension to areas of male employment. By the end of the war there were probably a thousand welfare workers in British industry.[32]

One reason why welfare work and other aspects of internal labour management developed slowly in Britain was because of the reliance of British firms on employers' organisations. Historically these played an important part in the development of labour management in Britain. Employers had long combined to deal with trade unions and to regulate wages and conditions. However, in the last two decades of the nineteenth century, as union strength grew, so employers' associations took on a more permanent form and moved from anti-union, 'free labour' strategies to develop conciliation and collective bargaining arrangements with unions. Their number grew from 336 in 1895, to 675 by 1898, and had doubled again to 1487 by the outbreak of the war. During and immediately after the war there was a further, and final, period of employer organisation growth. As a result, by the mid-1920s official figures recorded the existence of 2403 employers' organisations, many of them small local associations, but including also at least one major organisation in each British industry.[33]

Employers' organisations performed various functions. They were a way of keeping unions out of the plant and preserving management prerogatives by the use of collective employer power. Zeitlin's chapter in this collection discusses this role in the case of the engineering industry. They also performed a market function in that they were a way of countering and containing trade union wage claims. In homogeneous industries such as iron and steel, hosiery, and coal they were in addition a way of taking wages out of competition, bolstering up collusive product market arrangements, and reducing competitive uncertainty.

The impact of employers' organisations is discussed more fully below and in subsequent chapters. It remains to be noted here that as an innovative and formative type of managerial structure in British industrial relations their importance declined from the 1920s onwards. At first in the 1920s many small firms started to undercut national and district rates and to drop out of their associations. In the 1920s and 1930s some larger firms left their associations so as to experiment with their own internal labour policies. Thus, as Lewchuk shows for the engineering industry, employers' organisations were left defending and maintaining an industrial relations system which had crystallised around the First World War.[34]

The elaboration of management hierarchies in Britain was slow during the inter-war years. However, there was a further development of line management, with an increase in the number of foremen, along with production and works managers. There was some further growth in managerial accounting and production engineering specialisms. There was also a growth of work study with the introduction of formal Scientific Management techniques into British industry, not least through the agency of the Bedaux consulting company as discussed below. Welfare work, after being cut back in the immediate post-First World War recession, also slowly developed. In some firms welfare departments were upgraded to employment and personnel departments, their coverage being extended to male employees and to a widening scope of issues. By 1939 there were about two thousand welfare and labour managers in the United Kingdom. Once again, however, it was wartime pressures which accelerated this development, with the number increasing to about five thousand by the end of the Second World War.[35]

A company like ICI is interesting as a forerunner of some of these developments. ICI had established a central labour office in 1927. This was based at headquarters, was accorded high status within the company, and from the beginning reported directly to a senior board member. General labour policy emanated from the department and local factory labour departments mainly administered the system established at head office. The department dealt with the trade unions through a national industrial relations council in which directors and central labour staff met with trade union full-time officers. It also developed company-wide profit-sharing and staff status schemes and by the late 1930s was considering a company-wide job evaluation scheme. It is significant that ICI, having developed its own personnel organisation, left its employers' association in the mid-1930s.[36] Some other firms (e.g. Courtaulds, Ford, Dunlop, Pilkingtons) were experimenting on similar lines in the late 1930s, but it was really only in the post-Second World War period that internal management hierarchies on these lines developed and spread in Great Britain.

On structure, it might be concluded that labour management has developed through a number of stages – putting-out, subcontracting, internal bureaucratic hierarchies. Organisation into employers' associations constituted a separate, but extremely important, dimension in Britain. However, there was considerable overlap between the different forms and earlier stages continued to exist alongside later ones. A complex set of factors drove these developments. However, emphasis is here placed on three sets of factors; on market forces, especially the extension of the market and the structure and degree of competition; on changes in the overall structure of the firm and the growth of large multi-plant companies; and on pressure from the labour force and the need to control workers. These forced firms to develop tighter, more bureaucratic forms of labour management. Similar developments occurred in other capitalist economies and are examined in the second half of this volume. However, it will be seen that for the most part the speed of development was more rapid in the United States, Germany and Japan.

The strategies of management
The development of structural forms both reflected and facilitated changes in managerial strategies. Strategy is here taken to mean the plans and policies used by management to direct work tasks; to evaluate, discipline, and reward workers; and to deal with their trade unions. It might be objected that in this sense British employers and managers have not had strategies in industrial relations, but have merely reacted, within a very limited planning horizon, to market and other conditions and pressure from workers. This may seem to be the case when looking at employers over a short time period. It is true that most British firms in the period under consideration did not have written formal policies in the labour area. In addition, as has been shown, much was handed over to employers' organisations and lower level line management. However, this in itself could be said to constitute a strategy, if only one of delegation or indirect control. But when examined more closely, over a longer historical perspective, strands and patterns of strategies may be discerned.

Some of the typologies of strategies referred to above offer insights into the study of management in industrial relations. For example, Edwards's idea of a movement through stages from 'direct' to 'technical' and 'bureaucratic' forms is suggestive. It charts a development over time to systems of labour management based on internal hierarchies and complex, impersonal forms of governance. At the same time it allows that in certain industries earlier types of control may continue to predominate. Equally, Friedmans's typology of 'direct' and 'responsible autonomy' strategies is useful. It also allows for the differences between industries and within industries between core and peripheral firms. Where it argues that 'tight' and 'accommodative' approaches are a function of market conditions, it can be used to elucidate changes in management policy over time.

However, there are problems with any typological approach. They are often overschematic and deterministic, failing to convey the variety of strategies from which management can choose. Moreover they cannot always be transferred wholesale between different contexts. For example, Edwards's typology may work well for the United States; but his bureaucratic stage, in so far as it describes unilateral managerial systems of government, cannot be applied without modification to the British context where trade union membership has always been more widespread. Rather than seeking an elegant typology, it is probably more historically accurate to look at the problems and opportunities which have confronted management over time and at the mix of strategies with which they have experimented. The combination of strategies has been highly complex, and employers have searched in a zig-zag backwards and forwards movement between them. With this in mind, therefore, this chapter focuses on a number of strategic areas and within them looks at the search for policies. The areas chosen are divided analytically into work relations, employment relations, and industrial relations.

Work relations

By work relations is meant the way technology and social processes are organised at work. Historians and social scientists have long been interested in the division of labour within the work-place. However the study of this area has been enlivened in recent years since the publication of Braverman's *Labour and Monopoly Capital* in 1974. The argument is too well known to need stating in any detail. For the purposes of this introduction it might be summarised as follows. Over time employers have reorganised work so as to avoid reliance on workers with unique skills, to overcome production bottlenecks, and to control the labour process. As stated above, Taylorism and the Scientific Management movement are seen as crucial stages in the shift of the locus of production knowledge from the workers to the firm's management. According to Braverman, it was Taylor who most explicitly formulated the principles of capitalist work organisation and developed techniques for analysing and reorganising work. Taylorite principles are still seen as driving work organisation in capitalist society. Mechanisation and automation, as controlled by employers, are at the centre of such developments, but significant changes in work organisation may occur independently of the introduction of new techniques. The outcome of Taylorism has been the deskilling and homogenisation of work, making labour at one and the same time cheaper, more interchangeable and substitutable, and more amenable to control.

Around this thesis has developed a growing body of research, including historical studies. Some of these have leant support in the form of more detailed case studies of particular industries.[37] Other work has been more critical. It has been suggested that Braverman conflated theoretical and historical methods of analysis, never really tracing the experience of a group of firms or an industry over a long time period and in any detail. As a result he focused on changes in some types of work, but failed to see countervailing changes in other types. Equally he has been criticised for implying the notion of a golden age before Taylor when skilled workers truly controlled the production process. Likewise the criticism has been made that he left out worker resistance to management attempts to reorganise work.[38]

Here we wish to make a number of historical points, concerning the attitudes and practices of British employers. In the first place the importance of Taylorism and Scientific Management has probably been exaggerated in the British context. British employers were attempting to reorganise work relations on lines favourable to themselves long before the advent of Taylorism. Contingent on particular product and labour market situations, there were employer attacks on craft and other forms of worker control over the production process throughout the nineteenth century. These took a variety of forms. Zeitlin's chapter in this collection shows how in the key engineering industry there were attempts to reorganise workshop practices throughout the period he examines. These involved attempts to introduce piece-work, extend overtime working, and expand the number of handymen and apprentices. In turn, these moves were associated with developing structures – new styles of foremanship and the creation of employers' organisations. Yet even after the employers' victory in 1897–8 there was no general introduction of new machinery, and attempts at work reorganisation were for the most part slow, uneven, and piecemeal. This Zeitlin explains in terms of the crucial importance of product market structures and employers' investment decisions. Workshop reorganisation was therefore a continuing, but slow, process which did not result in any simple unilinear deskilling.

Formal Taylorist methods had little impact in Britain until the inter-war years. Then the Bedaux company played an important part in introducing time and work study, especially in the 1930s. However, the impact of this should again not be exaggerated. During the inter-war period only a relatively small proportion of firms experimented with such methods. Littler has shown that Bedaux was used predominantly by firms in new expanding industries, such as light engineering, chemicals, and food, drink and tobacco. It was most often used to enable work loads to be increased but within largely unchanged patterns of work organisation. Moreover, there was often management hostility, not least from lower level managers and traditional foremen who saw it as undermining their position. Equally, Lewchuk's article in this collection shows how British motor car firms were suspicious of Ford-type reorganisatiion and preferred to rely on piece-work and a mixture of traditional methods of coercion and paternalism. There was, therefore, no universal or uncontested acceptance by British management of Taylorite or later Ford-type techniques.

There was not only hesitancy on the employers' side, there was also opposition from workers to attempts to reorganise work relations. Especially where unions had some depth in the work-place and where product and labour market conditions favoured workers, management's prior intentions and the actual outcomes were often very different. Management did not always get its own way. Workers were able to resist, maintain some autonomy, and create new areas of control. Yet, this is not to deny that over time there was a reorganisation of work relations: but in Britain it was slow, uneven, and challenged. The transformation of work relations was therefore far more complex than is implied by Braverman's conceptualisation of a simple unilinear transition from craft to Taylorite forms of organisation. Employers had to use additional methods of management to control and motivate workers.

Employment relations

Broader aspects of employment relations therefore need to be considered. By employment relations is here meant the form of job structure and job tenure and the package of benefits, pecuniary and non-pecuniary, attached to jobs within an organisation. Labour economists have argued that within large firms there have developed internal labour markets, where workers are to some degree isolated from the external market and where complex wage and benefit hierarchies exist.[39] There have been a number of explanations offered as to when and why internal labour markets have developed. It has been argued that technology and production processes specific to firms create on-the-job training and firm specific skills. Along with these develop internal promotion systems and related wage and benefit ladders.[40]

However, from a different perspective, others have argued that employers have developed internal labour markets as a more or less conscious strategy aimed at ensuring labour supply, encouraging identification with the firm, and motivating and controlling workers.[41] Others have pointed to the importance of trade unions and collective bargaining as factors influencing the development of job property rights and seniority systems within organisations.[42]

Much of the literature has been American, and it is possible in the American context to provide some historical evidence to support the argument that in some large firms managements have more or less consciously developed internal labour markets as part of a control strategy. Stone and Edwards in particular have shown how historically some large American firms restructured job hierarchies and created internal job ladders and complex benefit systems.[43] Also, in the Japanese context, at least in the big firm sector, the system of life-time employment and seniority wages can be tracked back to employer initiatives in the early period of industrialisation. The chapters of Lazonik and Okayama in this volume provide further discussion of this.

The question arises, however, whether historically the argument can be extended to Great Britain. At first sight this might seem not to be the case. For blue collar workers the majority of British managements have pursued more of what Littler calls a 'minimum inter-action' strategy,[44] relying on local markets for recruiting labour and laying-off workers when demand falls. Within the firm this has usually been associated with close supervision, simple wage systems such as piece-work, and rudimentary benefit packages. Lewchuk's article, for example, describes the suspicion, on the part of British motor car employers, of American-fangled employment relations based on high day wages and job ladders. The outcome of this strategy has been a more instrumental and alienated relationship between management and labour in Britain. However, this picture needs to be qualified. In government employment, in public corporations such as the Post Office, and in the railway companies there developed, quite early, job structures and wage systems somewhat similar to those referred to by internal labour market theorists. Moreover, there is evidence that for certain key groups, whose supply and performance was particularly important for the firm, employers developed strategies along these lines. Melling's paper, in this volume for example, suggests that the mid-Victorian 'labour aristocracy' not only won autonomy and benefits, but were to some degree conceded these by their employers as a more or less conscious strategy. In particular, however, groups such as technical, clerical, and supervisory grades usually enjoyed various advantages: greater job security, sometimes company housing, staff status, pension and superannuation cover-age, and so forth. Paradoxically, perhaps, Melling also shows how apprentices and female staff were also the subject of special welfare provisions: this he explains in terms of employer attempts to influence labour supply, to discourage unionisation, and to enforce work discipline.

Both Melling and Lewchuk also remind us of the continued exis-tence of paternalism in British industry, the origins of which may be traced back to Arkwright, Peel, Dale, Owen, Salt and others. Recent work on the early and mid-nineteenth century has shown how pater-nalist and deferential relations pervaded many employment situa-tions. Joyce, for example, has admirably described a complex pattern of relations in the close-knit mill towns of mid-Victorian Lancashire: company-owned housing, the use by employers of family relations in the work-place, religious ties, and various forms of philanthropy and welfare provisions.[45] The aim of such paternalism was to obscure economic and power relations and, where possible, convert them into moral relations. However, 'Paternalism was a paying proposition, not least, to one degree or another, because it was paid for out of the wages and long hours of those who were its beneficiaries.'[46] However, traditional forms of paternalism had largely declined by the early twentieth century as ties of family ownership were weakened, as pro-duct and labour markets extended, and as workers' political and industrial loyalties were redirected away from their employers. Yet, as Lewchuk shows, 'human relations' ideas continued to have a currency in Britain throughout the period covered by this volume.

In Britain traditional paternalism was not however replaced by comprehensive corporate paternalism on Japanese or even, though to a lesser extent, on American or German lines. There were some approximations to this in a few large firms – Unilever, Pilkington, Cadbury. For example, ICI experimented with a mix of traditional and novel schemes. In 1928 they instituted a profit-sharing scheme, a traditional device for identifying workers with the firm, and one which has gone through periodic cycles of revival by management.[47] They introduced a works council system which offered a form of representation and participation via a consultative framework of committees, over which management kept firm control. More inter-esting and more novel, they also introduced a staff status scheme. Under this, manual workers with more than five years' employment were eligible for staff status. The main benefits were a weekly, instead of an hourly, wage, with elaborate arrangements for extra time at premium rates; the right to a month's notice; payment for certain holi-days; and payment for sickness of up to six months in any year. Promotion to the grade was at the discretion of management and was definitely designed to promote loyalty to the firm and tie workers to their jobs. As has already been stated above, in the late 1930s ICI was also beginning to consider a company-wide wage structure based on job evaluation. However, ICI remained somewhat of an exception. Moreover, alongside these employment policies it had also recognised trade unions and was developing collective bargaining arrangements with them.

Industrial relations

Finally, then, we turn to industrial relations, defined as covering management–union relations and the institution of collective bargaining. Flanders once referred to 'the inadequacy of any account of either the nature or the growth of collective bargaining which sees it only as a method of trade unionism and overlooks in its development the role of employers and their associations'.[48] However, it is still true that the employer interest in collective bargaining and employer strategies in industrial relations continue to be relatively neglected.

There are a number of strategic decisions an employer must take in industrial relations. In the first place he must decide whether or not to recognise an organisation of employees, what kind of organisation, at what levels, and for what purposes. The advent of a union involves some determination of the respective standing and rights of the parties. Second, he must decide on the kind of machinery through which to deal with the worker representatives and handle disputes. Third, the level of bargaining and the scope and form of bargaining has to be decided. Obviously the employer is not completely free to choose in these areas and is constrained by economic, legal, and political factors as well as by the nature of union organisation. However, it is certainly arguable that employer action and inaction have been a predominant factor shaping the development of the industrial relations system.[49]

Historically in Britain it might be said that employer recognition of trade unions developed along two trajectories. In the first place, where union organisation, or more often craft work groups, had established some autonomous regulation, recognition developed out of a *de facto* situation of informal worker control over various aspects of wages and work conditions. In the second place, recognition has developed out of situations of unilateral management regulation of work and employment relations, with recognition coming as a result of growing union organisation. In the former situation, employers played a large part in initiating and establishing collective bargaining with the classic objective of regaining control by sharing power with the union.[50] In the latter cases unions have had more purposefully to force employers into recognition. This is not to say that, where a measure of work group regulation preceded collective bargaining, employers willingly recognised unions and entered into bargaining relations. In such situations employers had calculated that the costs of fighting the union were too high and, indeed, there might be some positive benefits in recognition – though such benefits have probably usually only been perceived after the event. These are obviously broad generalisations and most situations evidence a more complex pattern. However, it might be said that trades such as engineering and other craft industries fall into the first category, while unions representing general and transport workers fall into the latter.

In the two decades before the First World War there was an extension of recognition along both trajectories. During and immediately after the war, with the massive rise in union membership, recognition was further conceded. The policy of British employers, as it developed, was recognition through their employers' organisations. This, it was intended, should strengthen their collective position, especially in regard to the scope of subjects for which the union was recognised. At the same time the hope was to exclude the union from the work-place by formalising relations at regional and industry level. As an aside it might be added that this aspect of employer strategy, involving as it did recognition by federated firms of all the unions recognised nationally, played a part in creating multi-unionism in Great Britain.

As part of the policy of constraining union activity within the work-place, there was little recognition of shop stewards, at least officially, before the Second World War. Engineering was one exception to this when in 1917 and 1919 shop stewards were given formal, though limited, recognition. In practice, however, in engineering and other industries, individual employers would recognise and deal with shop stewards when market conditions made this unavoidable. Along with opposition to shop stewards, there was also before the Second World War, strong opposition to recognising unions for clerical, technical and supervisory staffs. In these areas employer policies of 'forceful opposition' and 'peaceable competition' continued well into the post-Second World War period.[51]

Collective bargaining in British industry developed in the first place at district and regional levels and later was extended to national level. Negotiating machinery was usually *ad hoc* and open-ended. Subsequent to the official Whitley reports of 1917–18 on industrial relations, machinery was established at plant level in many industries, but the employers insisted that this was consultative in nature, and during the unemployment of the inter-war years this insistence was largely successful. In the British context considerable emphasis was placed by employers on dispute procedures, with cases passing through formal stages up to national level. Zeitlin describes how the engineering employers, after formally asserting their managerial prerogatives in 1898, used the disputes procedure as a way of enlisting union support to create industrial law and order. As in engineering, so in most other British industries, it would seem that the initiative for procedural agreements came largely from the employers' organisations.[52]

Substantive agreements on wages and conditions usually developed later than procedural arrangements. Before 1914 most substantive agreements were at district and regional level. Exceptions to this were early agreements in coal mining and shipbuilding, where from the 1890s and early 1900s respectively national percentage changes were made to district base rates. In cotton weaving what might be considered the first national substantive agreement in Great Britain was established in 1892. It was only with the further development of national markets and the extension of union membership, that national agreements developed elsewhere. During and immediately after the First World War, encouraged by the state, they became a common feature in most industries. From a union point of view they were a way of enhancing organisational security and helping weaker members. From the employers' point of view they had the advantage of co-ordinating employer resistance to wage demands and, in certain industries, taking wages out of competition, thereby reducing market uncertainty.

In an assessment of employer strategies a number of further points need to be made about the industrial relations framework which developed in Britain in the late nineteenth and early twentieth centuries and which continued through into the post-Second World War period.

First, the system as it developed was skeletal and largely kept like that by the employers. Certainly during the inter-war years they were able to fill the gaps at work-place level. But a corollary of this was that traditional work-place practices often continued, managerial rights could not always in practice be enforced, and movements in earnings at the work-place were in most situations never tightly controlled from national level.[53] In the tighter labour market situation of the Second World War and the post-war decades, when the balance of advantage shifted to the workers' side, the skeletal and fragile nature of the industrial relations system was revealed. Then, in the more competitive product markets from the late 1950s onwards, employers had to find ways of reducing their labour costs. Because the scope of markets was now more international and less amenable to collusive arrangements, the option of multi-employer strategies was less appealing. Firms were thus impelled to bargain about wages and work arrangements at plant level. Thus, on the whole, Clegg is probably correct to argue that, 'The main influences on the level of bargaining are the structure of management and the authority of employers' organisations.'[54] He might have added, however, that it was the extension of product markets and the increased competitive threat which lay behind changes in employer strategies and structures.

Secondly, it is too simplistic to see the development of British industrial relations institutions as part of an employer-initiated process of co-optation through the development of collective bargaining. Undoubtedly the growth of formalised and centralised industrial relations machinery in many industries constrained autonomous worker action and served to institutionalise conflict. However, in recent work there has probably been a tendency to overemphasise the degree of unilateral work group regulation in the earlier nineteenth century and to exaggerate the success, in the late nineteenth and early twentieth centuries, of employers' attacks on this in conjunction with a conciliatory union leadership.[55] Such an interpretation also neglects the fact that employers often had to be forced into collective bargaining, and it meant some loss of freedom and flexibility for them.

Finally, from a comparative point of view, the British system of industrial relations might have offered British employers certain advantages of stability and order. This was certainly commented on by foreign observers before the Second World War.[56] However, against this must be set the fact that the strength of work-place unionism and the rigidity of formal institutions were impediments to British employers, seriously restricting experiments with other strategies of work organisation and personnel administration. Moreover, the formal system was fragile and within it lay the seeds of the challenge from the work-place which re-emerged in the three decades following the Second World War. The attempt by British employers from the 1960s onwards to rebuild a new system of industrial relations based on plant and company arrangements and more sophisticated personnel administration has for historical reasons been hesitant and uncertain.[57]

Conclusions
This introductory chapter has attempted to outline the main areas which need to be considered in any historical study of managerial labour policies. It has argued that the structure of management and employers' organisations should be a central concern. In the British case a long-term, though hesitant, trend towards the elaboration of integrated internal hierarchies was identified. However, this developed at different times in different industries and even within the same industry. In other countries, as later chapters will show, somewhat similar trends occurred, though the speed of change was different. As

to strategies, it was suggested that some historically based typologies are useful. However, this chapter concentrated on three strategic areas – work relations, employment relations, and industrial relations. It argued that, confronted with problems and opportunities in the pursuit of their overall strategies, employers have experimented with various mixes of techniques and strategies.

In Chandler's original formulation of the strategy and structure relationship it was suggested that overall company stucture followed strategy. In so far as this framework can be adapted to the area of labour management, the relationship must be seen as more complex and dynamic.[58] The development of new strategies did indeed induce changes in management structure, but, in turn, the creation of new structures may facilitate the adoption of further strategies. They may also constrain strategic choices. Thus, rationalisation of personnel and production hierarchies within the firm developed simultaneously with the rationalisation of work and employment relations. Equally, strategies based on union recognition and procedural containment through collective employer action led to the establishment of permanent employers' organisations; these in turn facilitated the development of multi-employer strategies on wages and conditions; yet at the same time in Britain employers' organisations impeded the growth of internal industrial relations and employment policies at the level of the individual firm. The relationship between structure and strategy is highly interdependent.

In this introduction two main sets of explanatory factors have been stressed. First, emphasis has been placed on the nature of product and labour markets, especially their structure in terms of boundaries and the level of demand and competition in them. Second, workers' own objectives provide an essential element of the dynamic, both creating problems for management and obstructing managerial strategies. These two sets of factors re-occur throughout the chapters which follow. In addition, especially in the comparative articles, broader political and cultural influences are discussed.

In the following chapter Zeitlin deals with the strategies of employers in one of Britain's main industries, engineering, in the late nineteenth and early twentieth centuries. He argues that the development of an employers' organisation and the institutions of collective bargaining became a central part of management's labour strategy. However, he shows that at the work-place British engineering employers were unable to break fully the power of craft workers or to transform work relations in the direction of deskilling and mass production.

Chapter 3 by Melling deals with employment relations during the same period, in particular the use of various forms of welfarism, such as company housing, pension schemes, and profit-sharing arrangements, to secure co-operation and to control workers. It analyses the dimensions of paternalism and seeks to assess the extent of such policies, especially as applied to particular types of workers. The limitations and contradictions of these policies in the context of British industrial relations is emphasised.

Lewchuk in Chapter 4 takes up some of the points raised in the two previous chapters and focuses specifically on the British motor industry in the inter-war years. He argues that Ford-type work control strategies were never fully espoused by British motor car firms. Instead they placed reliance on ideological appeals for co-operation between capital and labour and on wage payment systems, in particular the use of piece-work, to control and motivate workers.

The next three chapters deal with similar aspects of employer structure and strategy in the other major capitalist economies. Lazonik in Chapter 5 examines the development of labour relations under monopoly capitalism in the United States. He reviews the American literature and recent debates about the labour process and employer strategies. The chapter emphases the importance of bureaucratic forms of personnel administration which developed in the inter-war years and also the broader cultural and political environment which conditioned relations between management and labour. In similar fashion Chapter 6 by Homburg deals with parallel developments in Germany. It takes the electrical engineering firm of Siemens as a case study and traces the development of bureaucratic forms of work organisation and personnel management in the inter-war years. Okayama in Chapter 7 then focuses on the Japanese engineering industry and traces the emergence of structures of labour management in twentieth-century Japan. She examines the development of bureaucratic paternalism and the origins of the modern Japanese system of employment and industrial relations.

Finally, Littler's concluding chapter presents a comparative analysis of managerial structures and strategies in the four countries covered by the volume. He broadens out the analysis and presents a theoretical model for examing the parallels and contrasts between the four countries.

Taken overall the aim of the book is to further the important task of analysing the development of management structures and strategies in the labour field. Together the chapters show the value of an approach which is both historical and comparative. Such an approach reveals something of the variety, continuity, and change in approaches to the management and control of labour.

Notes

1. One notable recent exception to this is the three volume study of Courtaulds by D.C. Coleman, *Courtaulds*, vols. I, II, III (1969, 1969, 1980).
2. Obvious exceptions here are S. Pollard, *The Genesis of Modern Management* (1968), and E.J. Hobsbawm, *Labouring Men* (1964).
3. This was certainly the view of the Donovan Report. See Royal Commission on Trade Unions and Employers' Associations 1965–1968, *Report* (1968).
4. A. Briggs, 'Trade Union History and Labour History', *Business History* (1966), p. 41.
5. For a useful comment on new approaches in labour history see D. Brody, 'The Old Labor History and the New', *Labor History* (1979).
6. See for example, for the United States, D. Nelson, *Managers and Workers* (1975), and for the United Kingdom recent work by J. Melling on welfare management and on foremen, ' "Non-Commissioned Officers"; British Employers and Their Supervisory Workers, 1880–1920', *Social History* (1980).
7. A useful volume, dealing mainly with Japan, is K. Nakagawa (ed.) *Labor and Management*, Proceedings of the Fourth Fuji Conference (1979).
8. G. S. Bain and H.A. Clegg, 'A Strategy for Industrial Relations Research in Great Britain', *British Journal of Industrial Relations* (1974).
9. R.A. Lester, *The Economics of Labor* (1964), pp. 209–10.
10. J.R. Commons, 'American Shoemakers, 1648–1826: A Sketch of Industrial Development', *Quarterly Journal of Economics* (1909).
11. O.E. Williamson, *Markets and Hierarchies* (1975).
12. O.E. Williamson, 'The Organisation of Work: A Comparative Institutional Assessment', *Journal of Economic Behaviour and Organisation*, (1980), and V. Goldberg, 'Bridges over Contested Terrain', *Journal of Economic Behaviour and Organisation* (1980).
13. See for example A. Chandler, *The Visible Hand* (1977), Introduction, and A. Chandler and H. Daems (eds.), *Managerial Hierarchies: Comparative Perspectives on the Rise of Modern Industrial Enterprise*, (1980). The latter contains a chapter by Williamson.
14. J. Woodward (ed.), *Industrial Organisation: Behaviour and Control* (1970), pp. 50–4.
15. For the best statements of 'strategic choice' see J. Child, 'Organisational Structure, Environment, and Performance: The Role of Strategic Choice', *Sociology* (1972), and G. Schreyogg, 'Contingency and Choice in Organisation Theory', *Organisation Studies* (1980).
16. H. Braverman, *Labor and Monopoly Capital* (1974).
17. S. Marglin, 'What Do Bosses Do? The Origins and Functions of Hierarchy in Capitalist Production', *Review of Radical Political Economics* (1974).
18. See Williamson (1980).
19. R. Edwards, *Contested Terrain: The Transformation of the Workplace in the Twentieth Century* (1979).
20. A. Friedman, *Industry and Labour* (1977).
21. A. Chandler, *Strategy and Structure* (1962), and *The Visible Hand: The Managerial Revolution in American Business* (1977).
22. Chandler and Daems (eds.) (1980).
23. See, for example, Lazonick in this volume.
24. This is the assumption in Marglin (1974).
25. For a useful account see C.R. Littler, *The Development of the Labour Process in Capitalist Societies* (1982).
26. D.F. Schloss, *Methods of Industrial Renumeration* (1892), p. 120.
27. P.N. Stearns, *Lives of Labour* (1975), pp. 169–79.
28. 'Industrial Reconstruction: An Employer's View', *The Athenaeum* (March 1917).
29. For more details see Zeitlin in this volume.

30. R.R. Locke, 'Cost Accounting: An Institutional Yardstick for Measuring British Entrepreneurial Performance circa 1914', *The Accounting Historians Journal* (1979).
31. E.B. Rawlinson, 'Some Notes on Cost Accounts', *The Incorporated Accountants' Journal*, n.s. (1910–11), p. 265.
32. M.M. Niven, *Personnel Management 1913–63: The Growth of Personnel Management and the Development of the Institute* (1967), esp. pp. 21–57.
33. For more details see, H.F. Gospel, 'Employers' Organisations: Their Growth and Function in the British System of Industrial Relations in the Period 1918–39' (London PhD, 1974), especially Ch. 1.
34. Ibid.
35. Niven (1967).
36. W.J. Reader, *Imperial Chemical Industries*, vol. II, (1979), esp. pp. 61–70.
37. See, for example, A. Zimbalist (ed.), *Case Studies in the Labor Process* (1979).
38. These criticisms are gathered together in some of the articles in S. Wood (ed.), *The Degradation of Work: Skill, Deskilling, and the Labour Process* (1982), and Littler (1982).
39. See, P. Doeringer and M. Piore, *Internal Labour Markets and Manpower Analysis* (1971), and R. Edwards, M. Reich, D. Gordon (eds.), *Labour Market Segmentation* (1975).
40. Doeringer and Piore (1971).
41. See, for example, Edwards (1979).
42. Goldberg (1980).
43. Edwards (1979), and K. Stone, 'The Origins of Job Structures in the Steel Industry', *Review of Radical Political Economics* (1974).
44. See Littler (1982), pp. 55–8.
45. P. Joyce, *Work Society and Politics: The Culture of the Factory in Later Victorian England* (1980).
46. Ibid. p. 146.
47. Reader (1979), pp. 61–70 for ICI. See more generally on profit-sharing Labour Department of Board of Trade, *Report on Profit Sharing and Labour Co-Partnership in the United Kingdom* (1912), Cd. 6496.
48. A. Flanders, 'Collective Bargaining: A Theoretical Analysis', *British Journal of Industrial Relations* (1968), p. 3.
49. At a general level, C. Kerr, J.T. Dunlop, F.H. Harbison and C.A. Myers, *Industrialism and Industrial Man* (1962), esp. Chs. 6 and 7, argue that the employer plays the main part in shaping the industrial relations system. It has already been suggested under note 3 above that this seems to have been the view of the Donovan Commission.
50. Flanders (1968).
51. See G.S. Bain, *The Growth of White Collar Unionism* (1970).
52. For a fuller discussion of this and supporting evidence see Gospel (1974), Chs. 4, 5 and 9. See also H.A. Clegg, *The System of Industrial Relations in Great Britain* (1970 edn), pp. 127, 201.
53. See Gospel (1974), especially Chs. 6, 7 and 8.
54. H.A. Clegg, *Trade Unionism under Collective Bargaining* (1976), p. 41.
55. See, for example, the otherwise excellent R. Price, *Masters, Unions and Men* (1980).
56. See, for example, F.E. Gannett and B.F. Catherwood (eds.), *Industrial and Labour Relations in Great Britain* (1939).
57. For the best contemporary survey, see, W. Brown, *The Changing Contours of British Industrial Relations* (1981). This deals with the development of managerial professionalism and plant and company industrial relations policies.
58. This point is also made about overall company strategy and structure by L. Hannah, 'Business Development and Economic Structure in Britain since 1880' in L. Hannah (ed.), *Management Strategy and Business Development* (1976).

2 The Labour Strategies of British Engineering Employers, 1890–1922[1]
Jonathan Zeitlin

The behaviour of British engineering employers has long occupied a prominent place in discussions of late Victorian and Edwardian economic and social history. As a leading beneficiary of the long Victorian boom, but increasingly challenged by foreign competition from the 1870s, engineering has often been treated as a microcosm of the trajectory of the British economy as a whole. Thus the introduction of new automatic machine tools in the 1890s, coupled with engineering employers' determination to wrest from skilled workers and their unions a broad recognition of managerial prerogative, has been seen as exemplifying both a progressive entrepreneurial response to foreign competition and an intensification of class conflict in the work-place resulting from the changing position of British industry in the world economy.[2] The employers' victory in the 1897–8 lock-out has in turn figured as a key moment in accounts of the 'employers' counter-attack' of the 1890s, marking a new spirit of aggressiveness; the 'Terms of Settlement' imposed on the defeated unions have likewise been taken as heralding an emerging model of economistic collective bargaining marking a decisive break with craft regulation.[3]

Yet despite this centrality of engineering employers to historical debate, there has been little systematic study of the evolution of their labour strategies in this period. In particular, despite indications of the survival of elements of craft regulation into the First World War, there has been little scrutiny of the extent to which engineering employers were able to use the leverage secured in 1898 to effect a thoroughgoing transformation of the division of labour on the shop floor. Drawing extensively on both employer and union sources, this paper seeks to redress the balance through a close analysis of employer strategies, both at the level of the individual enterprise and of organised collective action.

As we shall see in more detail below, a close analysis of the evidence reveals that despite their victory in 1898 British engineering employers failed, at least in the older sectors of the industry, to transform the division of labour in the direction of mass production. While they were able to subvert the long-term reproduction of craft regulation through such measures as changes in payment systems and in apprenticeship, they remained heavily dependent on skilled labour and thus vulnerable to a resurgence of craft militancy during boom periods. The explanation for this failure lies primarily in their avoidance of large-scale programmes of capital investment, which avoidance was in turn rooted in the fragmented structure of established enterprises, in the limited market for mass-produced goods in Britain, and in the possibilities of shifting into semi-protected markets in the empire and the underdeveloped world. At the same time, internal contradictions in the strategy pursued by the Engineering Employers' Federation and the opposition of skilled engineering workers combined to undermine the nascent structure of employer-dominated collective bargaining created in 1898, paving the way for a resurgence of craft militancy in the years preceding the outbreak of the war.

I

Engineering employers' turn towards wider organisation and confrontation with the unions in the mid-1890s must be seen in the context of a series of interrelated developments which were calling into question the existing structure both of the division of labour and of industrial relations. The gradual exhaustion of returns from an extensive development of the existing division of labour, the intensification of foreign competition, and new opportunities for mechanisation came together in the context of heightened conflict between employers and skilled workers over routine issues to precipitate a full-scale crisis in the existing pattern of industrial relations.

On the eve of a major wave of mechanisation and industrial conflict in the 1890s, both the division of labour in most engineering works and the pattern of relations between skilled workers and employers remained within a framework which had been established in the mid-nineteenth century. The 1830s and 1840s had been a period of rapid expansion and technical change for the industry, fuelled by demand from the textile factories and the railways. The introduction of non-apprenticed men and boys on new machine tools, coupled with the extension of piecework and systematic overtime, provoked bitter resistance from skilled craftsmen, and the late 1840s and early 1850s were punctuated by a series of disputes.[4]

But after the defeat of the newly formed Amalgamated Society of Engineers (ASE) in the 1852 lock-out by an alliance of London and Lancashire employers, changing market conditions made possible an accommodation between skilled workers and employers in the industry. After mid-century, demand for engineering products shifted from a rapidly expanding home market to more slowly growing markets overseas, bringing in its wake a movement towards less standardised production. The result was a shift from labour saving to labour using investment which persisted through most of the century. With the stabilisation of the pattern of investment came a stabilisation of the division of labour. The new machine tools of the 1830s and 1840s – the slide-rest lathe, planing, slotting, shaping, and drilling machines – had only been capable of routinising a portion of the engineering craftsman's work, and the expansion of demand for more sophisticated and less standardised products increased in turn the industry's reliance on new groups of more specialised craftsmen such as fitters, turners, and patternmakers. In this context, with the attenuation of pressures on employers to cut costs and undermine the position of craftsmen in the division of labour, the ASE and other craft unions experienced a rapid growth in membership and were able to re-establish a significant measure of craft regulation. Thus although the ASE had officially removed a fixed ratio of apprentices to journeymen and bans on 'illegal men', piece-work, and systematic overtime from its rule-book after its defeat in 1852, the enforcement of these aims was entrusted to the districts, which by the early 1860s were enjoying considerable success in containing these practices.[5]

By the 1870s and 1880s, however, signs of strain began to appear in this mid-century settlement, as the returns to a pattern of extensive growth diminished. There is evidence to suggest that labour costs were rising as a proportion of total costs as the increase in wage rates, particularly for skilled labour, began to outrun productivity growth in certain sectors.[6] The onset of the Great Depression in the 1870s, bringing a decline in overseas demand for engineering products, contributed to a squeeze on profits, as did the first stirrings of German and American competition.[7]

In the context of relatively stagnant demand, these pressures drove engineering employers to experiment not with new forms of capital-intensive investment, but rather with methods of cheapening and intensifying skilled labour within the existing division of labour, thereby reopening the whole range of issues whose conflictual importance had receded in the 1850s and 1860s. Foremost among these were the spread of piece-work and the intensification of supervision as methods of boosting output and speeding up the pace of work without commensurate increases in labour costs: nearly 17 per cent of ASE members were paid by the piece in 1891, and the figures were closer to 50 per cent in some districts.[8] The employment of non-apprenticed workers – known as 'handymen' or 'machinists – registered a parallel increase. At issue here were not the new automatic machine tools, such as turret lathes and milling machines, being developed in the United States; the number of such tools sold in Britain remained extremely small until the mid-1890s. Rather, employers promoted larger numbers of handymen on to the simpler types of existing machine tools such as planing and drilling machines and multiplied the number of 'fitters' assistants' and boys working alongside the men.[9] Similarly, this period saw an accelerated subversion of apprenticeship into a form of cheap labour, as the proportion of apprentices to journeymen rose sharply and the technical content of their training declined.[10]

Even the most purely economic of the union's achievements – the standard working day and the standard rate – were threatened by this assault on craft regulation. Systematic overtime once again became endemic in the industry, as employers sought to take the fullest possible advantage of upturns in trade during the overall depression, and to intensify the pressure on their work-force by keeping manning levels low. The cumulative force of these various tactics was to reduce the effective hold of district rates over earnings. Thus the 1886 wages census reported that outside of London and Manchester not only did average earnings for fitters and turners fall several shillings below the district rate, but some 15 – 30 per cent of these groups were earning either 10 per cent above or below (in this depressed context presumably below) average earnings.[11]

Such trends were most evident in those sectors where a significant degree of repetition production could be found, such as textile machinery, railway engineering, cycles, and armaments. The giant arms firm of Sir W.G. Armstrong, Mitchell & Co. provides perhaps the clearest example. In 1890 the firm employed *c.* 15,000 men in its naval shipyard, ordnance, and engine works. While its battleships and large guns remained custom-built products requiring skilled labour, large orders for shells and machine guns offered considerable scope for repetition production. Thus the firm made extensive use of machinists and its managing director wrote to the Webbs, 'I take as many apprentices as I dare'.[12] More original were the firm's methods of labour discipline and supervision. By 1890 Armstrong's had already developed an elaborate system of timekeeping, using individual time boards to monitor attendance and movements from day to piece rates. In shops engaged in repetition work, piece payment coupled with frequent rate cutting prevailed. But where the nature of work precluded piece rates or where the men were thought to be limiting output to prevent rate cuts, the firm introduced a special class of supervisors, known by the late 1890s as 'feed and speed' men whose duty was 'to keep moving through the shops in order to see that each machine is being kept at its proper speed and is producing the amount of work which it is known to be capable of turning out'.[13]

The stability of the pattern of investment, and with it the division of labour in engineering after 1850, had rested on two related economic conditions: the commanding position of British products in world markets and the limited demand for standardised, mass-produced goods. Both of these conditions were eroded with accelerating force in the 1890s, with the increasing penetration of German and American products, first into European and Third World markets and then into Britain itself, and with the diffusion of new American machine tools in the wake of the bicycle boom.

From the 1840s American manufacturers operating behind steep tariff walls developed a new generation of automatic and semi-automatic machine tools to cater for a burgeoning demand for mass-produced consumer durables – typewriters, small arms, agricultural machinery, sewing machines – for which the American market provided much greater support than did the British. While American machines and methods – turret and capstan lathes, milling and grinding machines, precision gauges – made it possible in principle to routinise a much larger proportion of skilled labour, their impact on British engineering practice before 1890 was minimal. Neither the diverse character of most engineering demand nor its slow growth had encouraged British employers to launch a major programme of capital-intensive investment, though both armaments and sewing machines offered a certain scope for mass production methods.[14] Hence, as Saul has argued, it was not until the bicycle boom of the mid-1890s that a broad-based demand developed in Britain for a product with standardised, interchangeable parts; and it was this demand which effected the diffusion of American machine tools, first within the cycle industry itself and then in the older sectors as well. An enormous surge in demand for cycles during the mid-1890s brought in its train a similar demand for the new generation of machine tools required to produce them. Imports of American machine tools consequently mushroomed, and British machine tool firms making the new products also prospered.[15]

Though the new machine tools were best suited to mass production, they were flexible enough to be used on less standardised work as well. The intensification of foreign competition, together with the example of the cycle makers, the falling prices of the new machine tools, and the improved network of distribution in Britain encouraged manufacturers in the older sectors of the industry to experiment with the new techniques. In most cases, this amounted to the piecemeal introduction of new equipment, rather than wholesale scrapping of existing machinery in the interest of a transformation of the division of labour. The process went furthest in those older sectors most involved in repetition work, such as armaments and textile engineering, but also touched marine engineering, locomotive building, and machine tools making itself. Though the practical consequences of the new techniques remained limited in the late 1890s, the result was nonetheless to call into question the position of skilled craftsmen within the division of labour.

This new wave of mechanisation inaugurated during the mid-1890s coincided with a period of intensified conflict between skilled workers and their employers. With the revival of trade from the late 1880s, skilled engineers launched a major offensive to regain ground lost to the employers during the depression. While disputes flared up in London and Lancashire, the movement was concentrated above all in the marine districts, whose connection with the sharp cyclical fluctuations of the shipbuilding industry encouraged workers to take the fullest advantage of the leverage afforded by a boom.[16] The storm centre of this movement was the north-east Coast, which by the early 1890s had become the best-organised district in the ASE. A newly formed co-ordinating committee of ASE districts in the region quickly obtained an advance of wages and a reduction of one hour in the working week; in 1890–1 it embarked on a campaign for the restriction of overtime which enjoyed some limited success despite a protracted lock-out.

Following a series of organisational reforms in the ASE in 1892 and the renewal of concern about unemployment with the downturn of trade after 1893, the focus of union militancy shifted to a national campaign for the eight hour day. By 1894, the eight hour day had been conceded in all government establishments, and major private employers had followed suit in a variety of engineering centres. Thus the union appeared on the verge of achieving a universal forty-eight hour week when the deepening of the recession halted the movement in 1895.

It was this resurgence of craft militancy beginning in the late 1880s which provided the impetus for the creation of a centralised national employers' federation in 1896. An earlier attempt to create a national association of engineering employers by Armstrong after the nine hours strikes in 1872 had foundered on conflicts of interest between inland and marine producers which caused the latter to hold aloof. But while the Iron Trades Employers' Association (ITEA) had members in some seventeen engineering districts, it remained a loose confederation of local employers' associations without the power to undertake national action.[17]

Co-ordination among the local employers' associations on the north-east coast had existed since the 1880s, and by the following decade employers throughout the region were operating a unified system of black-lists directed against union activists and known as the 'character note' system, whose abolition figured prominently among the demands of strikers in 1890–1. In the course of disputes with the ASE over restriction of overtime and demarcation in 1890–2, the north-east coast employers had developed the tactic of turning disputes at a single firm into regional confrontation by locking out union members in stages of 25 per cent per week. The extent of the north-eastern employers' alarm at developments on the trade union front can be seen most clearly from a memorandum written by Col. Dyer, managing director of Armstrong's and later president of the Engineering Employers' Federation (EEF), explaining the firm's decision to abandon plans for the construction of a plant which it believed would in principle be economic:[18]

> At one time we intended to lay down this plant; the drawings were ready and all arrangements made, but owing to the rapid succession of labour troubles in this district during the last few years, we have finally decided not to increase our works in any way or expend any more capital in developing them; indeed, the tendency is the other way and it is not improbable that we will gradually decrease them.

By 1895, the north-east coast branch of the ITEA had gone so far as to set up an elaborate mutual strike insurance scheme, whereby members could pay in so much per man employed per week and would receive a proportional amount from the general fund in the event of a shutdown.[19]

The final impetus towards national organisation came, however, from the Clyde, where engineering employers had formed themselves into a separate association after an unsuccessful attempt to form a national federation with the shipbuilders in 1889. With the revival of trade at the end of 1895, engineers sought to regain the wage reductions imposed during the preceding slump, and the ASE launched movements in a number of districts, including the Clyde and Belfast. The employers locked out 25 per cent of ASE members in their shops despite the willingness of the district committee to accept a lower rise than their counterparts in Belfast. Faced with this display of employer militancy, the ASE executive hastened to arrange a settlement.[20]

The success of coordinated action in the Clyde–Belfast dispute provided the spark for the formation of the EEF, which at first drew in the employers' associations of the major marine centres alone. The intensified conflicts of the early 1890s over routine issues such as overtime, apprenticeship, and demarcation, which were cumulatively perceived as a threat to managerial prerogative, had prepared the ground for this breakthrough towards national organisation. At the same time, the sense that the introduction of new machinery might provide the opportunity for a significant transformation of the division of labour likewise stiffened the employers' resolve. In contrast to employers' associations in some industries, the EEF made little attempt to regulate the product market but operated more as a sort of employers' trade union: its central aim, as stated in its rules, was to provide a framework for collective action in response to demands raised by workers and their unions over a range of issues from workplace organisation to wage bargaining.[21] Federation decisions were binding on local associations, which were prohibited from taking independent action on matters of general importance without consulting the executive, and central authority was given added teeth by the executive's power to subsidise firms for strike losses incurred while following its instructions.[22]

With the accelerated diffusion of the new machine tools after 1896, the problem of machine manning moved rapidly to the centre of the mounting tensions between the ASE and the Federation. The ASE realised from the outset that the capture of the new machine tools was essential if the position of skilled craftsmen were to be maintained, and a number of strikes against the promotion of handymen on to machines ensued. By late 1896, the Federation had decided to mount a co-ordinated resistance to union claims on machine manning, taking its stand on the principle that, 'the machines are the property of the employers . . . and they will therefore continue to exercise the discretion they have hitherto possessed by appointing the men they consider suitable to work them'.[23] Already in August, the EEF had threatened a national lock-out if the ASE executive did not force its members to end a strike over machine manning at one Glasgow firm. Though this confrontation was resolved by the departure of the handyman in question, a series of further disputes in various districts over machine manning, 'interference' with foremen, and restrictions on overtime, led the Federation to renew its threat of a national lockout in March 1897.[24]

While the more routine issues were quickly resolved through negotiation, the 'machine question' proved less tractable. In 1896 the EEF had been prepared to concede control over certain machines to the ASE – principally sliding and screw cutting lathes and large boring machines – in exchange for a free hand with the rest. But by the time of the machine conference in April 1897, this willingness to compromise had disappeared. The ASE executive, aware of the vulnerability of its position, was prepared to treat the machine question essentially as a problem of wages and therefore proposed the establishment of local joint committees under Board of Trade arbitration to adjudicate which machines should be worked at the skilled rate. These proposals would have proved extremely difficult to implement in practice, since the class of work rather than the type of machine was the key determinant of skill requirements. But in any case, the employers, conscious of their growing strength, had become committed to an unyielding defence of managerial prerogative.[25]

In the event, however, it was not the machine question itself which triggered off the national lock-out, but rather the resumption of the movement for the eight hour day outside the EEF's sphere of influence in London. A joint committee of engineering and shipbuilding trades, having secured the eight hour day from a majority of large London firms, announced its intention to bring round the intransigents with an overtime ban, to be followed by a strike. Faced with this ultimatum, the loosely organised London employers applied for membership in the EEF, and the Federation responded by threatening a national lock-out if the London strike notices were not withdrawn. The ASE held its ground and the lock-out began in early July.[26]

The history of the 1897-8 lock-out has been narrated at length a number of times, and it is my intention here merely to highlight certain aspects of the dispute.[27] Though the labour market was booming and the ASE's membership and financial resources had reached unprecedented heights, the union's underlying position was weak. Despite its numbers, the ASE had succeeded in organising only half of the 180,000 fitters and turners in the industry, not to mention the army of handymen capable of working the new machine tools. At the same time, the ASE's history of demarcation disputes and organisational rivalries left it isolated, as the other major craft unions held aloof. Ideologically and politically the ASE was likewise on weak ground as the employers were able to represent them in the press as enemies of progress and property in the context of a wider legal and industrial offensive against trade unions.[28]

The employers, by contrast, had achieved an unprecedented degree of collective organisation and had been preparing for a national lock-out since the previous year. The Federation had been energetically seeking to win over the firms associated with the ITEA, and the intensification of conflict over mechanisation and craft regulation had enabled them to draw in the Manchester association. The eight hours demand proved an ideal catalyst for the unification of the diverse sections of the industry in defence of 'the power to manage'. A substantial reduction in working hours would at a single stroke reduce productivity, raise costs, and undermine the competitive position of firms from all sections of the industry. At the same time, however, the Federation's growth from 180 firms at the outset of the lock-out to 702 firms at its conclusion depended in large part on the boycott imposed by the large Federated firms on those of their suppliers who refused to joint the conflict.[29]

At its peak, the lock-out involved some 45,000 men and a quarter of

ASE members, whose withdrawal was, however, insufficient to stop production. Some major firms ceased work completely, believing themselves dependent on an adequate quota of skilled workers; most continued operations at a reduced level, using blacklegs supplied by professional strike-breakers such as the National Free Labour Association and by promoting their labourers on to skilled work. Thus while the ASE was able to raise a considerable strike fund, the financial strain of supporting the locked-out men eventually became intolerable, and by November the ASE executive was investigating peace terms.[30]

Whereas during the previous national lock-out in 1852 engineering employers had sought the outright destruction of the unions, by 1897–8 a shift in strategy was discernable. To be sure, Col. Dyer waxed euphoric over the regime of managerial prerogative introduced by Carnegie at the Homestead works, while the head of the London employers' association hinted that the unions might find themselves excluded from the ultimate settlement between masters and men. But even the most sanguinary expostulations of employers' spokesmen made it clear that craft regulation rather than trade unionism *per se* was their principal target, and the EEF for its part insisted throughout the dispute that it aimed not to smash the ASE, but to establish managerial prerogative once and for all. The object of a national lock-out, in fact, was above all to coerce the ASE executive into forcing its members to abandon their efforts at craft regulation on a local level, hence the lock-out threats even in the case of strikes opposed by the national union.[31]

While sanctioning the right of trade unions to bargain for their members the employers were at the same time concerned to reserve as wide a margin as possible for their own unilateral determination, as can clearly be seen from the first 'Terms of Settlement' they proposed to the unions, which called for individual bargaining over piece-work and to a considerable extent over wage rates and overtime as well. These terms were rejected by the ASE executive and by ballots of the membership, so that after a public outcry against the threat to collective bargaining the EEF agreed to add a set of explanatory notes explicitly recognising the legitimate functions of trade unions.[32] The revised terms, signed in January 1898, nonetheless embodied the key principles of managerial prerogative. Employers were henceforth free to hire non-unionists; to institute piece-work systems at prices agreed with the individual worker; to demand up to forty hours overtime per man per month; to pay non-unionists at individual rates; to employ as many apprentices as they chose; and to place any suitable worker on any machine at a mutually agreed rate. In addition, the Terms of Settlement established a novel disputes procedure according to which no strike could occur without first going through a national conference between the union executive and the EEF. In this way, the Federation hoped to contain rank and file resistance to the re-organisation of the division of labour by forcing the ASE executive to discipline its members through the constant threat of a national lock-out.

II

In the immediate aftermath of the 1897-8 lock-out, engineering employers believed that they had removed the major barrier to that transformation of the division of labour in their workshops which alone could repel foreign competition. As the editor of a leading trade journal declared:[33] 'The master again became master in fact as well as in name . . . . The free selection of the most suitable labour thus secured has given the employers the full and productive use of the machines.'

Yet by 1914 it had become clear that despite important gains, engineering employers had failed, at least in the older sectors of the industry, either fully to displace skilled workers from their central position in the division of labour or to break the back of craft regulation as a significant constraint on their freedom of action in the workplace. To be sure, engineering employers continued to introduce automatic and semi-automatic machine tools at as fast a rate as they had in the 1890s, and were able to undermine the long-term future of craft regulation through the increasing employment of semi-skilled and female labour; the multiplication of apprentices and the subversion of the technical content of their training; and the rapid extension of payment by results. But ASE members were increasingly able to capture control of new machinery and 60 per cent of the work-force in Federated firms was still classified as skilled in 1914.[34] Productivity growth, which had fluctuated around a rising trend in the 1880s and 1890s, levelled off after 1900, and foreign producers continued to expand their shares of world markets: by 1913 the UK exported £34.8 million of mechanical engineering products compared to Germany's £37.2 million and the United States' £26.9 million.[35] Perhaps the most striking evidence of the limited transformation of the division of labour in this period can be found not in statistical series, but rather in the striking successes scored by a resurgent craft militancy from 1909 onwards, and in the continued dependence on skilled labour which emerged as a central aspect of the munitions crisis of the First World War.

Why did British engineering employers fail to take full advantage of the commanding position they had established in 1898 to effect a thoroughgoing transformation of the division of labour in the industry? The answer lies in a combination of the economic forces which shaped individual firms' investment strategies; the broader industrial relations strategy developed by the EEF; and the responses of the executive and the rank and file of the ASE.

Engineering manufacturers' approach to the division of labour in their works was largely determined by their investment strategies, which in turn depended in great measure on the structure of established enterprises, on the nature of their product, and on the movement of demand. A full-scale transformation of the division of labour in line with the best-practice engineering technology of the day involved extensive capital investment in new machinery and often required a major reorganisation of workshop layout or even a purpose-built plant if it were to be fully effective. Ambitious investment programmes of this kind were discouraged in the first instance by the fragmented structure of ownership which characterized most of the older sectors of the industry, as it did so many of the staple trades in Britain during this period. Outside of armaments and railway work, the older sectors of engineering were dominated by small and medium-sized firms, often family-owned and usually specialising in a particular type of product, with a larger penumbra of smaller and less specialised firms comprising the bulk of the industry.[36] Even when amalgamations resulted in the creation of larger, vertically integrated enterprises, these usually retained a federal rather than centralised structure, as in the case of Guest, Keen and Nettlefold, with little co-ordination among the constituent parts even in terms of finance and marketing. The highly competitive relations among individual firms, their lack of market power, their reluctance to seek outside finance, and their limited development of managerial hierarchies all combined to inhibit engineering manufacturers in the older sectors from embarking on expensive and risky programmes of investment aimed at the capture of new markets through a transformation of the division of labour in their works.

In any case, such a transformation would be profitable only where there was a predictable and rapidly rising demand for a standardised, mass-produced product, which in Edwardian Britain was concentrated primarily in newer, lighter sectors such as cycles, motor cars, and electrical goods, and in certain types of armaments. While in these newer sectors British firms would be unable to enter world markets unless they adopted the most advanced methods, in those sectors where foreign competition remained ineffective before the war – principally textile machinery, but other parts of the older sectors as well – there was little incentive for manufacturers to undertake a transformation of production. Since the short and medium-term profitability of individual firms always remained the principal criterion for their investment decisions, British manufacturers could even concede a steadily growing share of European markets to American and German competitors if they themselves could maintain reasonable profit levels by turning to markets in the empire and the rest of the underdeveloped world. Such tendencies were accentuated by the sharp shift of the terms of trade in favour of primary producers after 1900, which shift brought in its train a veritable Indian summer for the older sectors.[37]

At the same time, while the newer sectors grew rapidly up to 1914, prior commitments to established forms of lighting, power, and transport, together with the relatively weak demand for mass-produced goods in the home market, placed limits on their expansion and profitability.[38] In electrical engineering, profit rates rarely exceeded 10 per cent (one estimate put the average for the industry as low as 1.67 per cent), except in the better-established cable making sector, and often failed to cover capital costs for the firms concerned.[39] Similarly, while Daimler could achieve profit rates of over 50 per cent on capital at certain points before 1914, Armstrong-Whitworth and Vickers, both of whom invested in motor car manufacture before the war, failed to find the game worth the candle: their car subsidiaries made frequent losses and even in good years barely topped returns of 10 per cent on capital, compared to the 15–20 per cent earned by Armstrong-Whitworth's arms divisions in the same period. With British military spending on a rapid upward trend, Sir Andrew Noble of Armstrong-Whitworth was no doubt correct to say that there was more money to be made from building one river boat than from producing 6000 cars. Hence it is scarcely surprising that between 1898 and 1914 the capital of the heavy engineering companies flowed towards armaments rather than towards the new industries.[40]

In those large firms in the newer sectors where rapidly rising demand made possible major capital investments – as at Daimler, Siemens, or Armstrong-Whitworth – British manufacturers undertook rationalisations of factory layout and of the division of labour which pressed towards the limits of the new technology. In such cases, employers sought to appropriate to themselves and their supervisory staffs a greater share of the planning and direction of production and to enforce tighter workshop discipline. A separate tool-room was often established where skilled workers designed the jigs and fixtures necessary for repetition production, while also grinding tools to the appropriate angles for the rest of the work-force, tasks which had hitherto been the province of the individual craftsman working at his machine. Timekeeping also became increasingly important, together with new systems of supervision and incentive payment designed to speed up work. In many cases, a new type of supervisor, the 'feed and speed' man, was employed to select the optimum angles and speeds at which machines should be operated, usurping this traditional prerogative of the skilled worker; where incentive bonus systems were in force, a rate fixer might also set output norms and piece prices based on primitive methods of work measurement.[41] It should be remembered, however, that even in such advanced firms skilled craftsmen were still required in large numbers to design jigs and fixtures, to set tools for the less skilled, to repair and maintain the machinery, and even to perform production work where the nature of the job made mass-production methods impractical or uneconomical.

In the bulk of the engineering industry, however, the fragmented ownership of the firms, the structure of the market, and the nature of existing plant discouraged major retooling, so that innovation consisted rather in the introduction of new machine tools and work practices within a workshop organisation that remained structurally unchanged. Indeed, a close examination of engineering employers' conduct in the aftermath of their victory in 1898, based on case files of disputes over machine manning and payment by results in the EEF archive and on the reports of the ASE organising district delegates, suggests that their attempts to free themselves of craft regulation were more an extension of traditional strategies for work intensification and cost cutting than any break-through into a new rationalising or 'Taylorist' mode. These sources show that the main consequence of their victory was to enable employers to pursue more effectively those measures which had been set in motion before the lock-out but which had been impeded by local craft resistance. The promotion of handymen into skilled men's work, the extension of piece-work and systematic overtime, the subversion of apprenticeship into cheap boy labour dominated conflicts between skilled workers and their employers in the years after 1898 as they had before. The main novel element lay in employers' attempts to introduce new systems of supervision and incentive payment designed to boost output and reduce labour costs without major capital expenditure; even these grew out of methods already in force in some engineering workshops before the lock-out and tended in practice to degenerate into rate cutting exercises similar to those used in conventional piece-work.[42]

On the question of machine manning, for example, the evidence suggests that while handymen were promoted onto skilled men's work in significant numbers, the result fell short of a radical transformation of the division of labour. Thus, from the onset of the lock-out to mid-1898, EEF figures for such promotions in four districts comprising 121 firms reveal an average of 8.8 promotions per firm, with the number approaching 20.0 only in one inland district dominated by a few small firms.[43] During the years following the lock-out the typical machine manning dispute involved the promotion of a small number of handymen onto an isolated number of new machine tools or onto a rough part of fitters' work.

Engineering employers had long viewed piece-work as a key method of increasing output per man hour and lowering unit labour costs; with the relaxation of the ASE's opposition after 1898, they accordingly pressed forward the rapid extension of piece payment. By 1914, 46 per cent of turners and 37 per cent of fitters in Federated firms were paid by results.[44] But piece-work did not prove quite the royal road to efficient production that employers had envisaged, since it generated its own dilemmas, particularly in relation to the fixing of piece prices. Engineering workers believed that the additional effort involved in piece-work should be remunerated above the ordinary day rate and accordingly pressed for the initial price for each job to be fixed loosely enough for them to earn this bonus; often their strong shop floor organisation and intimate knowledge of the task enabled them to influence price fixing in this way. Once a particular task had been priced and worked for a period of time, however, it might become possible for the operative to turn out work at a vastly increased pace, and so earn a huge bonus if the rate were left unchanged. In such a case, the employer found his labour costs increasing proportionately with output and was therefore tempted to cut the rates. In turn, the workers, conscious that there was an implicit or explicit ceiling on piece earnings, operated a covert system of restriction of output among themselves to protect the rates.[45]

An alternative strategy which gained many adherents among engineering employers after 1898 was to replace simple piece-work with some form of 'premium bonus' system, whereby a maximum time was fixed for a task when it was assigned; if the worker completed the job in less than the time allotted, the proceeds were divided proprotionately between worker and employer. Depending on the system, the worker might receive one-half or one-third of the time saved, though the time wage was often formally guaranteed, marking an advance on most piece-work arrangements from the worker's point of view.[46] The theorists of the premium bonus systems argued that they would eliminate the tendencies towards restriction of output built into piece-work because 'no 'critical rate' of earnings looms in front of the [worker] to dampen his activity and lead him to slacken his energies'.[47]

Such descriptions of the rationale behind the premium bonus were not, however, completely convincing: in most such systems, the division of time saved between worker and employer shifted to the advantage of the latter as output increased. As those workers subjected to the system quickly realised, the premium bonus was intended to remove the need for rate cutting by building into the system of wage payment an 'automatic price breaker' restraining workers' earnings from increasing in direct proportion to output. In practice, moreover, the premium bonus often degenerated into a more old-fashioned form of rate cutting, since even under the Carlisle Agreement signed by the ASE and the EEF in 1902 a minor change in working practice could serve as the pretext for a sharp reduction in the time allowances. Similarly, the associated systems of work measurement meant that each man's individual performance could be ascertained and those not quite up to the maximum standard of efficiency weeded out.[48]

Generally speaking, the introduction of the premium bonus and tighter supervision and labour discipline went hand in hand, as various witnesses testified to the TUC joint committee's inquiry in 1909.[49] The systematic character of the changes involved emerges most clearly from the following account of the alterations in workshop practice introduced by a rationalising manager at the Thorneycroft works in Chiswick in 1905:[50]

> Hitherto, if a man deposited his check in the timekeeper's box within five minutes after starting-time, he could walk leisurely to his shop. Time recorders were installed in each department and we had to 'clock in' within two minutes or lose half an hour's pay. The plant started up before time, and we had to be at work as soon as the hooter stopped; discipline men marched round to see that we did. Charts indicating the feeds and speeds to be employed were fixed on every machine, and 'feed and speed' bosses, armed with 'feedometers', endeavoured to keep men and machines working to their fullest capacity. Emery wheels were taken from the shop, all tools being ground to theoretical angles by a skilled man. Men were forbidden to leave their job except when Nature demanded; labourers were sent for all tools and tackle. The lavatories were clean, but without doors and facing each other, with a perambulating inspector to see that no malingerer exceeded the seven minutes prescribed in a minatory notice.

While the principle of the 'progressive piece wage' had become relatively familiar to British employers by the early 1890s, its first application to British engineering workshops was developed by a number of Glasgow employers in the wake of the 1897–8 lock-out. By 1901, a number of large firms in various sectors had introduced some variant of the premium bonus, and after the Carlisle Agreement, its diffusion accelerated markedly. The 1906 wages census showed 4.6 per cent of all engineering workers on some form of the premium bonus, while an ASE survey three years later reported 9.2 per cent of its members working under such systems. As might be expected the large arms firms such as Vickers and Armstrong-Whitworth were most enthusiastic, although their example was followed by a considerable assortment of other engineering firms.[51]

It will be apparent that these new systems of supervision and incentive payment bore some affinity to the scientific management schemes taking root in the United States in the same period. But while British managers were acutely aware of American developments, most of the actual innovations introduced in their workshops had their roots in indigenous methods pioneered by the large arms firms, and even where some borrowing took place, as with the premium bonus, modifications were made to suit British conditions. British managers were on the whole suspicious of the systematic character of American theorising, reflecting not only the bias towards 'rule of thumb' methods in British entrepreneurial traditions, but also the limited possibilities for wholesale reorganisation of factory layout and other innovations. It was not generally possible to introduce the degree of standardisation American theorists recommended; similarly, British managers balked at the high supervision costs imposed by American practice and rejected above all the high-wage strategy which formed a central component of Taylorist, and later Fordist, thinking. Finally, they were rather less sanguine than their American counterparts about the possibility of inducing skilled workers to accept such innovations, a scepticism which would increase sharply with the resurgence of craft militancy in the run-up to the First World War.[52] Ultimately, British managers were unconvinced of the profitability of the American model; as one writer in the *Engineer* put it:[53] 'Unless scientific management enables us to produce more cheaply or more quickly than before, it is of little avail. We have yet to learn that British works managed on American lines have paid higher dividends than British works managed on British lines.'

While individual employers pressed home their piecemeal assault on craft regulation in their workshops, responsibility for maintaining the overall framework for managerial prerogative rested with the EEF. The Federation's approach to industrial relations in the decade and a half following the lock-out can best be characterised as a combination of strategic rigidity with tactical flexibility. On the strategic plane, the EEF remained committed to defending the central principles of the 1898 settlement, which guaranteed managerial freedom of action in workshop organisation; at the same time, the Federation sought to deploy its newly acquired collective strength to depress district wage rates in hopes of restoring British manufacturers' competitive edge in world markets.

The principal instrument of this double-pronged strategy was the new procedure for avoiding disputes inaugurated in 1898. Since no strike could 'constitutionally' take place until a deadlock had been reached at the national level, the Federation could use its national strength to choke off local flare-ups of craft militancy, as well as to stall district movements for wage advances until after the peak of the trade cycle had passed. Conscious of its dominant position and of the ASE executive's willingness to work within the Terms of Settlement, the EEF generally refrained from open threats of a national lock-out, preferring to isolate local resistance by bringing informal pressure to bear on the union leadership and by offering financial support to the firm concerned. Rule 48 of the EEF constitution stipulated that 'any member of a Federated Association who suffers a loss by the adoption of any measure necessitated by the Board shall be assisted by the Federation', with the normal practice being for the finance committee to make grants to the affected firm up to 45 per cent of the wages of the men on strike.[54]

The success of this strategy in the short run can be gauged from the outcomes of central conferences with the ASE and from the fate of unofficial strikes. Thus in none of the twenty-two machine manning cases discussed at central conference between 1898 and 1910 did the Federation make significant concessions to the demands of skilled workers. Similarly, the ASE executive refused official sponsorship to all strikes over machine manning or the premium bonus before 1912, and all of the major 'unconstitutional' strikes before that year proved unsuccessful. We can, moreover, identify certain cases where local craft resistance would almost certainly have been successful had it not been for the ASE executive's intervention.[55]

In this context, the Federation could afford to adopt a flexible line in negotiations with the ASE executive. Thus in certain particularly bitter machine manning disputes, it was prepared to recommend that employers minimise the displacement of old hands and give attention to the 'class of work' involved when making manning assignments. Similarly, it was willing to offer general but unenforceable guarantees against rate cutting on the premium bonus, to accept union amendments to the Terms of Settlement which called for greater mutuality in piece price fixing and representation of local officials at central conferences, and to trade a small decrease in hours for a reduction in the number of breaks in the working day. But where more significant issues were involved, as in the question of whether the 'current conditions' in force under the disputes procedure (until changed by a central conference) were to be those prevailing *before* or *after* a managerial innovation, the Federation remained an intransigent defender of managerial prerogative.[56]

An essential condition for the success of the EEF strategy was the determination of the ASE executive under George Barnes to work within the Terms of Settlement. Faced with the employers' determination to root out those vestiges of craft regulation which concerned the organisation of production, Barnes sought to convert the demands of his members into a form which could be made acceptable to employers by its concentration on questions of remuneration and collective bargaining. Hence Barnes saw in the premium bonus a means of protecting engineering workers against rate cutting and of securing them a share of the returns from increased output. As a new unionist, Barnes urged the ASE to 'accept specialisation' and introduced a new section for the less skilled; as a determined centraliser, he welcomed the enhanced control over local militancy built into the new disputes procedures, while fighting for amendments of the Terms of Settlement which would alleviate rank and file grievances.[57]

Despite its dominance over union policy in the decade after 1898, Barnes's strategy ultimately foundered on the combination of skilled engineers' defence of their craft status, the elaborate system of checks and balances in the ASE constitution, and the employers' determination to press forward a hard line on wages at the same time as a militant assault on craft regulation in the work-place. As their confidence returned in the years following the lock-out, ASE members in the districts resumed their pressure against the employment of handymen, enjoying considerable success where the firm involved was reluctant to refer the case to the EEF disputes procedure, while the premium bonus attracted even greater hostility. The union's own local officials generally supported the membership in their opposition to executive policy. A series of decisions by the delegate meeting and the final appeals court progressively circumscribed the executive's powers to withhold dispute benefit or order strikers back to work where it disapproved of their actions. The executive's inability to prevent major strikes against wage reductions on the Clyde in 1903 and on the northeast coast in 1908 precipitated Barnes's resignation, and with it the collapse of his conciliatory strategy.[58]

Barnes's departure exposed the contradictions in the employers' own strategy. Precisely because individual employers were determined to reduce unit labour costs through a mixture of traditional and novel methods rather than undertake a major programme of capital-intensive investment, they were rarely prepared to pay an effective premium to secure the consent of skilled workers. Wherever possible they preferred to employ the cheaper and more docile handymen, to evade the provisions of the Carlisle Agreement, and to depress real wages by pressing reductions when the trade cycle turned downwards while resisting advance in the up-swing. This approach left little possibility of success for the ASE executive's strategy of replacing the defence of craft regulation with rising wages obtained though collective bargaining. In this context, the joint pressures from the EEF and the union executive to centralise control over policy in the latter's hands resulted in the effective disintegration of executive authority.

With the erosion of executive authority after 1908, and the rapid tightening of labour markets after 1911, craft militancy among ASE members enjoyed a dramatic resurgence. Its effects could be seen first of all in an intensified militancy in machine manning disputes, which both mushroomed in number and proved vastly more successful from the skilled workers' perspective than at any time since 1898. More machine manning questions were raised by the ASE through the disputes procedure between 1911 and 1914 than in the previous twelve years taken together; for the first time ASE members won compromise settlements and even victories through the procedure in significant numbers, as their negotiators were rarely prepared to drop a machine manning case at any stage before the final failure to agree. The outcome of strikes on machine manning shows a similar pattern: where all previous strikes over machine manning had been defeated, the same was true in only two of ten cases in 1912–13, while four resulted in outright victories. Moreover, where previous strikes had been unofficial, the executive now sponsored three such strikes after the exhaustion of the procedure, all of which were quite successful. In several cases, large firms which had played a leading role in the assault on craft regulation were forced to accept limitations on their rights to promote handymen, as at Vickers in Barrow and at Dobson & Barlow in Oldham.[59]

This resurgence of craft militancy was by no means confined to the machine question, but extended to the reorganisation of the division of labour more broadly, singling out the premium bonus for special opprobrium. A TUC committee had called for the abolition of the premium bonus in 1909, and with the upturn in trade after 1911, local militants began to take matters into their own hands. Thus Vickers was prevented from introducing the system at its Sheffield works, while a 'Taylorist' experiment at Lever Bros resulted in the dismissal of an American manager after a mass meeting in protest; similarly, movements were launched against the premium bonus where it had already been established, as at Armstrong-Whitworth and in the east of Scotland.[60]

By 1912, this revived craft militancy had captured the ASE executive itself. In 1912 the old executive was replaced by a new one committed to the vigorous defence of craft regulation. Its first act was to ballot the membership on the abolition of the Terms of Settlement and the Carlisle Agreement, proposals which obtained huge majorities from the membership. At the end of 1913, the executive issued notice of its unilateral termination of these agreements and demanded the opening of negotiations for the forty-eight hour week. Constrained like its predecessor to establish some *modus vivendi* with the powerful EEF, the executive concluded a new agreement with the employers covering only the disputes procedure, but this was presented to the membership as an interim rather than a binding agreement.[61]

The dramatic resurgence of craft militancy in the ASE from 1908 onwards posed a major challenge to the tactics developed by the EEF in the years following the lock-out. But despite the setbacks experienced in local struggles over the division of labour, even where the Federation put its full financial weight behind the resisting firm, its leaders were not yet prepared to abandon the tactics which had produced such handsome results during the preceding decade. Long experience under the disputes procedure had bred a habit of negotiation among employers that was not easily broken, and the broad coalition necessary to sustain a national lock-out was difficult to mobilise in the context of a boom which tipped the balance of power in favour of rank and file militancy.

The EEF was therefore prepared to discuss amendments to the Terms of Settlement with successive ASE executives, while refusing any binding concessions on matters of principle. At the same time, it cautioned its members to follow procedures strictly and avoid unnecessary provocation of the union. Even when the new ASE executive unilaterally abrogated the Terms of Settlement and the Carlisle Agreement, the Federation's initial response was to reopen negotiations rather than threaten a general lockout.[62]

But even as the EEF was maintaining its traditional tactics through negotiations with the ASE, it was also strengthening its hand for a possible confrontation by drawing up plans for a mutual strike insurance fund. A scheme of this kind had flourished among ITEA members on the north-east coast during the mid-1890s, but had faded away with the advent of the more centralised EEF. George Barnes's failure to force the north-east coast strikers back to work in 1908 provoked the first efforts of employers in the district to revive the concept of a strike insurance or 'indemnity' fund on a national scale, but it was not until the revival of craft militancy had begun to threaten the foundations of the 1898 settlement that the Federation became prepared to implement it. The scheme itself was ultimately established in 1913.[63]

Thus, despite its initial cautious and moderate response to the changing industrial climate, the EEF was not prepared to see all that had been won in 1898 slip away. Sentiment was mounting among engineering employers for a renewed confrontation with the ASE, and the managing director of one of the more aggressive Scottish firms was doubtless correct when he observed in 1917 that:[64]

> The position just before the outbreak of the war was that, by consistent disregard of the Terms of Agreement, many of these provisions, though officially effective, had become inoperative, and these inroads on the powers of management in the shops had become so serious that, had war not intervened, the autumn of 1914 would probably have seen an industrial disturbance of the first magnitude.

III

While pressures for a renewed confrontation between the EEF and the

ASE over managerial prerogative were mounting before 1914, it required the radically intensified industrial conflict of the war and immediate post-war years to bring them to their culmination in the 1922 lock-out.

Following J. Hinton, historians have focused on dilution as the central flashpoint of wartime industrial unrest and have seen state intervention in the war economy as shaped by an alliance between a 'servile state' and the employers dominated by the latter's priorities.[65] A growing body of recent research strongly suggests, however, that both of these propositions are mistaken. Thus, careful studies of wartime industrial unrest on Clydeside have shown that conflicts over dilution, though significant, were overshadowed by other sources of workers' discontent with state intervention in industrial relations, such as restrictions on labour mobility, the operation of munitions tribunals, the extension of payment by results, the suspension of demarcation rules, and the lag of wages behind wartime inflation. Similarly, employers initially appear to have seen wartime state intervention as an occasion to roll back the pre-war gains of the unions not by pressing for far-reaching dilution schemes to transform the division of labour, but rather by using the provisions of the Munitions of War Act as a cover for the unilateral expansion of managerial prerogative and by demanding draconian restrictions on trade union activity. But in any case, the urgent demand for war material prompted state officials to strike compromises favourable to the unions, and employers were generally excluded from any influential role in the formation of state labour policy, as they repeatedly complained at the time.[66]

Nor did wartime dilution bring about a durable transformation of the division of labour in engineering. Whereas pre-war changes in the division of labour represented the response of private employers to the pressures and opportunities of the market, dilution was undertaken by the state in order to meet its immediate wartime needs. The resultant freedom from market constraints permitted the temporary development in munitions works of a division of labour more advanced than anything that had existed previously, even in the newer sectors of the industry.[67] But the specialised character of war production meant that this transformation of the division of labour was not designed to meet the long-term needs of British engineering manufacturers, and dilutees were concentrated on work which had little direct connection with pre-war output. Whereas pre-war developments had advantaged semi-skilled men at the expense of skilled craftsmen, wartime dilution involved an influx of large numbers of women and hence resulted in a temporary up-grading of the skills of most engineering craftsmen which enabled them to extract effective guarantees of the retoration of pre-war practices. Since most dilutees were engaged in the production of armaments, they flooded out of the industry with the cessation of wartime demand for munitions. Of the 819,000 women working in the industry in 1918, only 221,000 remained by 1921, as compared to 172,000 in July, 1914.[68]

If the war, then, marked no major watershed in the distribution of engineering skills, it had significant indirect repercussions on the struggle between skilled workers and their employers. The closing years of the war and the reconversion boom which followed saw an unprecedented explosion of industrial conflict and union growth. The EEF disbursed £93,000 from its indemnity fund between 1914 and 1922, of which £53,079 was spent in 1919 alone, a year in which strike days in the engineering, shipbuilding and metal industries reached four times their highest pre-war level. The ASE grew from 170,000 members in 1914 to nearly 300,000 in 1918; the new Amalgamated Engineering Union (AEU) had 450,000 members at its formation in 1920.[69] With this expansion of union numbers came a parallel expansion in bargaining power and combativity on the shop floor; the unions won the long-desired forty-seven hour week in 1919, and influential voices were raised among the growing network of shop stewards calling for the replacement of managerial authority with elements of workers' control. These painful and expensive experiences of engineering employers with the intensified shop floor militancy of the period – coupled with their frustration at government-enforced settlements during the war, which they believed to have favoured the unions – reinforced the determination that had been building up in the EEF before 1914 to restore the eroded hegemony of managerial prerogative in the work-place through a second confrontation with the unions.

With the onset of a severe recession in 1921, the employers moved onto the offensive. The EEF had expanded rapidly in influence and numerical strength, growing from 714 member firms in 1914 to 1469 in 1918 and 2600 in 1921. While pressing home a drastic and largely successful attack on wartime wage gains, the Federation also became increasingly aggressive on questions which it considered to touch on managerial prerogative, including machine manning, the payment of apprentices, and the regulation of overtime, all of which were the subject of local disputes in 1921. Early that year the EEF threatened a lock-out over these issues. In the event, it was AEU members' rejection of the Federation's claim that employers should be entitled to decide unilaterally when overtime should be worked and to introduce changes in working conditions before the exhaustion of the disputes procedure, that led the Federation to lock out all AEU members in March 1922. With unemployment running high, the EEF felt so sure of itself that it threatened to lock out forty-six other engineering unions unless they signed the memorandum defining managerial functions rejected by the AEU. By May 1922, the AEU's funds had dropped from £3,250,000 at its formation to £32,572. In June, the membership, recognising the futility of further resistance, voted to accept the EEF's revised definition of managerial functions, known as the York Memorandum.[70]

The Federation's victory, though more complete than in 1898, did not lead automatically to an effective transformation of the division of labour capable of restoring engineering manufactureres' position in world markets. In the short-term, employers had been able to slash their wage bills and to force the unions to recognise their authority in the work-place. But depressed demand for engineering products, coupled with sharpened foreign competition, rendered the barriers to rationalisation in the older sectors more severe than before 1914. Thus employers in these sectors confined themselves to those measures which required little capital investment, eschewing further mechanisation in favour of wage cuts, short-time work, extensions of payment by results, the promotion of the semi-skilled on to existing or replacement machinery, and the reduction of total capacity through mergers and amalgamations.[71] It was only in the newer sectors, such as motor cars and electrical goods where demand was rising rapidly and the unions had been driven almost entirely off the shop floor in 1922, that the employers secured large productivity gains through the wholesale introduction of new techniques such as the assembly line. Even there, however, employers appear to have relied more on payment by results and less on technological and organisational change than their American and German counterparts.[72]

The completeness of the employers' victory in 1922 and the persistence of mass unemployment in the older sectors ruled out any speedy revival of craft regulation comparable to developments after 1898. But the undisputed hegemony of employers in the work-place rested more on the broader state of the labour market than on the sophistication of their labour strategies. Hence the transition to fuller employment after 1936, coupled with the stabilisation of the labour force in the newer sectors, paved the way for a sharp revival of shop militancy, albeit with a changed centre of gravity and altered organisational forms.[73]

IV

A number of central points emerge from this account of British engineering employers' labour strategies. The first concerns the necessity of carefully situating these strategies within the broader economic context which shaped the decisions of individual employers in particular sectors. Too often, historians influenced by teleological models of economic development have assumed that the conjunction of foreign competition with mechanisation and organisational change will necessarily produce a rapid transformation of the division of labour. But as we have seen, engineering manufacturers were to varying degrees discouraged from a major turn towards mass production by structural features of the long-term development of the British economy, particularly the fragmented structure of established firms, the relative weakness of mass demand in the home market and the opportunities to evade foreign competition by moving into non-European markets where Britain's imperial position and early domination of the world economy gave them privileged access. Thus while British engineering employers mounted militant defences of managerial prerogative and were quick to introduce new techniques on a piecemeal basis, they generally eschewed, at least in the older sectors, the sort of major capital investment which would have been essential for a full-scale transformation of the division of labour.

It was this context, too, which shaped the wider strategies of the EEF. Just as much as trade unions, employers' associations are complex coalitions of often conflicting interests, particularly in so heterogeneous an industry as engineering. The original formation of the Federation, and even more the two national lock-outs of 1897–8 and 1922, depended on a combination of long-term pressures and short-term opportunities which overcame the divisions among employers oriented towards disparate product markets. Hence, despite its considerable resources and authority, the EEF executive was obliged to adapt itself to the investment decisions and labour practices of its constituents, and the major contradictions in its overall strategy can be traced to this source. Thus the demands of engineering employers for a downward pressure on wages undercut the Federation's efforts to neutralise craft resistance through the disputes procedure and the promotion of economistic collective bargaining, and it is this dilemma which helps to explain the paradox of long-term stagnation for the bulk of industry despite the successful assertion of managerial prerogative in repeated contests with the unions.

Notes

1. I am pleased to acknowledge the generous access to its archives provided by the Engineerng Employers' Federation. I am also grateful for valuable comments on earlier drafts to M. Dintenfass, H. Gospel, J. Lovell, J. Melling, A. Reid and S. Tolliday.
2. For the progressive response of British entrepreneurs, see S.B. Saul, 'The American Impact on British Industry, 1895–1914', *Business History* (1960); Saul, 'The Market and the Development of Mechanical Engineering, 1870–1914', *Economic History Review* (1967); Saul, 'The Machine-Tool Industry in Britain to 1914', *Business History* (1968a); and Saul, 'Engineering' in D.H. Aldcroft (ed.), *The Development of British Industry and Foreign Competition, 1875–1914*

(1968b). For the intensification of work-place conflict, see K. Burgess, *The Challenge of Labour* (1980), esp. chapter 3.

3. H. Clegg, A. Fox and A.F. Thompson, *A History of British Trade Unions, 1889-1910*, vol. 1 (1964), Chapters 2 and 4; K. Burgess, *The Origins of Industrial Relations* (1975); and R. Price, *Masters, Unions and Men* (1980).

4. K. Burgess, 'Technological Change and the 1852 Lockout in the British Engineering Industry', *International Review of Social History* (1969); and Burgess, 'Trade Union Policy and the 1852 Lockout in the British Engineering Industry', *International Review of Social History* (1972).

5. Burgess (1975), pp. 25-41; J.B. Jefferys, *The Story of the Engineers* (1946), pp. 16-17, 55-8; M. and J.B. Jefferys, 'The Wages, Hours and Trade Customs of the Skilled Engineer in 1861', *Economic History Review* (1947); J.H. Zeitlin, *Craft Regulation and the Division of Labour: Engineers and Compositors in Britain, 1890-1914*, (Warwick University PhD 1981 hereafter cited as Zeitlin *Thesis*), pp. 38-50, 96-102.

6. Royal Commission on the Depression of Trade and Industry in 1886: *Second Report*, P.P. 1886, XXII, app. IV; and *Third Report*, pp. 1886, XXIII, qs. 10, 963-7.

7. W.A. Lewis, *Growth and Fluctuations, 1870-1913* (1978), pp. 34-57; Saul (1968b); R. Floud, 'The Adolescence of American Engineering Competition, 1860-1900', *Economic History Review* (1974); I.W. McLean, 'Anglo-American Engineering Competition, 1870-1914', *Economic History Review* (1976).

8. Royal Commission on Labour, Group A, *Minutes of Evidence*, P.P. 1893-4, XXXII, app. XLVI; Jefferys (1946), pp. 100-1; Zeitlin, *Thesis*, pp. 105-8.

9. Saul (1960), (1968a) and (1968b); Floud (1974); Zeitlin, *Thesis*, pp. 110-12.

10. R.C. on Labour, app. XLVI, and testimony of ASE witnesses in ibid.; Webb Coll. EA XVI f. 6; Zeitlin, *Thesis*, pp. 113-17.

11. R.C. on Labour, app. XLVI; 1886 Wages Census, P.P. 1893-4, LXXIII; Zeitlin, *Thesis*, pp. 128-9 and table 5.

12. Col. H. Dyer to B. Potter, 15 October 1891, Webb Coll. EA XXI, f. 18; ASE *Quarterly Report*, June 1894.

13. Committee on the Organisation and Administration of the Army (Morley Committee), *Minutes of Evidence*, P.P. 1887, XIV, especially qs. 8998-9016; W.G. Gordon, *Foundry, Forge and Factory* (1890), p. 34; D.F. Schloss, *Methods of Industrial Remuneration* (1898),p. 15; S.C. on Government Contracts, *Minutes of Evidence*, qs. 2468, 2506, 2536; B. Taylor, 'The Machine Question and Eight Hours', *Cassier's Magazine* (1897); for a similar description of these supervisors from a trade union perspective, see R.C. on Labour, qs. 23, 157.

14. For the capacities of the new technology see N. Rosenberg, 'Technological Convergence in the American Machine Tool Industry, 1840-1910', *Journal of Economic History* (1963); Saul (1960), esp. p. 22; and R. Floud, *The British Machine Tool Industry, 1850-1914* (1976), chapter 2. For the limited impact on British industry before the 1890s see the various articles by Saul cited above and Floud (1974).

15. Saul (1960), (1968a), (1968b); Floud (1974); A.E. Harrison, 'The Competitiveness of the British Cycle Industry, 1890-1914', *Economic History Review* (1969); J. Blackman and E.M. Sigsworth, 'The Home Boom of the 1890s', *Yorkshire Bulletin of Economic and Social Research* (1965).

16. ASE, *Monthly Report*, December 1889, and *Quarterly Reports* June and September 1894; Webb Coll. EA. XVI, f. 6, pp. 42-53; and B.M. Weekes, *The Amalgamated Society of Engineers, 1880-1914* (Warwick PhD 1970), chapter 1.

17. E. Wigham, *The Power to Manage: A History of the EEF* (1973), chapter 1.

18. Webb Coll. EA XXI, f. 18.

19. Details of the scheme are given in a letter from B.C. Browne (Hawthorn, Leslie & Co.) to A. Smith (Secretary, EEF), 15 May 1912, EEF I (4) 1.

20. Clegg, Fox and Thompson (1964), p. 82; Wigham (1973) pp. 20–4.
21. See Clegg, Fox and Thompson (1964), chapter 1. On the local level, however, where product and labour markets might be more homogeneous, there is some evidence that district associations of the EEF did attempt to fix the prices of some products, as in the textile engineering districts of Lancashire. It also seems clear from post-war discussions about wage policy that EEF districts sought to prevent their members from paying wages above locally agreed levels except through systems of payment by results: see Lewchuk in this volume.
22. EEF, 'Conditions of Federation' (1896), reprinted in Wigham (1973), app. B, pp. 280–1.
23. Letter from EEF to ASE December 1896, quoted in Weekes (1970), p. 84; cf. also EEF, *Executive Minutes*, 26 November 1896 and Wigham (1973), p. 33.
24. On the dispute at Dunsmuir and Jackson's, see EEF, *Executive Minutes*, 24 August 1896; Weekes (1970), p. 83; and Wigham (1973), pp. 32–3.
25. EEF, *Executive Minutes*, 13 August 1896 and 12 March 1897, *Conference between the ASE and the EEF on the Machine Question, April 1897.*
26. ASE, *Monthly Journal and Report*, June–July 1897; ASE, *Notes on the Engineering Trades Lockout* (1898); Wigham (1973), pp. 38–43; Weekes (1970), pp. 190–2.
27. See R.O. Clarke, 'The Dispute in the British Engineering Industry, 1897–8', *Economica* (1957); Weekes (1970), chapter 4; Wigham (1973), chapter 2; Jefferys (1946), pp. 144–8; Clegg, Fox and Thompson (1964), pp. 161–8.
28. Jefferys (1946), p. 292; Burgess (1975), p. 47; ASE (1898), pp. 4, 20–7; Clarke (1957); Zeitlin, *Thesis* pp. 197–200.
29. EEF, *Executive Minutes*, 24 April and 26 November 1896, 21 March 1897; EEF, *List of the Federated Engineering and Shipbuilding Employers who Resisted the Demand for a 48 Hours Working Week, 1897–8* (1898); EEF, *Executive Reports*, 1897–8, passim; F.W. Hirst, 'The Policy of the Engineers', Economic Journal (1898), p. 127; ASE, *Monthly Journal and Report*, July 1897. For a sample of employers' views see the articles and letters reprinted in ASE (1898) and *The Engineers' Strike: A Series of Articles Reprinted from 'Engineering'* (1898).
30. Royal Commission on Trades Disputes and Combinations, *Minutes of Evidence*, P.P. 1906, LVI, q. 2574; EEF, *Executive Report*, 35, 13 August 1897; S.Z. de Ferranti, 'How to Win a Lockout', reprinted in Wigham (1973), app. C; Clegg, Fox and Thompson (1964), pp. 163–4; G. Alderman, 'The National Free Labour Association', *International Review of Social History* (1976); Jefferys (1946), p. 147.
31. See the strike at Dunsmuir and Jackson in 1896. Dyer to the *Times,* 5 September 1897, reprinted in ASE (1898), pp. 74–5; A. Siemens to *Daily News,* 7 October 1897, quoted in Clegg, Fox and Thompson (1964), pp, 164–5; *Engineering,* 24 September 1897.
32. For the text of the employers' terms and the debate over the threat to collective bargaining, see ASE (1898), pp. 116–26, 133–7, 148–52; Clegg, Fox and Thompson (1964), pp. 166–7; Zeitlin, *Thesis*, pp. 202–6.
33. L. Cassier, 'The British Engineers' Strike of 1897–8: Its Lessons and Results'; *Cassier's Magazine* (April 1900), p. 495.
34. M.L. Yates, *Wages and Labour Conditions in British Engineering* (1937).
35. E.H. Phelps Brown and M. Browne, *A Century of Pay* (1968), pp. 174–95; Floud (1976), pp. 187–9. For market share see Saul (1968b), p. 229.
36. While there is no good study of the structure of firms in engineering, see Saul (1968b) and Board of Trade, *Report of the Departmental Committee on the Position of the Engineering Trades after the War*, P.P. 1918, XIII; for the special case of machine tools, where the general complaint was that firms were insuffi-

ciently specialised, see Saul (1968a); Floud (1976), chapter 3; and D.H. Aldcroft, 'The Performance of the British Machine-Tool Industry in the Inter-war Years', *Business History Review* (1966). Except for the arms firms, which combined steel making and naval shipbuilding with ordnance work, no engineering firm figures among Payne's list of the fifty largest British firms in 1905. See P.L. Payne, 'The Emergence of the Large-Scale Company in Great Britain, 1870–1914', *Economic History Review* (1967); and L. Hannah, *The Rise of the Corporate Economy* (1976), chapter 6, especially p. 97; and H. Gospel, 'The Development of Management Structure and Strategy' in K. Thurley and S. Wood (eds.), *Management and Industrial Relations* (1983).

37. See Saul (1968b), especially pp. 195–205 and Saul (1967); Lewis (1978), chapters 4–5; P.L. Cottrell, *British Overseas Investment in the 19th Century* (1975), esp. pp. 11–15. For a similar overall argument to that advanced in the previous two paragraphs, see E.J. Hobsbawm, *Industry and Empire* (1969), pp. 187–9.

38. For the growth of the new sectors, see Jefferys (1946), p. 120; Saul, 'The Motor Industry in Britain to 1914', *Business History* (1962). For obstacles to their further development, see I. Byatt, 'Electrical Products' in D.H. Aldcroft, *Development of British Industry* (1968); R.E. Cotterall, 'Electrical Engineering' in N. Buxton and D.H. Aldcroft (eds.), *British Industry between the Wars* (1979). On the more general weakness of mass markets in Britain, see J. Saville, 'Some Retarding Factors in the British Economy before 1914', *Yorkshire Bulletin of Economic and Social Research* (1961); and L. Hannah, 'Visible and Invisible Hands in Great Britain', in A. Chandler and H. Daems (eds.), *Managerial Hierarchies* (1980).

39. I. Byatt, *The British Electrical Industry, 1875–1914* (1979), pp. 156–7; Cotterall (1979), p. 248.

40. See Lewchuk in this volume; R.J. Irving, 'New Industries for Old? Some Investment Decisions of Sir W.G. Armstrong, Whitworth Company, 1900–1914', *Business History* (1975).

41. For broad descriptions of the implications of the new techniques, see D.S. Landes, *The Unbound Prometheus* (1972), pp. 292–323; Jefferys (1946), pp. 124–5; Saul (1960), pp. 28–9; J.W.F. Rowe, *Wages in Practice and Theory* (1928), app. III; C. Littler, 'Deskilling and Changing Structures of Control' in S. Wood (ed.), *The Degradation of Work* (1982).

42. Zeitlin, *Thesis*, pp. 357–71.

43. EEF, *Emergency Reports,* 1 June and 13 September 1898; Zeitlin, *Thesis*, pp. 357–8 and table 9.

44. Yates (1937), p. 117.

45. For an extremely explicit discussion of rate cutting, see the testimony of the managers of the various departments of the Woolwich Arsenal to the Morley Committee in 1887.

46. For descriptions of the various systems, see G.D.H. Cole, *The Payment of Wages* (1925), chapters 5–6; W.F. Watson, *The Worker and Wage Incentives* (1934); Yates (1937), pp. 85–8; and Weekes (1970), pp. 117–19. For a contemporary account, see the articles reprinted from the *Engineer* (1902) as *The Premium System of Paying Wages* (5th edn 1917).

47. J. Slater Lewis, 'The Labour Factor in the Intensity of Output', *Engineering Magazine* (November 1899), pp. 203–4.

48. TUC Joint Committee, *Report on the Premium Bonus System* (1910), pp. 25, 31, 34, 62, 73.

49. TUC Joint Committee (1910), pp. 34–5.

50. Watson (1934), pp. 10–11.

51. Schloss (1898), chapter 6; Jefferys (1946), p. 130; Weekes (1970), p. 178; P.P. 1911, LXXXVIII, part I; TUC Joint Committee (1910), pp. 11, 73–5; and the list of cases in the EEF Archives, Series P.

52. For a critique of the over-systematic approach of scientific management, see

Engineering, 1 January 1907; on high supervision costs, see *The Engineer*, 14 November 1913, p. 521; on fears of worker resistance, see ibid. and D. Smith and P.L.C.N. Pickworth, *Engineers' Costs and Economical Workshop Production* (1914).

53. *The Engineer*, 14 November 1913, p. 521. For general discussions of the reception of scientific management in Britain, see Weekes (1970), chapter 5; M. Barenbert, 'The Reception of Scientific Management in Britain' (unpublished paper, Harvard University, 1976); Littler (1982); and Littler, 'Taylorism in Britain in the Inter-war Years' (paper presented to SSRC Conference on Business and Labour History); and Lewchuk, in this volume.

54. EEF, *General letter* 171, 30 April 1913; *Emergency Committee Report* 75, 30 April 1913.

55. Zeitlin, *Thesis*, tables 10–11.

56. EEF, *Central Conference*, case 294, p. 66 and case 11, p. 27; EEF, *Executive Report*, 229, 4 April 1900: 'Request by the ASE, SEMS and UMWA for Amendment of the Terms of Settlement'; *Verbatim Report of Conferences between the EEF and the ASE, SEMS and UMWA, December–May 1900*; EEF Archives A (2) 5–9: verbatim transcripts of further conferences *re* amendments to the Terms of Settlement, 1906–7; EEF, *Executive Minutes*, 1905–7, passim.

57. G.N. Barnes, 'The Uses and Abuses of Organisation among Employers and Employed', *Engineering Magazine* (January 1901); Zeitlin, *Thesis*, pp. 372–406

58. ASE ODD reports in the union's *Monthly Journal and Report*, 1898–1904, passim; and Zeitlin, *Thesis*, pp. 367–77, 387–405; R. Croucher, *The ASE and Local Autonomy, 1898–1914* (Warwick MA 1971); Weekes (1970), chapter 6.

59. Zeitlin, *Thesis*, tables 10–11; 'Verbatim Transcript of Local Conference, Barrow in Furness, 13 February 1913'. EEF Archives M (6) 8; EEF, *Executive Report for 1913; Central Conference*, case 306, p. 68.

60. TUC Joint Committee (1910); S. Pollard, *History of Labour in Sheffield* (1959), p. 232; ASE, *Monthly Journal and Report, January 1913; EEF, Central Conference,* case 681, p. 136; and cases 1436 and 1439, pp. 298–300.

61. Weekes (1970), chapter 8; 'Verbatim Transcript of Special Central Conference between the ASE and the EEF, 13 February 1914', EEF Archives A (4) 6; EEF, *Executive Minutes*, 7 February 1913, 16–17 April 1914.

62. EEF, *General Letters* 176 and 181, 13 November 1913 and 14 April 1914; EEF, *Executive Minutes*, 13 October 1913.

63. For details of the scheme see the various letters and drafts in EEF Archives I (4) 2; *Minutes of Executive Board Meeting*, 16 May 1912; EEF, *General Letters* 171 and 175, 30 April 1913 and 1 October 1913, EEF Archives I (4) 2.

64. J.R. Richmond (Weir's), *Some Aspects of Labour and Its Claims in the Engineering Industry*, Presidential Address to the Glasgow University Engineering Society (1917).

65. J. Hinton, *The First Shop Stewards' Movement* (1973).

66. J. Melling, ' "Non-Commissioned Officers", British Employers and their Supervisory Workers, 1880–1920', *Social History* (1980); and J. Turner, 'The Politics of the Business Community During the First World War' (unpublished paper, Bedford College, 1980).

67. See the official *History of the Ministry of Munitions* (8 vols., 1920–4), esp. IV/2, pp. 74–5, 79.

68. G.D.H. Cole, *Trade Unionism and Munitions* (1923) esp. p. 196; Hinton (1973), pp. 63–4; B. Drake, *Women in the Engineering Trades* (1917), pp. 8–9; Yates (1937), pp. 146–7.

69. EEF Archives I (4) 12; Hinton (1973), p. 37; Jefferys (1946), pp. 191, 194; Wigham (1973), pp. 121–4; Jefferys (1946), pp. 218–22.

70. Wigham (1973), pp. 121–4; Jefferys (1946), pp. 218–227. For an account of the lock-out and its consequences in Conventry, see F. Carr, *Engineering Workers and the Rise of Labour in Coventry, 1914–39* (Warwick, PhD 1979), chapter 4.

71. See Zeitlin, *Thesis*, pp. 466–72.

72. Carr (1979), chapters 4–5; R.C. Whiting, *The Working Class in the 'New Industry Towns' between the Wars: The Case of Oxford* (Oxford, DPhil 1977), chapters 2–4; R. Church, *Herbert Austin* (1979), pp. 98–101; and especially Lewchuk in this volume.

73. See my 'The Emergence of Shop Steward Organisation and Job Control in the British Car Industry; A Review Essay', *History Workshop Journal* (1980), and the literature cited therein.

3 Employers, Industrial Welfare, and the Struggle for Work-Place Control in British Industry, 1880–1920
Joseph Melling

One of the deficiencies in the study of employers, in labour and business history, concerns the welfare services they have provided. Although acknowledged to be highly untypical, the tracts produced by those self-acknowledged pioneers of modern enlightened management, the Nonconformist foodstuffs manufacturers, continue to exercise a significant influence on the minds of historians. P. Mathias points out how the Quaker confectioners and similar progressives were able to provide welfare in their sheltered domestic markets and with a work-force benefiting from a hygienic environment in which to produce goods for mass consumption.[1] Other writers have traced the origins of such humane and benevolent regimes to the experiments carried out by industrialists as different as Arkwright, Peel, Dale, Owen, and Salt, though there is less agreement about the degree of philanthropy which market pressures permitted.[2] The danger of accepting contemporary ideology as factual account is often recognised, but there remains little analysis of the meanings of 'paternalism' or the definitions of 'welfare' itself.

Those works which attempt to situate welfare provision in a wider perspective of economic development usually disagree over the basic functions of non-monetary services. Liberal economists characteristise early forms of social amenities as relics of pre-industrial (and pre-bourgeois) society, whilst more radical interpretations portray such 'fringe benefits' as the rational response of efficient capitalist management to the labour needs of the enterprise.[3] Much more work has been carried out in Germany and the United States on such employer policies, ranging from the initiatives of Siemens and Krupp to the model settlements of Carnegie, Morgan and Pullman.[4] Yet there are similar unresolved questions in these countries. Liberal German scholars have tended to cite the authoritarian predilections of Stumm and his contemporaries as evidence of the 'feudalisation' of the industrial bourgeoisie, whilst a new school of historians argues strongly against the suggestion that Germany was anything other than a dynamic and economically progressive (if politically authoritarian) industrial state.[5] The absence of a feudal heritage poses rather different questions in the American context, whose pace of industrialisation paralleled that of Germany after 1870. It is also true, however, that the traditionalist areas of the southern United States were probably more pronounced welfarist regions than either the East Coast or Midwest states long after the Civil War ended.[6]

The limited debate on welfare provision, therefore, raises some fundamental questions about the origins of industrial capitalism and the character of labour relations. In the British case, serious discussion of such issues has been hindered by the imprecise usage of terms such as 'paternalism', which suggest at once the patriarchial care of an individual capitalist and the traditional inequalities of pre-bourgeois society. One recent study of Victorian England suggests that the 'paternalism' of Lancashire's cotton towns derived precisely from these ideas and practices at the level of culture and politics – establishing a powerful continuity during the transition to industrial society.[7] Welfare services were only one expression of the successful integration of paternal care in the large family firm, male domination in the family economy of the factory itself, and bourgeois supremacy in the voting of a deferential proletariat. Whilst recognising certain features of hierarchical dependence at both the work-place and in politics, it is difficult to accept the emphasis given to a particular strand of bourgeois ideology in such accounts. Most importantly, there is insufficient attention to the definitions of both welfare and paternalism, which is essential for the effective comparison of industries or national economies.

Definitions and Functions of Industrial Welfare

Industrial welfare may be defined quite simply as the provision of a service by an employer upon a non-wage basis for his employees. This implies a nexus beyond the wage contract, though it does not confine the groups serviced to the manual wage earning sector. There are three ways of approaching welfare provision: empirically, purposively, and functionally. Empirical approaches define welfare in terms of the range and content of amenities, though the attempts at comprehensive surveys leads to an extremely loose understanding of boundaries between areas of welfare.[8] Purposive analyses attempt to outline the motives for provision, ranging from the employer's need for labour to his efforts in supplementing state schemes.[9] Functional models outline the objective functions which welfare seems to fulfil in the firm or an industry, irrespective perhaps of the intentions of the employers or the nature of the service.[10] It is arguable that we need an insight into each of these facets of welfare before a full description of its significance in private enterprise is possible.

None of these approaches, however, can be considered adequate until they are located in the wider context of production and economic development, generated by a particular set of market relations. At the same time it is vital that these relations be set within a specific historical period rather than relying upon abstract models of costs and benefits in provision. The provision of industrial housing, for example, dates from a period when unfree bond labour was used in coal mines and mineral workings in colliery districts.[11] Such services evolved alongside the emergence of market relationships between capital and labour.

It is with the supply and efficiency of labour that the industrial employer is primarily concerned in the provision of services, seeking to create and regulate a pool of willing workers. Thus the supply, efficiency, and discipline of labour were continuing themes in welfare administration after the development of market relations. Services are provided where wages contracts cannot accomplish this formal and immediate subordination to the employer. They may be supplementary to wage payment, but are rarely incidental or optional extras and cannot be considered as peripheral factors in most cases. The ways in which these calculations of labour needs were phrased by employees were neither theoretical nor neutral estimations of optimum requirements. Persistent resistance by labour to regulation in the market and at the work-place signified deeper antagonisms over the control of labour and the fruits of production, overshadowing management strategies to improve output or increase efficiency.

Economic Advance, Work-Place Conflict and the Context for Welfare

Recent literature on work-place conflict and control has challenged many of the assumptions found in classical Marxist accounts of technical change, including the notion of a progressive deskilling and subordination of the work-force.[12] Historians tend to emphasise, in the manner of Stinchcombe, the large number of sectors where craft administration of production has persisted as a result of fluctuating market conditions and physical constraints on close supervision.[13] Such qualifications seem particularly appropriate in studies of late-Victorian and Edwardian industry, where Britain enjoyed a relative abundance of skilled workers trained in a variety of handicraft or operative techniques.[14] Contemporary observers tended to argue that the appearance of machinery to deal with the heavier physical tasks only increased the need for an all-round knowledge and the ability to organise work. This nurturing of 'mental culture' in the workshop developed alongside the manual skills needed by the journeymen, which could only by gained by practical experience.[15] One writer identified the shipbuilding industry as an exemplary case where a very large proportion of skilled hull construction was 'still done by hand, and, in the nature of things, must continue to be so'.[16] Even if the customs of craft administration sustained the influence of the trade societies, most employers could not contemplate a comprehensive restructuring of work or the work-force under such conditions.

The strength of craft controls was evident in the prevailing system of apprenticeship and technical training in major skilled occupations before the First World War. Improvements in technical education from the 1880s were mainly seen in the spread of evening and (more rarely) day classes which supplemented, rather than superseded, established craft training under the journeymen at work. As late as the First World War the director of the most advanced apprenticeship school then existing, acknowledged that general understanding of industrial processes could not suffice without practical workshop experience of the trade.[17] It is significant that his arguments focused on the moral and educational influence of such classes and – like welfare amenities in general – technical schools had become part of the 'human factor' philosophy of management, which argued that the 'human element is the most important factor in every undertaking'.[18] His audience reminded the speaker that 90 per cent of all factory boys would remain workmen all their lives, tempering his enthusiasm for what was seen as elaborate provisions.[19]

The conservatism of many employers during the war itself only confirms the impression of a resilient craft apprenticeship, where even an advanced sector like engineering encouraged the diversified all-round training which enabled boys to deal with specialised as well as standardised work.[20] Whilst a growing number of firms realised the advantages of formal instruction which gave journeymen the ability to read blueprints with greater literate (rather than practical) knowledge, the low costs of using craftsmen to train adolescent workers whilst completing jobs was a strong disincentive to radical change.[21] Throughout the early and middle decades of the twentieth century there is undeniable evidence of employers' tacit support for a 'traditional' mode of apprenticeship which provided skilled men even at the price of union influence over trade entrants.[22] The existence of trainee labour also offered one simple means of effective dilution, with the more aggressive firms expanding their apprentice ratio in periods of growing competition or union weakness.[23] There were complicated costs and benefits to be derived from the existing craft practices which managements calculated with regard to labour relations as well as market environments.

For these and other reasons the issue of work-place supervision became a cause for growing concern amongst industrialists as firms sought greater flexibility in the deployment of men and machines. In American industry, it is true, foremen enjoyed comparable power and influence before the advent of mass production and Taylorism, though the foreman's empire was under imminent threat of invasion by the turn of the century.[24] British supervision in the craft trades demanded considerable technical expertise and organising ability, involving the application of complex drawings and calculations to the job in hand. The foremen were invariably promoted from the ranks of journeymen and there is evidence from a wider variety of trades that foremen often occupied prominent positions in craft societies, enforcing collective practices with or without their employers' knowledge.[25] It was this contrast with American industry, where foremen were more rarely attached to trade unions, that disturbed Colonel Dyer of Armstrong-Whitworth.[26]

Faced with an accumulation of restrictions on their powers of workplace organisation, British employers made a series of efforts to improve the general efficiency of their concerns, with initiatives in different sectors noticeable from the 1880s. Innovations were perhaps most dramatic in the locomotive, armaments and machine tool sectors of engineering. As early as the 1840s the great locomotive works at Crewe and Swindon were noted for their detailed organisation and specialist division of work, with the Crewe works covering 85 acres and employing 6000 men and boys by the 1880s.[27] It was at this stage that gifted managers such as F.W. Webb carried administrative and financial, as well as industrial, reforms into effect at the great works – with an increase of timekeeping and inspection personnel to supplement the trade foremen now working to prepared payment systems.[28] Even more impressive were the changes made at the plants of large armaments manufacturers such as Armstrong, which consciously assumed a leading managerial and strategic role on several occasions during these decades. Military equipment necessarily stood in the forefront of precision designing and quality finishing, though the arms manufacturers were keen to reduce labour costs on rougher machine work by introducing piece-work and handymen.[29] The serious conflict at the Maxim–Nordenfelt works indicated the extent of management encroachments on the domain of craft administration and the resistance to pacing of repetition work.[30] Even in the craft-intensive sectors of marine engineering, employers such as Benjamin Browne were insisting on the need to reduce costs during the austere climate of mounting competition from abroad.[31]

These attempts to improve output and profitability lacked the general coherence that could only come from shared experiences of market conditions and labour problems across industries, though the extent of technological diffusion and convergence of working methods should not be overlooked. Amidst the varying tactics and initiatives of different industrialists, it is possible to chart the spread of more *systematic* management that fell short of the formulae offered by Taylor but marked a significant advance in the British context. Lacking the abstract principles of industrial organisation or mechanical motion developed by subsequent theorists, various employers introduced useful improvements by empirical observation. As one speaker noted during a discussion on scientific management in 1917, it would be a mistake to assume that employers had neglected questions of workshop organisation:[32] 'An inference of that nature would be a libel on many firms and managers, for although the methods involved had not been universally adopted, there were without doubt, many who had very successfully applied some systematised methods of management, which deserved to be called scientific.' It was the vitality of craft and union resistance in the face of such efforts by many individual firms which convinced large numbers of industrialists of the need to enforce managerial prerogatives by collective action. The stronger and larger firms in the metal working trades led the movement to integrate regional associations in national federations during the decade following 1889. With the emergence of a strong managerialist leadership inside the new federations went the creation of a dedicated secretariat, composed of able professionals, such as Allan Smith, trained in legal firms and well-equipped to deal with union negotiators or the ruffled sensibilities of individual employers. These business officials advised employers, such as Colonel Dyer of Armstrong, striving to translate particular enterprise practices into Engineering Employers' Federation (EEF) policies and thereby offer a solid front to the craft societies. This resulted in the peculiar emphases given to EEF strategies during its early months of existence, as Dyer pressed on his fellow employers the vital importance of the machine question and their 'right to appoint any man they might choose to the machines in their shops'.[33] It had also implications for the conduct of the great 1897–8 struggle, as Zeitlin and others have shown.[34]

The movement amongst employers for an assertion of management power was not confined to engineering, nor to sectors with a rapid pace of mechanical innovation at the work-place. Within a few years of the employers' victory over the Amalgamated Society of Engineers (ASE), the shipbuilding associations were discussing a similar offensive in the craft-dominated shipyards, with Andrew Noble advising the Tyne employers that any review of wage rates or yard management should be made with 'the experience of the Engineering Employers before them'.[35] There followed two years of internal debate amongst the shipbuilders, culminating in the deliberations of 1904, as the original handful of proposals developed into twelve detailed arguments on various aspects of management, including principles of business prerogatives, rating of workmen, payment systems, apprenticeship, supervision and machine tool manning.[36] Although the shipbuilders encountered almost insuperable problems of occupation demarcation and craft control, they made significant gains on apprenticeship ratios, premium bonus and introduction of machine tools before and during the First World War.[37]

One vital element in the ability of the craft societies to reconstitute their defences after management encroachments was undoubtedly the provident benefits which the unions administered. Some union historians have argued that the conduct of financial management and distribution of trade benefits formed the major responsibilities of national officials throughout the later nineteenth century, and leaders such as Robert Knight certainly preferred to accumulate reserves than engage in costly strike actions.[38] This delicate balance rested on the assumption that union funds were protected against civil actions, thereby encouraging voluntaryism in thrift provision as well as collective bargaining. The controversies surrounding the Taff Vale decision, and the legal guerilla warfare which characterised the succeeding years, abruptly ended this equilibrium and influenced both business and union strategies. Clyde employers such as John Inglis now favoured legal protection (or verification) of management powers under contractual obligations, with Inglis writing to Hunter of the Tyneside employers in 1902, that:[39]

> I think some of us are disposed to exaggerate the difficulty of coming to an arrangement on the subject of yard management – and for my part I believe the Union leaders only require to be convinced that they have a united body of employers to face – they are all fearful of their funds and will not squander them in a contest where all honest men will consider them in the wrong.

Leaders such as Inglis were sternly prepared for a war of attrition which would exhaust the societies financially as well as morally, helped by the uncertainties and anxieties now surrounding their legal status. Before they approached the unions, the same employers went on to take the highest legal advice on their proposed conditions of management. The discussion of the foreman question took a considerable time, with counsel dubious about the stipulation of non-unionisation as a pre-condition for employment of supervisors.[40] During ensuing debates on the foreman problem, various industrialists pressed for an extension of an engineering benefit scheme that offered a serious alternative to society benefits, whilst Andrew Noble had noted the value of free foreman labour at Elswick engineering shops.[41]

Throughout such campaigns, the northern industrialists were able to articulate a philosophical as well as economic case for freedom of contract and liberty at the work-place. The draft memorandum of Allan Smith emphasised this aspect to such a degree that Hunter objected to its expressions of generosity. Inglis added the postscript:[42] 'I am quite in accord with Mr. Hunter . . . [that] there is no need for us to appear as philanthropists first and business men afterwards – we benefit the workmen incidentally but our motives are selfish to begin with.' The same sobering corrective could be applied to the evaluation of employers' welfare projects in these decades. Industrial benefits did not suddenly appear with the onset of work-place conflict or systematic management, any more than they sprang from the enlightened imagination of Cadbury or Rowntree. During the 1870s, Sir Joseph Whitworth had explained to a group of London foremen the profit bonus scheme operating at his concern since 1874, whereby employee shareholding could resolve many of the fears associated with the growth of limited liability and remote direction of companies.[43] What is significant about the spread of benefit schemes after 1880 are the qualitative and administrative developments linked to the rise of employers' organisations and the ascendancy of a determined managerialist leadership within the ranks of the employers. It is interesting that, after absorbing the Whitworth interests in their growing empire, the Armstrong employers should have promoted their own profit sharing facilities along with a superannuation scheme for supervisors, which attracted controversial attention during the 1897–8 struggles as the foremen resisted the pressures of management to leave their unions in favour of the company amenities.[44] Dyer probably used this scheme as the model for a benefit society financed and operated by the new Federation, serving as a client body with representation for foremen as well as management. This growing coherence of business welfare policies and their integration with a wider programme of reforms brought about through collective action signifies a new departure in management thinking that contributed to the debates on the 'human element' at the work-place, reflecting a growing concern with the retention of legitimacy and the assertion of work-place control. The following discussion of the engineering industry does not form an archetypal *or* an isolated case, though the strategic and ideological importance of struggles in that sector were appreciated by contemporaries – whether employers in neighbouring trades or unions sustained by benefit provisions.

Employers and Welfare in the Engineering Industry, 1880–1920

The fundamental requirement of industrial employers possessing capital remained that of an adequate labour supply. A powerful factor in the exercise of management authority was labour market domination, though this market was inevitably sectionalised in accordance with the division of labour itself. The examination of industrial disputes after the 1870s suggests that conflict between masters and men was neither confined to periods of strong competition nor to issues of technical innovation. Subordination and resistance took place on a variety of fronts and affected a wide range of groups. Even where industrialists were successful in introducing innovations, there were often serious difficulties for management in their efforts to maintain hierarchical authority whilst restructuring the work-force and concentrating responsibilities.

Whilst it is possible to define industrial welfare in terms of the labour need of employers, their own perception of labour utilisation changed in accordance with work-place conflict as well as the rationalisation of production. The analysis of the objective functions of welfare cannot be undertaken in accordance with some schematic model of economic progress, but must be set in the specific conditions of each industry and the apparent motives of a welfare scheme's architect. Engineering firms were not only aware of the relative costs and benefits attached to different welfare services, but also the importance of the groups catered for and their influence over work-place relations. The following discussion of services places welfare in the broad chronology of innovation and conflict within the engineering industry after the 1870s.

Probably the earliest and most substantial form of welfare investment by engineering employers was the housing schemes financed in new railway settlements such as Crewe, Swindon and Springburn in the middle decades of the nineteenth century. The great joint stock enterprises were capable of funding hundreds of dwellings, though were careful to attract skilled permanent workers and showed a notorious disregard for the accommodation of the temporary labourers.[45] During the 1850s the railway and engineering company at Crewe had completed over 700 houses, but showed little interest once the most important employees were provided for as speculative building surged ahead.[46] Similar comments can be made about the great armaments firms at Clydeside, Tyneside, Barrow and elsewhere, though shipyards and marine engineers continued to construct dwellings well into the twentieth century.[47] Only the largest of companies could contemplate substantial projects and were usually reluctant to invest such resources in housing property after 1870, particularly when skilled tradesmen were able to pay reasonably high rent to private landlords or purchase their own cottages. The scope offered for the coercion and manipulation of engineers in company housing also made such schemes unpopular with workmen, particularly in times of trade depression.[48]

After 1870 the opportunities for distributing benefits amongst the skilled tradesmen diminished rather than increased with the advent of managerial sophistication. Independent friendly societies spread rapidly even in company-dominated settlements such as Crewe, and the craft societies cemented their position by offering a range of social benefits to the trade fraternity.[49] Indeed, during the debates on society functions in the 1860s and 1870s employers were divided over the wisdom of supporting the more acceptable thrift functions of the 'new model' unions such as the ASE. One commentator on the controversy over strikes and union funds argued for a separation of friendly and trade purposes that would prevent an aggressive leadership using accumulated subscriptions to finance strikes.[50] This duality of union administration survived the legristration of the 1870s and the provisions for registration with the government official responsible for friendly societies, though George Howell argued strongly against any restriction of union fraternal services.[51] It is certainly true, however, that the scale and stability of society benefits acted as a powerful deterrent against leaving the union and helped the engineers to retain their membership even after the disastrous defeat of 1897. When in retreat or divided over trade policies, union leaders could improve the attraction of membership by publicising benefits and could support journeymen withdrawing from unpopular work in specific firms.[52] During the intense struggles of 1897, and again from 1906, the question of the legal and friendly status of trade societies was again raised in the trade journals patronised by employers. As one article commented in 1907:[53] 'the wealthier of our Unions are provident societies as well as Trade Unions, and the wealth which is used to fight the employers is very often . . . contributed for a purpose which is foreign to the legitimate aim of a trade union, and ought not, strictly speaking, to be used in industrial warfare'. The Taff Vale judgement and judicial hostility during the pre-war years placed union resources in jeopardy far more effectively than friendly society regulation, but union administration remained largely intact on the eve of war.

One consequence of union vitality was the renewed interest in benefit schemes and profit-sharing arrangements during the 1880s and 1890s in the engineering industry. Workshop provident agreements, or 'shop clubs', had been a feature of early industrialisation as workpeople sought to protect themselves against sickness, old age or death by regular contributions to an informal friendly scheme. Employers often sponsored such initiatives from thrift or co-operative societies on their premises by providing facilities for meetings or holding the funds at a small interest.[54] For the employers, such schemes had the considerable advantages of providing an alternative method of self-help to that involved in trade unionism, and costing very little beyond limited donations or goodwill. It also gave the lesser skilled work-people an opportunity to subscribe to a club and receive benefits previously associated with craft societies. Even the spread of new unions for non-trade groups did not remove this important benefit function associated with an individual work-place, given the slight emphasis on social services in these organisations.[55]

After the 1870s there appears to have been a resurgence of interest in such workshop societies, which were able to register under Friendly Societies legislation as official 'shop clubs' from 1876. The growing number of texts on workshop management for employers often advocated the introduction of sick funds, thrift associations and pensions, one writer observing that[56] 'These valuable institutions are now happily attached to a large number of workshops . . . their management may be useful, both to employers, under whose auspices they should be conducted, and to the workmen in whose interests they are maintained.' Such advocates of systematic management and rigorous work-place organisation also recognised the importance of autonomous initiatives amongst the workers and insisted that the schemes should be introduced and administered by the employees, with the management providing practical support by stipulating compulsory membership to all incoming workers.[57]

This last condition would have made such a scheme ineligible for registration with the Friendly Society officials, given the statutory exclusion of 'closed' benefit shops without membership options.[58] Any society directly dependent on outside support from a business-man for its financial success was also denied registration, though during the 1890s a succession of officials testified that many of the 24,000 registered societies were in fact sustained by such means.[59] The thousands of unregistered shop societies were undoubtedly operating on such an irregular basis before 1914.[60]

In the engineering industry, firms engaged in the building of loco-motives were often well placed to institute such schemes, including the sick clubs seen at Crewe in the mid-century.[61] As one of the most tightly regulated sectors of the economy, railway enterprises were usually familiar with legislative enactment and drafted their own pro-posals for parliamentary control of the industry. Amongst the provisions for working conditions were the 'statutory societies', imposing compulsory membership of work societies administered according to private acts rather than Friendly Society rules.[62] The great workshops of locomotive employers were able to rival the provisions of 'new models' despite the vitality of craft unionism, and complemented the hierarchy of authority with graded benefits. When the shop management came to increase output by retiring older and less efficient workers, the provisions for pensions and superannuation also helped to ease out those being retired.[63]

Welfare innovations at this period were not confined to either locomotive engineering or simple shop clubs. In 1882 the London engineering firm of Waterlow introduced a comprehensive provident scheme to cover different grades of employees and the contingencies of death, retirement, sickness and urgent need. Participation in the administration of these services was as much a part of the plan as the joint contributions, though management maintained an influential voice in welfare policies.[64] During the 1870s Armstrong-Whitworth, with over 16,000 employees in their armaments and engineering plants, introduced a profit sharing scheme for more than 2200 workers.[65] In character with the general cycles of interest in such projects, this scheme appeared at a critical period of industrial conflict following the famous 1871 troubles at Tyneside.[66] It was one such firm that complained during the 1897 conflict about the attitude of the ASE to a profit-sharing bonus which has been paid for five years to engineering workers. Despite the sense of grievance expressed by the employer in a trade journal of the time, it is clear that profit-sharing was offered partly as an alternative to wage increases, when:[67]

> the ASE interfered, having pronounced a boycott against profit sharing as tending to weaken the loyalty of the men to the union . . . the system had to be dropped, because the men, though under a 12-months' engagement, demanded the same advance as was being given in other shops in the trade where there was no bonus. They struck the shop until their demand was conceded, preferring the dictates of the men to the terms of a co-operative partnership with their employers.

By the outbreak of war only a handful of the large employers introducing profit-sharing had succeeded in sustaining their bonus schemes, though it was this survival rate rather than total number of schemes or employees involved that presents such a contrast with the most successful of profit-sharers – the gas companies.[68] The great concerns in locomotive and armaments production were simply unable to convert their key manual workers to the cause of industrial co-partnership in times of greatest conflict. This determined resistance amongst the tradesmen reduced the scope for more comprehensive friendly benefits before 1914, though it did not exclude important initiatives by many larger concerns. The war itself provided another major impetus to management welfare as employers strove to increase output substantially and reduce the endemic conflict at their works.

Finding the Government opposed to outright prohibition of all alcoholic sales in munitions districts, Clydeside industrialists were persuaded by the Liquor Control Board and Welfare Section of the Munitions Ministry to provide alternative attractions to lunch-time drinking.[69] Canteens and restaurants at large engine shops and shipyards were partly financed under allowances against excess profits duty, as were selected housing schemes designed to attract key workers into the armaments and shipbuilding centres.[70] At the same period there was a widespread interest in house magazines, which projected an image of the firm and work-place relations acceptable to management – thereby providing an alternative to the information distributed in such magazines as the ASE's monthly *Journal*.[71] These innovations represented collectively a significant area of management activity, but they cannot be considered an important element in work-place control of adult male labour. Premium bonus was pursued by employers far more energetically than profit bonus; rigorous supervision was far more popular with them than improved working conditions. Faced with the impressive union organisation of their work-force, industrial managements concentrated their services upon three groups strategically important to the division of labour after 1880: apprentices, females, and intermediate grades of staff workers. In this they were at least moderately successful.

At a period when employers were seeking to dilute the proportion of journeymen in their work-force and effectively cut trade rates for machine work, apprentices were a key group in the regulation of work. Engineering employers insisted on a special and personal relationship to their trainee workers, although the formal indentures system was much less comprehensive by the late nineteenth century. During major disputes, including that of 1897–8, management expected apprentices to stay at work under the supervision of trade foremen. The skilled societies, on the other hand, mounted a serious campaign to restrict apprentice ratios during the 1890s and introduced union 'clubs' to advise younger workers ineligible for full membership. Manchester engineering firms complained to the Employers' Federation, that journeymen 'threaten our boys into joining the clubs, by refusing to show or assist them in doing their work, and when the boys have joined they become indifferent'.[72] Industrialists saw this as yet another example of unjustified interference with managerial prerogatives and a method of restricting output.

In this situation, facilities such as technical education classes assumed a strategic as well as an economic significance in such sectors as marine engineering. Larger and more progressive advocates of strong management, including the Thames firm of Yarrow, recognised the value of formal instruction in promoting acceptable attitudes as well as practical expertise.[73] Sir William Beardmore, owner of the great engineering, shipbuilding and armaments interests at Glasgow, emphasised the necessity of exploiting new scientific methods at all levels of industry.[74] The traditional reliance on the practical experience of the workshop and shipyard was gradually giving way to a serious campaign to improve technical classes, provided these did not conflict with the short-term perceptions of profitability.[75]

The coming of war and the radical regrading of labour entailed a substantial increase in the effort and responsibilities of apprentice labour, as employers avoided strict observance of government circulars (with the tacit approval of dilution officials) by placing apprentices on trade work and allocating apprentice tasks to dilutees.[76] Apprenticeships were reduced to five years and immigrant workers transferred from the Highlands to the engineering shops early in the war.[77] The younger workers responded by organising their own version of a central shop stewards' committee, requesting a sharp increase in rates and demanding clear recognition by employers and the state.[78] After the crushing of this challenge to Clydeside employers, management took a more serious interest in the welfare proposals of Robert Hyde and his boys' welfare supervisors at the Munitions Ministry.[79] The employment of large numbers of adolescents outside the apprenticeship system (and the lapsing of many indentures during the war), underlined the value of effective welfare supervision. In 1916 the Fairfield Engineering and Shipbuilding Co. at Govan, scene of the most bitter disputes in the previous year, appointed a special supervisor to direct the 2000 boys employed there. Despite initial resistance from the young workers, this proved a success and influenced the growing support for Hyde's policies.[80] When the ex-clergyman set up his Industrial Welfare Society in 1918, Sir William Beardmore agreed to act as chairman and Stephen Alley assisted the institute's activities – including the publication of the *Boys' Welfare Journal*.[81] The commitment to welfare both as a moral force as well as a practical means of technical improvement remained a strong theme in the literature of the period.[82]

Engineering continued to be one of the most male-dominated sectors of production throughout this period, with little more than 170,000 women employed in the metal industries as a whole (or one tenth of the male work-force) in 1914.[83] There were perhaps a thousand in marine engineering on the outbreak of war, with approximately the same number in small arms production during the first year of fighting. Their numbers expanded rapidly, however, with almost 31,000 in general engineering by mid-1915 and 125,000 employed there a year later. The sheer scale of female dilution should not be underestimated, even if we can qualify earlier generalisations about the precise character of 'deskilling'.[84] By the end of the war about one-third of a million women had flowed into the heavy industries, concentrating in the munitions area of engineering production, and with 13,000 females entering Clyde engine shops during 1916 alone.[85]

Here again the craft societies were caught with an ambiguous and divided set of policies on dilution procedures, as tradesmen concerned themselves not with integration of women so much as 'getting them out as easily as possible', once the war was over.[86] Both the guarantees given under the munitions legislation of 1915–16 and the various circulars of the Munitions Ministry were not sufficient in themselves to win over craftsmen accustomed to skilful maneouvring by such employers as the dilution official William Weir.[87] After the divisions between local shop stewards and the deportation of the leadership at Beardmore's Parkhead works, female dilution on the *employers'* terms and with management supervision went ahead. Here was the crucial issue: engineering workers attempted to control directly female labour by means of everyday overlooking and an arrangement with their union. Beardmore introduced a special welfare supervisor for the female employees and it was her energetic espousal of the management cause that brought matters to a head in 1916. In doing so, she precipitated the defeat of the stewards and the destruction of strong union organisation amongst the female shell workers.[88] The same welfare supervisor later summarised her role as attending to the health and well-being of the employees, thereby 'attaining the best possible results for the employer'.[89] Such attitudes were reinforced by the professional literature which appeared on the subject, though more critical comments on middle-class morality applied in factory welfare work soon followed.[90]

The impression given by much of the literature emanating from acknowledged welfare pioneers at this period is usually that of the appreciative and contented female workers passively receiving the services administered for them.[91] This is misleading as a portrait of attitudes amongst engineering workers. The bitter hostility aroused by welfare supervision was clear even to sympathetic parties after the experiences of wartime administration.[92] By adopting an anti-union policy, many middle-class supervisors provoked the greatest resentment amongst the women in their charge, which was exacerbated by a predilection of some superintendents to interfere in the private lives and morals of the employees.[93] These responses were gradually expressed in the form of trade union opposition to certain forms of welfare, which strengthened the position of those supervisors seeking to establish a genuine professional independence for social workers from management.[94] One lady supervisor at the Armstrong-

Whitworth works, for example, insisted that welfare should be completely divorced from considerations of efficiency and the pressures to improve output.[95] This trend towards establishing welfare work in autonomy from works management was defeated by determined opposition from employers and state officials.[96]

Although female and adolescent workers are seen generally as the groups most protected by state legislation and most catered for in the provision of business welfare, their benefits were completely overshadowed by those introduced for senior male employees. Technical and clerical workers were accorded the courtesy befitting 'non-manual' staff for much of this period, though it was the supervisors who attracted the consistent attention of their employers during the years of change and conflict in engineering. Foremen were traditionally favoured with such privileges as sick pay and periodic *soirées* with the principals of the firm, though were not usually paid for overtime once they had reached full staff status.[97] When shop clubs or accident funds were organised with the support of the management, it was the foremen who served as officers and trustees either appointed by employers or elected by the men.[98]

As with their apprentices, engineering masters insisted on the strict loyalty of foremen to management and rejected any suggestion that trade societies should interfere in this personal bond. With the spread of systematic management and the rise of work-place conflict after the 1870s, there was a renewed emphasis on the vital role of the foreman in the maintenance of managerial authority.[99] In their campaign to assert managerial prerogatives during the 1890s, engineering employers began to 'discover' unacceptable invasions of business freedom and unprecedented interference with their supervisory staff.[100] These transgressions culminated in the intimidations during the 1897–8 dispute, when the Employers' Federation heard that:[101]

> A grave and novel feature in the present dispute has been the attitude of the ASE towards foremen – heretofore exempt from trade agitations. The complaints which have reached the Executive Committee of the Federated Employers are very numerous, of the coercing and terrorising of foremen into restricting work; of compelling foremen to strike; and of driving foremen out of the Society, after contributing to its benefits for many years.

The fact that many reports suggest a collusion on the part of foremen in the limitation of output, and that the same deplorable example of interference (including one from a Glasgow firm which is probably Weir), are reproduced again and again in press and circulars indicate the rhetorical element in this propaganda campaign.[102] At the same time, it is undeniably true that the bitter antagonisms of this period, as much as the rationalisation of production and hierarchies, placed a serious strain on the workshop supervisors.[103] This was as evident at locomotive and marine engineering plants as the great armaments shops at Elswick or Clydeside, until there appeared open hostility between foremen and workmen during the hectic acceleration of output in the war years.[104] During the restructuring of the work-force and the renegotiation of hierarchical relationships, it was the foremen who acted as agents of management whilst striving to preserve their own freedom of action.

The significance of supervisory workers at this time is impressively demonstrated in the investment made by many firms in housing their senior foremen. Whereas most engineering employers could not contemplate accommodating their skilled tradesmen in company dwellings, given the scarcity of resources for substantial building projects, they were prepared to undertake the construction of canteens and restaurants as well as cottages for their deputies.[105] Company housing at Crewe and Swindon had always reflected the gradations of the workplace in its location and standards, but management seemed even more determined to accentuate the distance between staff foremen and tradesmen in the selective housing of the pre-war years.[106]

One of the major difficulties which employers faced in converting foremen to the justice of their cause was the close contact which supervisors continued to have with both men and unions. Promoted from the ranks of the highly skilled, under-foremen and foremen were usually loathe to commit themselves entirely to a management that might reduce them 'to the tools' without compensation. Departure from the trade societies would mean loss of contributory benefits as well as reducing their prospects of future employment in a union shop, even if the supervisor felt detached enough from his trade to implement unpopular policies on machinery, manning, payments and so forth. In this light, management interest in provident schemes after the 1870s can be seen in terms of a general struggle for superiority in benefit administration as one aspect of work-place control.

Evidence can be found in the more general shop club schemes introduced in the 1880s, including that of Waterlow where there was a sharp distinction between 'overseers and sub-foremen' on one side and work-people on the other.[107] Many of the profit-sharing projects designed at this time were also restricted or graded according to supervisory status. Sir Joseph Whitworth told a gathering of London foremen in 1877 that his ambitious co-partnership arrangements had created a situation where twenty-three members of management and supervisory staff held over 90 per cent of the £25 shares. The foremen also received a profit bonus on all net profits beyond 5 per cent, which offset the disadvantages of impersonal administration associated with a limited liability venture.[108] An aggressive initiative was taken once again by the Armstrong empire, headed by Colonel Dyer who shared Weir's admiration for American managerial methods. In 1897 a trade journal reported that the Elswick foremen were in revolt against a works superannuation scheme, 'which seemed to contemplate that all foremen give up their connection with the several unions to which they belong'.[109] Like the earlier profit-sharing proposals, this experiment was met with suspicion amongst the journeymen and their overlookers.

It was during the crisis of 1897–8 that the supervisory issue became a matter of Federation policy in the engineering industry, being discussed at both regional and national levels for the first time. Earlier disputes in 1852 and 1871 had thrown up supervisory associations independent of the trade societies and subsequently patronised by employers, but they never proved popular or prosperous enough to rival the benefits and security offered by craft unions.[110] Industrialists again found that many foremen left the works in sympathy with a major strike, whilst others heeded the instructions of the ASE and refused to instruct or supervise non-trade labour during 1897–8.[111] Well before the strike actually threatened the London masters, Colonel Dyer raised the question of a client union in the shape of a Foreman's Benefit Society:[112]

> The Chairman referred to the urgent necessity for such a Society and to the important bearing it would have in protecting Employers' interests. Its importance had been still further impressed upon him by a recent lengthened visit he had made to the United States and he explained the satisfactory arrangements . . . whereby the foremen he found were invariably unconnected with any Society of men.

Despite the premature death of Dyer shortly after the conclusion of the struggle, plans went ahead and each district association was asked to appoint a supervisor as one of the Foreman's Mutual Benefit Society (FMBS) trustees in order to qualify for Friendly Society registration.[113] The west Scotland engineering firms were strongly in favour of supervisory recruitment to the scheme though the attempts by aggressive managerialists like Weir, Jackson and Henderson to enforce compulsory membership on employing firms was narrowly defeated in 1904.[114]

The limitations on the new Benefit Society, even supported by steady contributions and serviced by the resources of the Dyer Memorial Fund, were also clear by the outbreak of war.[115] Traditional welfarists such as Dennys of Dumbarton were won over to the client organisation along with progressive innovators like Stephen Alley, but there were difficulties in prising foremen away from the established unions.[116] The ASE in the north-east and on Clydeside fought tenaciously to retain foremen in the ranks of the union, whilst many industrialists were slow to recognise the need for energetic promotion of the masters' Foreman's Society amongst their supervisors.[117] Even the industrial leadership in west Scotland could not prevent their underforemen joining strike movements before 1914, even if shipbuilding employers formally supported the scheme after 1905.[118] There was a steady growth in benefit distribution and discretionary grants to deserving foremen or dependents, but a minority of supervisors were enrolled before the war.[119]

Many employers seem to have complemented this organised commitment to a national scheme with the sponsorship of foremen's clubs in their own workshops during the 1890s.[120] Another district organisation set up in 1897 was the West of Scotland Foreman Engineers and Draughtsmen's Association, as a semi-professional body patronised by employers and management as well as supervisors and technical staff. Its membership and benefits were as limited as their counterparts in other regions of Britain, but it certainly served to inculcate ideas of professional qualification and formal training for nonmanual employees.[121] A decade after its foundation, the Association were listening to a manager of Simon at Renfrew advocating improvements in shop methods and appliances, whilst the Foremen's Mutual Benefit Society hosted a speaker from Vickers-Maxim who criticised the ingrained conservatism of the engineering workman.[122]

None of these initiatives severely undermined the position of foremen holding union cards, or prevented the spread of autonomous trade unionism amongst supervisory and drawing office staff during the First World War. The Association of Engineering and Shipbuilding Draughtsmen extended its base from John Brown and other marine engineering establishments during 1916–17, largely in response to deteriorating working conditions and the erosion of differentials. Their employers made a belated effort to persuade draughtsmen into joining the FMBS, 'or some other Approved Society in preference to the Draughtsmen's Association', with little success.[123] Drawing office staff clearly recognised the disadvantages of entering either a client society or a friendly club which would neutralise their efforts at independent representation. As renewed unrest over wage demands and trade card exemptions swept engineering plants in the autumn of 1917, foremen themselves made the first move towards autonomous organisation in areas like Clydeside.[124] As management tried first to repress the movement and then to concede wage increases combined with advertisements of FMBS benefits, recruitment to the supervisory associations spread in engineering and shipbuilding.[125] The ASE retaliated to management promotion of the FMBS by virtually outlawing the masters' society, though their relationship with the Scottish Foremen's Protective Association and the National Foremen's Association remained decidedly uneasy at this period.[126] In the aftermath of the Penistone dispute of 1920 and the great confrontation of 1922 throughout the engineering trades, the employers decided to recognise supervisory organisations on the condition that they maintained a considerable distance from the manual unions and negotiated separately.[127] They continued to vigorously support the FMBS, however, which continued to expand beyond the Second World War in the face of union hostility to employers' societies.[128]

Conclusions

Any serious analysis of industrial welfare must consider its impact on labour relations as well as its place in the development of business enterprise. The fundamental concern of the employer in providing services beyond the wage contract was the creation and domination of local labour markets. Under capitalist production, this market relationship itself implied a conflict of interests crucial to the understanding of business welfare. Unfortunately, the pervasive ideology of benevolent management – disseminated by employers schooled in the arts of advertising and public promotion – continues to influence present orthodoxies in business history.

The case of engineering suggests that a major theme in welfare innovation was the struggle for work-place control in the decades after 1880. It is fruitless to focus exclusively upon the machine question in the engineering or other trades: struggles took place over a wide number of questions and involved a variety of employer strategies. Larger firms favouring technical improvements and systematic management were often strong advocates of welfare reforms in industry, though the conditions of administration were more significant than the character of the provision as such. Only by encompassing the diversity of questions where the issue of work-place control and managerial authority arose can we appreciate the significance of different schemes. Employers were primarily concerned to increase output and efficiency by intensifying supervision and restructuring the labour force in such a way as to reduce overall costs. Resistance to management appeared in the restrictions imposed on labour market entry as much as in the limitation of effort at the workshop machine. Industrialists were able effectively to break this resistance in the three great confrontations of 1897–8, 1915–16 and 1922, but there was no inevitability about the alignment of forces or the precise character of the results.

In the struggles with labour and the design of welfare schemes, employers thought primarily in terms of the groups catered for and the purpose in sight rather than the type of service available. After more general schemes were tried with little effect, industrialists and their managers concentrated on the employees most vulnerable to additional benefits. In the case of engineering, women, apprentices and supervisory or technical staff offered the best prospects of weakening trade society regulation in the labour market. Particularly crucial was the attitude of the foremen during the crises of the 1890s and First World War, hence the employers' aversion to 'interference' with their supervisors and apprentices. At both enterprise and association levels, more adventurous masters introduced schemes directly related to their labour strategies – whether the profit-sharing and superannuation schemes at Elswick or the endorsement of FMBS activities in west Scotland.

The experience of welfare policies in different branches of engineering illustrates the inadequacies of many notions of 'labour' and 'work-place control'. Wage relationships clearly extended throughout the management hierarchy, as did forms of labour subordination and working autonomy. For the foreman, draughtsman, clerk or manager, 'the work-place' existed as much as for the manual employee, even if their precise relationship to the owners varied. The effective functioning of this hierarchy depended upon the legitimate exercise of authority within the limits prescribed by intermediate groups as well as management and workers. Industrial relations had to be consistently negotiated throughout this hierarchy as well as across the shop floor, and the everyday contact of foremen and labourers made this hierarchical connection essential to the success of the enterprise.

The fact that even such selective welfare initiatives did not meet all the expectations of their originators should not obscure the real contribution which employers did make to the extention of workplace welfare. Too many firms possessed too few resources to devote to extensive benefit schemes, hence the reliance upon the sponsorship of thousands of shop clubs at their works. When fully formed projects were initiated by larger firms, their character and the conditions of their birth usually militated against widespread acceptance. Independent trade unions and autonomous friendly or thrift organisations were simply too powerful by the 1880s to be uprooted by business welfare. Such schemes were effective at crucial periods in limiting unrest amongst certain key grades, but even here they often provoked hostility and failed to stifle the growth of independent new unions amongst supervisors, draughtsmen and women workers.

Culturally and politically the scope of employers' services was almost inevitably limited by these decades. The virtues of thrift and self-help possessed their own ambiguities, but there was very widespread resentment at the suggestion of charity or benevolence attached to the work-place. Employees were seldom interested in a gift relationship or the patronage of superiors, as the reactions to wartime welfare supervision demonstrated. Politically there was also a powerful tradition, dating from the great operative societies in Birmingham during the era of the First Reform Act, of highly politicised benefit societies. Rather like the co-operative movement and fraternal lodges, they became increasingly institutionalised under Friendly Society regulation but they also retained an autonomous importance in working-class culture which prevented any simple incorporation by employers. Trade union pressure during the middle decades of the nineteenth century also averted any attempt to divorce friendly and trade functions in their administration, even if concessions were needed before Friendly Society registration of unions was permitted. Many industrialists discouraged the spread of trade unions by supporting the spread of autonomous shop clubs, though here again their unequivocal successes were limited.

There is considerable evidence that workers in Britain resented the description of any scheme in which they participated as 'paternalistic', and it is unlikely that many employers perceived their industrial role as a patriarchial or paternal one. The liberal tradition tended to justify work-place hierarchies in terms of a meritocratic leadership as well as a functional necessity, though employers and work-people alike showed little sympathy for the traditional inequalities of aristocratic society during the formative decades of their class development. Ideals of service to society and mutual responsibilities between master and man did survive into the late nineteenth century and were perhaps complemented by religious conviction, but there is nothing to equal either the authoritarianism of Stumm or the comprehensive commitment of Pullman or Carnegie.

Before ascribing these variations to the cultural peculiarities of the British, it is important to recognise the atypical qualities of celebrated individuals and the objective conditions of rapid industrialisation which each economy experienced after 1870. What the Arkwrights, Strutts, Fieldens and Fosters had undertaken over the decades of consolidated growth, the Krupps, Siemens, Morgans and Hillmans had to provide in years or even months. Their economies did not possess either the skills or the strong tradition of organisation which the British working class enjoyed, nor was the divide between industrial and political representation (painfully achieved in Britain after 1850) as explicit. Without a range of substantial benefits distributed via older societies, mobile and immigrant workers were more susceptible to business welfare than in Britain. Yet by the 1890s the German labour movement and the American unions were openly opposing company unions and closed welfare schemes. There was a resurgence after the First War, partly motivated by directly political objectives, but employers never enjoyed the comprehensive domination of the work-place or the neighbourhood implicit in the term 'paternalism'.

Notes

1. P. Mathias, *The First Industrial Nation* (1969), pp. 374–5.
2. D. Owen, *English Philanthropy 1660–1960* (1962), p. 381 and passim.
3. See the contrasting A.G.P. Elliott, 'Company Welfare Benefits' in G.L. Reid and D.J. Robertson (eds.), *Fringe Benefits, Labour Costs and Social Security* (1965), and A. Fox, *Man Mismanagement* (1974), pp. 58–9.
4. E.C. McCreary, 'Social Welfare and Business: The Krupp Welfare Program, 1860–1914', *Business History Review* (1968); J.R. Hay, 'The British Business Community, Social Insurance and the German Example,' in W.J. Mommsen (ed.), *The Emergence of the Welfare State in Britain and Germany* (1980).
5. G. Eley, 'Capitalism and the Wilhemine State: Industrial Growth and Political Backwardness in Recent German Historiography, 1890–1918', *Historical Journal* (1978), p. 741; D. Geary, 'Employer Policies towards Labour in the Kaiserreich, 1871–1914' (1981), mimeo.
6. D. Nelson and S. Campbell, 'Taylorism versus Welfare Work in American Industry', *Business History Review* (1972); S.D. Brandes, *American Welfare Capitalism, 1880–1940* (Chicago, 1976).
7. P. Joyce, *Work, Society and Politics: The Culture of the Factory in Later Victorian England* (1980), particularly chapters 6 and 8.
8. R.M. Titmuss, *Essays on 'the Welfare State'* (1969); A. Briggs, 'The History of Changing Approaches to Social Welfare' in E.W. Martin (ed.), *Comparative Development in Social Welfare* (1972), pp. 10–11.
9. J.R. Hay, 'Government Policy towards Labour in Britain, 1900–14: Some Further Considerations', *Journal Scottish Labour History Society* (1978), p. 47.
10. A. Briggs, *Social Thought and Social Action: A Study of the Work of Seebohm Rowntree* (1961), p. 129, for rather different argument on scale and welfare.
11. M.J. Daunton, 'Miners' Houses: South Wales and the Great Northern Coalfield, 1880–1914', *International Review of Social History* (1980).
12. W. Lazonick, 'Industrial Relations and Technical Change: The Case of the Self-Acting Mule', *Cambridge Journal of Economics* (1979), pp, 237–9; also Lazonick's essay in this collection.
13. A.L. Stinchcombe, 'Bureaucratic and Craft Administration of Production', *Administrative Science Quarterly* (1959), pp. 170, 179–80.
14. C.K. Harley, 'Skilled Labour and the Choice of Technique in Edwardian Industry', *Explorations in Economic History* (1974).
15. F. Smith, *Workshop Organisation* (1878), pp. 7, 57.
16. L. Nixon, 'The Building of a Ship', *Cassier's Magazine* (1898), p. 396.
17. Departmental Committee on Juvenile Education, *Summaries of Evidence* (1918) Cd. 8577; evidence of A.P.M. Fleming of British Westinghouse Electric Co., p. 14.
18. A.P.M. Fleming, 'Apprenticeship Training . . . for Engineering Apprentices', *Transactions Institute Engineers and Shipbuilders in Scotland* (1917–18), p. 78.
19. Ibid. p. 125, for Professor A.L. Mellanby in discussion.
20. C. More, *Skill and the English Working Class* (1980), pp. 154–7.
21. Ibid. pp. 186, 208–11.
22. D.J. Lee, 'Craft Unions and the Force of Tradition: The Case of Apprenticeship', *British Journal of Industrial Relations* (1979), pp. 37–8.
23. D.C. Cummings, *A Historical Survey of the Boilermakers' and Iron and Steel Ship Builders' Society, 1834–1904* (1905), pp. 192–3; S. Price, 'Rivetters' Earnings in Clyde Shipbuilding 1889–1913', *Scottish Economic and Social History* (1981), pp. 60–1, for an example.

24. D. Nelson, *Managers and Workers: Origins of the New Factory System in the United States, 1880-1920* (1975), pp. 34-5, 42.
25. Cummings (1905), pp. 138, 143, 155-6, etc.
26. Engineering Employers' Federation, *Minutes*, 13-28 August 1896, for some discussions and Dyer's views.
27. W.H. Chaloner, *The Social and Economic Development of Crewe* (1950), pp. 41-2, 67-8; *Foreman Engineer and Draughtsman* 1 August 1882, pp. 122-3.
28. A. Williams, *Life in a Railway Factory* (1915), pp. 102-3, 304; Chaloner (1950), pp. 42, 74.
29. Thomas Emerson, Works and Private Diary (1871), Newcastle Record Office MF 941: 23-4 February 1871, for one Elswick foreman.
30. B. Weekes, 'Craft Unionism and Primitive Democracy', unpublished draft (1980), University of Warwick; see also Zeitlin essay in the present collection.
31. North West Engineering Trades Employers' Association, *Minutes*, 28 February 1910; for comments on foreign competition: Sir B.C. Browne, *Selected Papers on Social and Economic Questions* (1918), pp. 50-1.
32. J. Richardson, 'The Question of Scientific Management', *Transactions Institute Engineers and Shipbuilders in Scotland* (1917-18), p. 180 for comments of John Halloway in discussion.
33. Engineering Employers' Federation, *Minutes*, 13 August 1896.
34. Zeitlin essay in the present collection.
35. Clyde Shipbuilders' Association, 'Conditions of Labour and Yard Management', Strathclyde Regional Archives, TD 241, 12/1 (TD 241 12/1 hereafter); Letter of Andrew Noble to Tyne Shipbuilders' Association, 22 December 1902, copy in C.S.A. file.
36. TD 241 12/1; Letter of Biggart (secretary of CSA and NWETEA), to Robinson of Tyne S.A., 1.10.1902; 'Memorandum on Conditions of Management . . .' for subsequent development of management prerogatives.
37. Price (1981), pp. 60-1, for rivetters' experience; see J. Melling, 'Employers, Industrial Housing and the Development of Company Welfare Policies . . . 1870-1920', *International Review of Social History* (1981), for some further discussion of shipbuilding firms.
38. J.E. Mortimer, *History of the Boilermakers' Society, 1834-1906* (1973), pp. 168-9.
39. TD 241 12/1; letter of John Inglis to G.B. Hunter, 29 December 1902.
40. TD 241 12/1; memorandum submitted for opinion of legal counsel, with annotations to foremen clause dated 20 January 1904.
41. TD 241 12/1; minutes of Edinburgh meeting of special Joint Committee of Shipbuilding Employers' Federation, with resolution on foremen by G.B. Hunter and C.D. Doxford of North East Coast; letter of Noble to Tyne S.A., 22 December 1902.
42. TD 241 12/1; letter of G.B. Hunter to Allan Smith, with postscript annotation by J. Inlis, 6 October 1903.
43. *Foreman Engineer and Draughtsman*, April 1877, p. 59.
44. *Engineering*, 'Notes', 30 July 1897, p. 150.
45. Chaloner (1950), pp. 45, 146.
46. Ibid. pp. 46-51.
47. Melling (1981), for details.
48. Chaloner (1950), p. 50, for events in 1848.
49. Ibid. p. xix.
50. J. Stirling, *Unionism: With Remarks on the Report of the Commissioners on Trades' Unions* (1869), p. 46: 'if you would preserve your union funds for sickness and old age, beware of wasting them on strikes and lock-outs'.
51. G. Howell, *The Conflicts of Capital and Labour* (1878) (1890 edn), p. 478; for a desultory and inconclusive discussion see C.G. Hanson, 'Craft Unions, Welfare Benefits and the Case for Trade Union Law Reform, 1867-75', *Economic History*

Review (1975), p. 245 and passim, and Comment by P. Thane in *Economic History Review* (1976), pp. 617-19.

52. Cf. K. Burgess, *The Origins of British Industrial Relations* (1975).
53. 'Trade Union Wealth', *Engineering Times*, 23 May 1907, p. 607.
54. J. Ward, 'Memoir of the late William Denny', *Transactions of Institute of Engineers and Shipbuilders in Scotland* (reprint 26 April 1887), p. 269 for one important example.
55. J. Melling, 'Industrial Strife and Business Welfare Philosophy' *Business History* (1979), for context of 1889 and the new unions.
56. Smith (1878), p. 41.
57. Ibid. pp. 42-3.
58. Royal Commission on Labour, *Minutes of Evidence of Representatives of Co-operative Societies and of . . . Public Officials*, C. 7063 (1893) (hereafter C. 7063): Evidence of Ludlow (ex-Registrar of Friendly Societies), q. 1838; P.H.J.H. Gosden, *The Friendly Societies in England* (1961), p. 62.
59. C. 7063, q. 1838; evidence of E.W. Brabrook (Registrar of Friendly Societies), q. 1277-80.
60. Ibid. qs. 1284-8, 1331; 1384, for Brabrook's comment that 'the accounts of the Society are kept by a mere entry in the books of the company.'
61. Chaloner (1950), p. xix, for shop clubs at Crewe; British Caledonian 'Speech by Sir James King to St Rollox festival' (1896) in BR CAL 4/152: 'You have a Friendly Society and we, the Directors, have great pleasure in subscribing somewhat liberally towards it.'
62. C. 7063, q. 1760, for Ludlow's comment: 'I am not aware of any case in which the employed have a share in the management of the fund, so far as it proceeds from the employer.'
63. K. Lee, 'The Human Element in Industry', *Ways and Means* (1920), p. 204, for a statement at a later period.
64. *Foreman Engineer and Draughtsman* 2 October 1882, p. 163, for details.
65. Labour Dept of Board of Trade, *Report on Profit Sharing and Labour Co-Partnership in the United Kingdom* (1912), Cd. 6496 (hereafter Cd. 6496), figures tabulated from separate schemes 1865-1912.
66. Ibid. p. 11, for gas companies and p. 70 for opinion of one employer on the significant increase in productivity; R.A. Church, 'Profit Sharing and Labour Relations in the 19th Century', *International Review of Social History* (1971), p. 3 and passim for cycles of interest in profit-sharing.
67. *Textile Mercury*, 27 November 1897, pp. 419-20.
68. Cd. 6496, p. 15 shows 21 firms in engineering and shipbuilding with 17,336 employed but only four schemes survived, as against 33 survivors of 34 innovators with 28,246 employed in gas industry totals.
69. CSA, *Minutes*, 13 June 1915.
70. Ibid. 30 August 1915; Health of Munitions Workers' Committee, *Memorandum No. 3: Report on Industrial Canteens*, Cd. 8133 (1915), (hereafter Cd. 8133), p. 6, para. 7; *History of the Ministry of Munitions* (1921-2), vol-V, part iii, p. 12.
71. *The Linthouse Magazine* vol. 1, no. 3 (March 1920), for one acceptable account of the 'old days' of close relationships.
72. Engineering Employers' Federation, 'Fourth Series of examples of restriction and interference', Webb Collection LIX No. 13, p. 3, para. 1; also p. 3, para. 2, for foremen and apprentices.
73. P.L. Robertson, 'Technical Education in the British Shipbuilding and Marine Engineering Industries, 1863-1914', *Economic History Review* (1974), pp. 225-6, 232-3 and passim.
74. Sir William Beardmore, 'The Influence of Scientific Research on Industry', *Institute of Engineers and Shipbuilders in Scotland* (reprint May 1916), p. 6-8.
75. CSA, Minutes, 29 August 1912, for some objections to evening continuation classes.

76. NWETEA, *Minutes*, 17 July 1916, for the collusion of Lynden Macassey in such strategems.
77. *Ibid*. 24 November 1914, 22 February 1915.
78. *Ibid*. 13 March 1916.
79. *Ibid*. 17 July 1916 to 22 January 1917, for visits of Robert Hyde to Clydeside; Health of Munition Workers' Committee, *Memorandum No. 2: Welfare Supervision*, Cd. 8151 (1915) (hereafter Cd. 8151), p. 7, para. 12.
80. Fleming (1917–18), pp. 123–4, for the contribution by Thomas S. Campbell of Fairfields.
81. Sir William Beardmore, ' "Welfare" as a Business Asset', *Journal of Industrial Welfare* (1920), pp. 29–30, for example; E. Sidney, *The Industrial Society, 1918–68* (1968), p. 7 and passim for background to foundation of Society.
82. Fleming (1917–18), pp. 79–80, for training in citizenship as well as workmanship.
83. *Report of the War Cabinet Committee on Women in Industry*, Cmd. 135 (1919), p. 10.
84. *History of the Ministry of Munitions* vol. IV, part iv, app. 1, table B, p. 146.
85. Ibid. vol. VI, part iv, p. 51; W.R. Scott and R. Cunnison, *The Industries of the Clyde Valley During the War* (1924), p. 85.
86. Askwith correspondence with W.H. Beveridge of 1916, quoted in I.S. McLean, 'Labour in Clydeside Politics, 1914–22' (DPhil. thesis 1971), p. 97; *History of Ministry of Munitions*, vol. IV, part iv, p. 117.
87. NWETEA, *Minutes*, 23 May 1916 to 15 February 1917.
88. NWETEA, *Minutes*, 23 March 1916; McLean (1971), p. 118.
89. Cmd. 167, *op. cit.*, p. 213, evidence of Miss Jean Lindsay.
90. E.M., 'The Training of the Welfare Worker', *The Englishwoman* (1916), pp. 240–51.
91. E. Cadbury, *Experiments in Industrial Organisation* (1912), gives both the impression of enlightened 'human factor' management and Christian duty.
92. Gertrude Tuckwell, 'Workers and Trade Unions', *Welfare Work* (September 1921), for first-hand account; S. Webb, *The Works Manager To-day* (1917), p. 142–3 for views of Mary MacArthur.
93. Ibid.
94. Cmd. 167, evidence of Rose E. Squire (Principal Lady Inspector of Factories), that: 'With better training the welfare worker should get rid of her prejudice against trade unions'.
95. Ibid. Miss Jayne's evidence, p. 209.
96. Ibid. evidence of Dr E.L. Collis (Rowntree's successor at the Ministry of Munitions Welfare Section), p. 206; cf. J. Lee, *Principles of Industrial Welfare* (1924), pp. 67–8, for welfare in general system of management control.
97. Clydebank Engineering and Shipbuilding Company, Wages Account (1893–9), for significant increases in both holiday entitlement and sick pay distribution.
98. W.J.M. Rankine, *A Memoir of John Elder* (1871), for foremen in the Elder shipyard accident fund.
99. Smith (1878), pp. 17–19, 32–4, and passim; C.L. Goodrich, *The Frontier of Control* (1920) (1975 edn), p. 120, for contemporary radical perspective.
100. Federation of Engineering and Shipbuilding Employers (FESE), 'First Series of Examples of Restriction and Interference', Webb Coll. LIX No. 10 (4 November 1897), p. 2, Nos. 1–2, for 'interference' over machines and shop stewards.
101. Ibid.; FESE, Webb Coll. LIX No. 17 (14 January 1898), p. 1.
102. FESE, Webb Coll. LIX No. 17 (18 November 1897), p. 2, para. 2; FESE, Webb Coll LIX No. 17 (27 November 1897); *Textile Mercury* 27 November 1897.
103. Williams (1915), p. 56–7, 302–5, for an ambiguous account by the author of changes in supervisory authority at the Swindon workshops.
104. Lord Balfour of Burleigh and Lynden Macassey, *Report on the Clyde Munition Workers*, Cd. 8136 (1915), p. 4, para. 8; *Report of the Commission of Enquiry*

into Industrial Unrest: Scotland, Cd. 8669 (1917), p. 4, para. 6.
105. Melling (1981).
106. Chaloner (1950), p. 48–51, including demand of eight works foremen for superior company housing.
107. *Foreman Engineer and Draughtsman*, 2 October 1882, p. 163.
108. Ibid. April 1877, for speech at 24th Annual Dinner of London Association, p. 59.
109. Quoted in J.F. Clarke, 'The Foreman – A Neglected Figure in the History of Industrial Relations?', *North East Group Labour History Society Bulletin* (1975), p. 28.
110. J. Newton, 'Origins and Objects', *Foreman Engineer and Draughtsman* (1876), p. 148–9.
111. FESE, 'Interference with Foremen', Webb Coll. LIX No. 17, p. 2, para. 8, for copy of letter from Glasgow ASE committee to foremen in Clyde engine shops.
112. Engineering Employers' Federation, *Minutes*, 19 December 1896.
113. NWETEA *Minutes*, 29 November 1898.
114. Ibid. 4 October 1899 to 19 April 1901; 27 April 1903 to 27 December 1904.
115. Dyer Memorial Fund Executive Committee, *Report of the Committee* (1898 and 1899), for some details.
116. *Denny Dumbarton, 1844–1932*, Dennys (1932), p. 87; Alley & Co., *Minutes*, 9 September 1907.
117. NWETEA, *Minutes*, 26 April 1899, 27 December 1904.
118. CSA *Minutes*, 19 April 1906 to 7 February 1908; 25 October 1905, for CSA affiliation.
119. NWETEA, *Minutes*, 30 August 1916, when the FMBS needed £2000 to capitalise the Fund at £13,500; see Engineering Employers' Federation, *Minutes*, 16 December 1896, for early examples of direct grants when loyal foremen at Dunsmuir & Jackson rewarded for their efforts.
120. J.B. Jefferys, *The Story of the Engineers* (1946), p. 128 and passim.
121. 'Clyde Foremen Engineers', *Engineering Times*, 14 March 1907, p. 293 when membership was reported to be 166.
122. 'Developments in Engineering', *Engineering Times*, 28 February 1907, p. 253, when James McKechnie of Vickers-Maxim at Barrow was speaker.
123. NWETEA, *Minutes*, 27 March 1917.
124. Ibid. 18 December 1917, for response of Biggart and the local association.
125. Ibid. National Foremen's Association, executive council, *Minutes*, 19–20 January 1918 NFA 1/1/1, for general context of supervisory organisation.
126. A. Richardson, *The Manpower of the Nation*, (1916), p. 131; Goodrich (1975), p. 129.
127. Glasgow and West Scotland Association of Foremen Engineers, *Paths to Peace in Industry* (1930), p. 19; G.S. Bain, *The Growth of White-Collar Unionism* (1970), p. 40–1, 57, 133.
128. 'Should Foremen Belong to a Trade Union?', *The Times*, 4 January 1960, for reputed membership of 60,000 in Foremen and Staff Mutual Benefit Society, including an increase of 6000 in 1955–60.

4 Fordism and British Motor Car Employers 1896–1932[1]
Wayne Lewchuk

A wealth of research has made it increasingly obvious that the relationship between capital and labour is one of the most important factors which explains changes in the organisation of production and the machinery used in production. This thesis has been cogently argued by Braverman.[2] He suggested that the relationship between capital and labour in a capitalist economy forced capital to adopt new production methods. Further research has pointed to a number of weaknesses in the basic model.[3] Two particular areas are explored in this article. The first is the simplistic formulation of the relationship between capital and labour. The second is the dichotomisation of machine methods from all of the other strategies available to management to improve productivity.

The article will examine how the relationship between capital and labour was transformed by the rise of managerial capitalism in Britain. It will be argued that direct control as proposed by Braverman did not seem a viable alternative to British management. Perceptions of class relations were such that payment by results and the cultivation of common interests between capital and labour, both nationally and within the firm, were seen to be potentially more profitable than direct control through mechanisation. It will be shown that it was labour not management which was the most vocal in calling for Fordism, and that it was management and not labour that expressed the strongest reservations about the system.

Direct Control as the Ultimate Capitalist Technology
The basic equation of Braverman's model is that capital purchases labour for a specified time period, but of an unspecified intensity. No distinction is made whether or not labour is purchased on the day rate system or on the system of payment by results. The intensity of work becomes a point of conflict between capital and labour, as one wishes to maximise effort and output, while the other wishes to minimise

effort. Capital is forced to design new systems of management and machine technology that increase its control over labour productivity. The new technology has three characteristics. The responsibility for conceiving how work should be done is taken away from those who actually perform the work. Workers are granted higher real wages in exchange for the reduction in their control over production decisions. Finally, the system naturally gravitates towards increasing mechanisation, as the control function is built into the machines.

For Braverman, Fordism, or direct control, became the ultimate means by which management gained control of the production process and the level of effort. Under Fordism, the worker forgoes any say in how work is done and accepts a level of effort dictated by close supervision and machine pacing. Labour accepts this system in return for wages paid on the day rate system that are relatively high in comparison with other opportunities available. It was Fordism's use of machine pacing which caused Braverman to see it as an advance over the control system employed by Scientific Management. He wrote, 'Machinery offers to management the opportunity to do by wholly mechanical means that which it had previously attempted to do by organisational and disciplinary means.'[4]

This approach has been criticised for focusing exclusively on machine pacing as the means of controlling labour effort. It has been argued that the antagonistic relationship between the two classes might be altered by alternative strategies. Friedman has argued that capital has the alternative of adopting responsible autonomy as a method of increasing labour output.[5] The difference between direct control and responsible autonomy is that with the latter the worker retains a greater degree of control over production decisions. This is possible because the workers are expected to act responsibly towards their employers. This raises the important question of how labour and capital assess their relationship to each other and whether or not that relationship can be consciously altered. This is seen to be particularly important if class antagonism is to be used to explain the process of mechanisation. The obvious alternative hypothesis is that if the antagonistic relationship between capital and labour can be mediated to minimise the negative impact of productivity, will this reduce the degree of mechanisation?

Palmer was one of the first to comment on Braverman's nearly exclusive focus on Fordism and direct control.[6] He was particularly critical of how Braverman had singled out machinery for special treatment as *the* strategy of management at the expense of the other aspects of production such as administrative systems, organisation of work, paternalism and welfarism. Management was forced to adopt more sophisticated systems of management because labour was able to resist early forms of direct control. Noble, who has examined these changes in the United States, argues that one of the main objectives was to alter the relationship between capital and labour so as to increase productivity.[7] Burawoy has also argued that Braverman's analysis of the relationship between capital and labour was deficient. He has suggested that the relationship between the two was more complex than simple antagonism, and that there were many reasons why at times they had common interests, whose importance might be amplified when viewed through the appropriate ideological screen. He wrote, 'History suggests, however, that the outcome of class struggle mollifies the opposition of interests and frequently coordinates the interests of labour and capital.' Burawoy's arguments build an extra dynamism into Braverman's analysis, and force us to examine the factors which influence the relationship between capital and labour and ultimately the form of machine technology. In his words, 'The capitalist mode of production is not just the production of things, but simultaneously the production of social relations and also the production of ideas about those relations, a lived experience of ideology of those relationships.'[8]

Payment Systems and the Relationship between Capital and Labour
It was indicated in the introduction that payment by results played an important role in the strategy of British management. Payment systems can be divided into two main groups, day-work and piece-work. With day-work systems, labour receives a fixed wage which is unaffected by short-run variations in an individual's output. With payment by results, wages are directly affected by changes in the level of productivity. There are many different types of payment by results systems. We are interested in the difference between ordinary piece-work where wages are directly proportional to output and 'progressive' systems where the gains from productivity increases are shared between capital and labour. Of the progressive systems, the premium bonus has been the most commonly found.

One of the problems for capital with ordinary piece-work systems was that capital did not benefit from reduced labour costs as productivity increased, unless rates were cut. This led to regular bouts of rate cutting which prompted labour to restrict output, hence defeating the objective of the payment system. In an attempt to overcome this problem, premium bonus systems were developed in the last decade of the nineteenth century. Under this sort of system, labour shared any earnings above the norm with capital. The standard division was half and half. The aim of the new system was to reduce the likelihood that capital would resort to cutting prices; it was hoped that this would eliminate the practice of restricting output on the part of labour. It was argued that,

> Every increase in earnings is necessarily accompanied by a corresponding decrease of cost, and if the premium be such as to give these a satisfactory relation, the workman may be assured that there will be no limit set to his earnings. . . . The very purpose of the plan is to avoid this by so dividing the savings between employer and employee as to remove the necessity for cutting the rate, and hence enable the workman's earnings to be limited only by his own ability and activity.[9]

For British management, which had little faith in scientific rate fixing, there remained a second problem with all systems of payment by results. Because prices could not be fixed accurately, workers with loosely timed jobs earned unacceptable high wages, as well as disrupting the existing scale of relative wages. Rowan, a British employer, introduced his own version of premium bonus to overcome this problem. The Rowan system, through the formula given below, limited the maximum bonus rate to 100 per cent.[10]

$$\text{Rowan Bonus} = \frac{\text{time saved}}{\text{time allowed}} \times \text{time actually taken}$$

The most important feature of premium bonus systems, for the sake of this study, is their attempt to foster common interests between labour and capital by reducing the need for rate cutting. According to Brown, British management turned increasingly to premium bonus systems in the period after 1900. They were seen as a direct substitute for the system of Scientific Management which Taylor proposed as the solution to the productivity problem.[11] Between 1886 and 1914 there was a significant increase in the number of workers paid on systems of payment by results. For turners, the number increased from 7 to 46 per cent, and for machinists it increased from 11 to 47 per cent of the total work-force.[12]

The question of whether there are important differences between day-work and piece-work has yet to be resolved. Braverman, and more recently Littler, have argued that it is not so much the payment system used which is important, but rather how the level of effort is enforced. This is a view which is supported by a number of contemporary writers on payment systems. Schloss argued, 'There exists underlying the method of time-wage, no less than that of piece-wage, a more or less definite quantitative basis, a fixed money value being placed upon the output capable of being produced . . . at a certain speed.'[13]

The conclusion that there are no real differences between day-work and payment by results seems to be seriously at odds with the important role attributed to payment by results by contemporary managers and union representatives as well as historians studying this period. Hobsbawm suggested that incentive wage payment systems played an important role in breaking down the existing work norms based on custom.[14] Leading managers, journalists, and employers' associations all strongly promoted incentive payment systems, while labour, particularly the rank and file, resisted it where they could.[15] By the late 1920s, payment by results was seen to be such an important element of the British management system that the Engineering Employers' Federation (EEF) considered expelling members who wanted to move to day-work systems.[16] This forces us to explain why British managers saw payment by results as such a critical component of their strategy.

The Rise of Managerial Capitalism and Capital's View of Labour
The emergence of a managerial class and the science of management occurred well after the initial industrial revolution. Some writers have suggested that their appearance late in the nineteenth century marks a second industrial revolution.[17] In Britain, these changes were influenced by the increase in the scale of production caused by the concentration of capital, the loss of Britain's monopoly position in world trade, and the rise of powerful labour organisations. Within such an environment, the new managers came to see the restriction of output by labour as the major barrier to the continued prosperity of British capitalism. As firms grew, management was forced to develop new methods of controlling labour. Urwick, in his study of British management systems, summarised the changes occurring as follows,

> With the advent of the modern industrial group in large factories in urban areas, the whole process of control underwent a fundamental revolution. It was now the owner or manager of a factory, i.e. the employer . . . who has to secure or extract from his employees a level of obedience and/or co-operation which would enable him to exercise control.[18]

If in the United States, the policies of these early managers were shaped by the belief that labour was innately lazy, in Britain the chief concern was that labour was organising to change the existing system. Prior to the First World War some elements of labour had started to become aware of an alternative to capitalism. Rolls Royce was one firm which became sufficiently concerned about the possibility of socialistic agitation that they considered building a duplicate works in France in case private production became impossible in Britain.[19] The extent to which sections of the working class saw their interests diverging from capital's led to a growng debate amongst employers and the new managers on how best to convince the workers that it was their self-interest to co-operate with capital. Treatises by Cadbury and

Leverhulme signalled the growing awareness amongst employers of a labour problem.[20] During the war, this debate was intensified, leading ultimately to Whitleyism as one proposed solution to the capital labour problem.[21]

At an address to the British Electrical Federation in 1919, E. Garcke suggested that one of the most important changes which the war had caused was labour's increased consciousness of its power. This had forced British management to accept that capitalism could only continue if labour was granted a larger share of output.[22] H. Cox, in a speech to the Institute of Civil Engineers, went even further. He argued,

> We shall get no real progress until you can demonstrate to the working class as a body that their individual and collective interest lies in more efficient production. If we solve the moral problem, I see no limit to the progress of our country. For as soon as you have secured the concurrence of the workman, it will become possible to develop immensely the efficiency of our manufacturing processes, so as to obtain an increased output at less cost, while paying higher wages.

Many of the British spokesmen on managerial methods argued that it was in capital's self interest to grant higher wages, Sir M. Fitzmaurice, a representative of this movement, supported his position with a quote from Burke, 'The question with them is not whether you have the right to render your people miserable, but whether it is not in your interest to make them happy.'[23]

As well as the need for higher wages, British management came to see the 'human element' as a critical factor in improving productivity. They viewed their concern for the human element as being incompatible with either Scientific Management or Fordism. Sir Robert Hadfield, a prominent steel entrepreneur, advocated higher wages, shorter hours, and a factory system which stressed the personal interaction between management and the workers. He associated direct control and Scientific Management with increased impersonalisation. 'I believe that I shall have every reasonable foreman with me. The personal touch will do more than all the system.'[24] The president of the Institute of Automobile Engineers also criticised Scientific Management. 'The human element was of far greater importance in England than in America.'[25] This concern with the motivation of workers, punctuates the writings of a large number of managers. Reeves, the former chief draughtsman at Crossley, rejected Scientific Management because of 'the awkward spirit characterising the workers of say the Northern Midlands'.[26] Pullinger rejected flow production, partly because the quality of output might be reduced but also because alternative means were being used to improve labour productivity. He wrote,

Our operatives must have instilled into them the idea that their work is an art, and that it is a high privilege to be able to operate machine tools and produce beautifully finished interchangeable parts. . . . A great deal more efficiency and interest can be obtained from employees if those in charge treat them in a kindly sympathetic manner, taking interest in their work, pointing out to them the directions in which they can improve, and giving them a word of encouragement.[27]

The instalment of the first president of the Institute of Automobile Engineers, Sir H. Fowler, was the occasion of a debate on post-war managerial problems. The need to overcome labour's resistance to capital through improved human relations was given priority over the need for new machine methods. Fowler proposed, 'As a rule in speaking on such subjects, it is usual to deal first with the machine and then with the man. I think this is reversing the importance of the subject and so propose first of all to deal with the human side.' He asserted that previously these questions were considered to be of secondary importance. Now he felt it necessary to pursue the study of industrial psychology and advocated the creation of a chair in psychology. R.E. Crompton, a former president of the Institute, agreed that there was a need to pay more attention to understanding the workers. He viewed large-scale production as being incompatible with good labour relations and argued for a shift away from the large units created by the war.

To me it is unthinkable that these huge concerns at the present time, with the number of men that come in from other shops, can be managed on any principle of knowing the feelings of the men. . . . I have always thought the ideal thing would be smaller towns, each town having one or two small factories, everyone living as neighbours in one district, the employers, the foremen, and the men, having their houses and their gardens near to one another's, all interested in everything their neighbours are doing.'[28]

The above statements, even if they were mainly rhetorical, which is unlikely as they represent exchanges between managers rather than between managers and workers, indicate that British management was conscious of the problem of the worsening relationship between capital and labour. When the post-war industrial strategy was formed, the lack of co-operation on the part of labour was foremost in management's mind. This is reflected clearly in one writer's interpretation of the different emphasis aspects of Scientific Management should have in Britain. He wrote in 1919, 'British Scientific Management aimed at the elimination of all waste. . . . The idea should be men, machines and minutes; get the men right first, then the machinery and after that they could go for the minutes.'[29] Very few spokesmen supported a policy of direct control and machine pacing as the solution to the productivity problem. Instead, the motivation of labour received the most attention, and attempts were made to show labour that it was in their interest to co-operate with capital. In doing this, improved versions of payment by results would become the key to managerial strategies. To understand why this policy was followed we must look briefly at the defeat of direct control during the First World War.

The Defeat of Direct Control and the Strategy of Coventry Management

The failure of British management to gain complete control of the production process, even during a war crisis, was critical in leading post-war management to reject direct control as a viable strategy. The EEF did try to create the conditions for a Ford-style industrial strategy in the initial negotiations over relaxation of pre-war customs. They proposed that the unions should refrain from contesting any changes in the areas of machine manning, demarcation, non-union labour, female labour, and overtime. They promised to return to pre-war conditions after the war, but in making this promise realised that it was highly unlikely that such drastic changes could ever be fully reversed.[30] When these negotiations collapsed, the Government was forced to intervene and introduced the Munitions of War Act 1915.

The Munitions Act differed from the EEF proposals. Only customs which directly reduced output were challenged. Of equal importance, management was not given the sole authority to decide which prac- tices reduced output. The government became the final arbitrator. Unlike direct control, which eliminates the need for management to confer with labour, the Munitions Act had actually increased the need. Increasingly these consultations took place at the point of production and a new level of labour representation emerged, one which was directly opposed to the principles of direct control, namely the shop steward.

In Coventry, the proposals that stewards would represent all grades of labour in a department and that they would be elected by all of the workers in a department can only be understood in relation to earlier attempts by skilled and unskilled workers to co-operate in protecting their interests.[31] Individual stewards on works committees would have represented both skilled and unskilled workers in the department which elected them, hence the term 'all-grades'. Hinton has argued that these committees were ineffective and undermined the more radical unofficial movement. While we agree that these committees in the end proved ineffective, they were seen at the time as a serious chal- lenge to managerial authority and are representative of the new role which British labour wished to have regarding decisions affecting the work-place.[32]

Even though the local Coventry unions had attempted to respond to wartime changes by appointing more stewards and forming works committees, there is little doubt that it was the unofficial shop stewards' movement which set the pace and direction of change.[33] In April 1917, the unofficial movement brought out the workers at Hotchkiss in an attempt to gain official recognition. The Ministry of Munitions intervened and forced the Coventry Engineering Employers' Association and the Coventry Engineering Joint Committee to accept elected shop stewards. Neither group was excited about the idea. Unions such as the ASE had consistently opposed elected stewards. The employers were concerned that these committees would spread to other Coventry shops. The Coventry Employers' Association informed the EEF that, 'We view with great concern the recognition of shop committees of this nature, as they are generally controlled by extreme men whose aim it is to secure election on shop committees.'[34] Later in 1917 they agreed to accept shop stewards but only on the following condition: 'The shop stewards shall not interfere with the proper exercise of authority by foremen and chargehands.' Works committees would be consulted on any changes in general working conditions, but it was, 'to be understood that the introduction of an improved method of manufacture is not in itself to be regarded as a change in general working conditions'.[35] The Association also reserved the right to approve all shop stewards. A national agreement on shop stewards was reached in 1917, but it contained neither works committees nor stewards who represented more than one grade of labour. The Coventry unions rejected this agreement and it was not until 1919 that they accepted an agreement which embodied their basic demands. But by 1919, any type of works committee was unlikely to insulate labour from the effects of post-war unemployment.[36]

At the national level, the Federation's experiences with the shop stewards' movement and the demand by the national executive of the ASE for an Engineers' Charter which would have resulted in all workers earning the skilled rate led the Federation to question whether or not they continued to have the right to manage.[37] According to Sir A. Smith of the EEF, the employers, 'are asking ourselves now, Mr. Brownlie, whether the works are to be carried on by your district committees in session in the firm's premises, or whether the management is still to have some say in the direction of the factory under ordinary work. . . . The recent discussions strike at the whole system of industry as carried on today.' Later he argued, 'At the moment we are at the head because we own the factories and this work is ours. You may be in the future at the head, and then we shall have to bow to it, but until that alteration takes place we are going to manage the factories.'[38] For

Sir A. Smith, day-work had become unworkable in Britain and payment by results was necessary.

It is idle for us to suggest to you that these machines should be on time . . . unless you are prepared to give us the production which is required for the industry by the personal inducement of payment by results, then I am afraid there is absolutely no hope for these proposals going through.'[39]

The Coventry Employers' Association were given an opportunity to move to day-work at the end of the war. But they argued that there was simply no way they could depend upon labour to produce the goods, nor did they have the authority to enforce the desired level of output.[40] The issue came to a head in late 1918 when Humber wanted to return to pre-war work. The Coventry Employers' Association were given three options by the local ASE. They could maintain payment by results on existing prices if they would accept higher recognised bonus rates of between 50 and 100 per cent. Payment by results could also be maintained if they agreed to raise pre-war piece prices. The final alternative was to accept a day wage system of hourly rates.[41] The acceptance of the last alternative, favoured by the ASE, would have forced Coventry Association members along a path similar to the Ford system. They would have had no choice but to accept the responsibility for controlling the level of productivity. It is interesting to note, that the final agreement, known as the Humber Agreement, accepted the first proposal, pre-war prices but with much higher recognised bonus levels. In doing this, the Coventry Association Members adopted a strategy which made the worker's productivity a major factor in his weekly wage. It seemed to them the best strategy in light of the relations between capital and labour in Coventry.

The national concern amongst employers about their right to manage and the rejection by the Coventry Employers' Association of day-work are indications that the necessary pre-conditions of Fordism or direct control might not have existed in the 1920s. We would argue that the members lacked confidence in their actual or even potential managerial control to risk a high wages high output strategy. Detailed studies of individual firms and their strategies will make it even clearer how the capital labour problem and the political climate in Britain pushed British management away from Fordism and towards other managerial strategies.

Rolls Royce and Management by Consent
Rolls Royce had had a long history of quasi-paternalistic relations with its workers and had recognised the importance of workers' attitudes as a factor determining labour productivity. During the war, they accepted that most factory work was dull and monotonous and

that the maintenance of output levels would depend upon management getting labour to accept such conditions in return for other benefits.[42] When they decided to convert their works from aero production to vehicles in 1919, they intended to reorganise on mass production lines. They employed 8000 workers at the time and planned for a weekly output of 135 chassis. Wormald, the works manager, stressed the need for careful organisation and good labour relations. He argued that mass production was only viable with a 'contented work force willing to co-operate'.[43]

Shop steward committees set up in 1911 were given a role in the transition process. They were consulted about the general policy the firm should follow. Even though the managers had pretty well decided what their policy was going to be, the fact that the consultation took place at all indicates a rather sophisticated strategy designed to make the workers feel they were an important part of the firm. A committee of design and production engineers was made responsible for implementing the changes. This committee analysed the work process to determine the best way of doing a job. The workers were then offered an opportunity to comment on management's suggestions. This, according to Wormald, resulted in a compromise. 'A job is turned out which satisfies the Management as regards quality and the employees as regards the method to carry it out.' Working in conjunction with this committee was an efficiency committee composed originally of foremen but with labour representatives after 1921. This committee was made responsible for keeping a check on speeds and feeds, jigs and tools, and ultimately became a pricing committee. One of the tasks of the committee was to employ the best workmen to show others how to do jobs. Wormald suggested that, 'The result of the efficiency committee's labour has been a very appreciable advance in production, and, what is equally important, a better feeling in the shops, the men seeing that we were out to improve conditions all round and were working in their interests as well as ours.'[44]

C. Johnson, a Rolls Royce director, wanted to integrate the workers' interests even more thoroughly with the firm's interests. In 1918 he proposed that the firm should allocate 200,000 ordinary shares to the workers (one-quarter of the total issued shares). He also suggested that the workers should elect two representatives to sit on the board of directors. Lloyd concluded that Johnson, 'appreciated more fully than most the extent to which restrictionism on the part of labour is a reaction against the factory system and that dissatisfaction with the actual distribution of income between capital and labour is a symptom rather than a cause of revolt'.[45] The board rejected such radical proposals. Instead they encouraged workers to buy shares on an instalment plan which was not overly successful. One of the direct results of Johnson's suggestions was the creation of a welfare fund which received 50 per cent of all profits after the shareholders received a 10 per cent dividend. The welfare committee, of which Wormald was the chairman, provided a wide range of activities.

Steps were also taken to reduce boredom in the shops by moving workers between jobs. Wormald condemned 'the over-specialisation of the workmen', and pointed out that 'the drudgery of being confined to one operation and one machine for any length of time must necessarily pall'.[46] The programme, which was begun in 1919, was intended to improve relations between capital and labour under the conditions of mass production.

> Though a machine is specialised and will never do anything else, we endeavour as far as the trade union restrictions allow, to move a man from job to job so that he may become a first class mechanic. This scheme is opposed to the ordinary idea of mass production where a man does one job all his life and never anything else. . . . [This] eventually makes him an automaton and kills effort . . . The men, seeing we are concerned in their well-being and development, take more interest in the work, and this factor also aids production.[47]

The radical nature of this policy can only fully be appreciated when it is realised that a major justification for lower wages according to the EEF was the reduction in skill levels which mass production allowed.

On paper, the Rolls Royce system was represented as a workers' utopia, in which an enlightened management benefited through increasing productivity. In reality, the system did not work so perfectly. Despite their commitment to make all workers skilled craftsmen, the firm continued to employ a large amount of unskilled labour in the lowest wage brackets. In 1920, when they attempted to introduce new machines with unskilled workers, the unions successfully resisted this deskilling.[48] In the same year, there was a strike over the sacking of a man. Negotiations between the two sides indicated that sacking was a common form of discipline. It also emerged that the shop steward system was creating a lot of tension amongst managers. The firm reported that,

> Continually for some time past, the shop stewards movement, as it is now constituted at Rolls Royce, is a direct menace against discipline and management, and the whole of the supervisors of Rolls Royce have decided that it is impossible to carry on, unless they are allowed to supervise their jobs without this tyrannical treatment meted out by the shop stewards.[49]

These events suggest that, despite the attempts by Rolls Royce to get the workers to identify with the firm's interests, the actual capacity of the workers to influence decisions was limited. This is further reflected in the extent to which factory operations were co-ordinated by management and by the tendency for the execution of work to be separated from its conception. Decisions about how long a job should take, which machine a job should be done on, and by which operators were, for the most part, determined in offices separated from the work-place. A cost department was employed to collect the available information on costs and was used to keep a constant check on productivity. The control department was responsible for keeping track of material in hand, material needed, and inventories of finished parts.[50]

Building upon their wartime experiences, machine tasks were simplified and divided into small components suitable for unskilled labour. Machinery was used extensively to ensure interchangeability of parts. The machines tended to be standard types rather than special purpose, but extensive jigging and tooling made mass production possible. The most noticeable difference between the Rolls Royce factory and other factories with comparable output, such as Standard, was the absence of a movement towards flow production.[51]

It is obvious that the Rolls Royce management had been able to gain control of many of the production decisions affecting the workers. But there was an important difference between Fordism and the Rolls Royce strategy. Management at Rolls Royce attempted to legitimate its control by consulting the workmen even though this consultation had little effect on actual events. They encouraged workers to adopt the company's objectives, gave them a direct interest in profits earned, and tried to reduce some of the distasteful aspects of repetition work. They did not try to adopt assembly lines or flow production in machine shops to control the pace of work, nor could it be said that they followed a high wages strategy.

Vauxhall and the Movement towards Direct Control

Vauxhall showed a greater tendency than most British firms to move in the direction of direct control and Fordism. It is of interest that this policy was actively pursued only after they left the EEF in 1921. Their success under this strategy is questionable as profit levels were very low and eventually they were taken over by General Motors in 1925. The pre-war manager of the firm, L.H. Pomeroy, had been a strong advocate of managerial control and the limitation of the workers' involvement in production decisions. He believed that the drawing office should be made the nerve centre of managerial organisation from which all instructions should be issued and all information collected.[52]

Vauxhall's isolation from both the London and the Midland engineering centres seems to have been to the workers' advantage prior to

1921. They were able to force the firm to use fully rated skilled men on capstan lathes, milling and grinding machines. In Birmingham, semi-skilled labour was used exclusively on capstans, and 75 per cent of the work on milling and grinding machines was done by semi-skilled labour. The firm's machine department was as advanced as any with a large selection of American tools including continuous loading, grinding and boring machines.[53]

The firm returned to private work in 1919 under conditions similar to their pre-war organisation. The premium bonus system was in use and, according to A.J. Hancock, the works manager, there was an excessive amount of skilled labour. They had also accepted a works committee based on the EEF's agreement with the unions. Hancock complained that production costs were excessive, with the cheapest Vauxhall selling for £1750. When the market for motor vehicles collasped in 1921, the firm took drastic action. The factory was closed for six weeks during which each of the 6000 jobs was studied, timed, and assigned to a specific grade of labour. The premium bonus system was dropped on the rationale that management had taken the responsibility upon itself for determining output levels. Hancock saw his task as one of managing a repetition factory on a semi-automatic basis. The firm also withdrew from the EEF over the question of works committees which they argued interfered with management.[54]

These changes in managerial philosophy, which signalled a move towards direct control, were not accompanied by major changes in the organisation of production on the shop floor. Machines continued to be organised along functional lines rather than in departments designed to produce a single component. Chassis were erected on the stationary principle rather than on an assembly line. In 1925, when the first assembly line was set up, the firm employed 1400 people and produced thirty vehicles per week. There were nine assembly stations on this line, and chassis were moved forward once every hour. A large amount of special purpose machinery had been installed, but much of it was used for only a few hours each week. This was justified on the grounds that special-purpose machines produced more accurate work than standard machines.[55]

In 1921, when the firm dropped the premium bonus system, they moved to day-work. But by 1925, they were forced to modify the payment system to provide a bonus to induce labour to co-operate. However, the managers stressed that the new system was not a return to payment by results and preferred to call it an efficiency system. The workers received a base rate, plus a supplement stated as a percentage of the base rate. This percentage was supposed to reflect management's assessment of the worker's value to the firm. It was based, for the most part, on quantity and quality of output. Decisions regarding work pace continued to be the responsibility of management. The workers were not offered the choice of a slower work pace and lower pay. 'Experience shows that in the majority of instances the work is actually done in this time. Where this is not the case, an explanation is required and an investigation made to determine the cause of the discrepancy.'[56]

When General Motors took over Vauxhall in 1925, they radically reorganised the machine and assembly departments. The factory was divided into twenty-three self-contained departments. All machines were organised on the line principle and assembly was done on tracks. Each department and assembly area was co-ordinated to produce one component every twenty minutes. This completed the translation to direct control begun by Vauxhall managers in 1921. Hancock, who remained with Vauxhall after the take-over, was made the head of planning. He argued that all machines should be organised in lines and that, wherever possible, mechanised tracks should be used to act as 'quantity per hour gauges'. One further change was made in the payment system. The original efficiency system had been based on the individual's value to the firm. This was changed to a group system in which the bonus was related to the department.[57]

Morris Motors: Direct Control and Advanced Forms of Machine Pacing

Of all the case studies, the methods used at Morris Motors in Coventry went the furthest in the direction of direct control, including the use of machines to control the pace of work. In the early 1920s, automatic transfer machines were installed in a number of departments using techniques well in advance of anything being used in motor factories in Britain or the United States.

Morris had all of his engines produced by Hotchkiss in Coventry. The firm had been the centre of the unofficial shop stewards movement in Coventry during the war. Taylor, the chief engineer, described the workers on munitions work as difficult. In 1918, when engine production began, the work-force was divided into two groups. The less co-operative workers remained on the munitions contracts which were paid on ordinary piece-work and yielded high bonus levels. The rest of the work-force was segregated and placed on engine production. Taylor would have preferred to place this section on straight day-work, but felt this was impractical because of the workers' attitudes. They were placed on a group incentive scheme which provided for a fixed bonus of 50 per cent if output levels were achieved. In Taylor's words, 'Some incentive to effort was necessary as the system was not sufficiently advanced to enforce the production requirements'.[58] In a further attempt to gain labour's co-operation during a period of rapid technological change, the work force was subjected to a propaganda campaign informing them that the firm intended to increase output and earnings in the future. Sometime before 1922 the workers were placed on ordinary piece-work at enhanced bonus rates. Management claimed that their policies had produced a 'feeling of confidence and satisfaction with the responsible officials'. This might seem to be supported by the absence of any record of a dispute at the company.[59]

By May of 1923, when Morris purchased the Hotchkiss factory, most of the elements of flow production had been adopted. Each department was self-contained and produced either one major component or several smaller parts. The engines and the gear boxes were assembled on hand-powered lines. The delivery of parts to all sections of the plant had been made automatic and thus shortages and bottlenecks appeared whenever something went wrong.[60] Woollard became general manager of the new factory and set out to increase output and productivity.

Attempts were made to link machines together using either hand conveyors or automatic transfer mechanisms. The first department to be reorganised was the cylinder block department. A common bed was constructed upon which all the machines were placed in line. The machines were linked by a series of conveyors. The blocks were moved forward by hand and inserted into the fixtures by hand. The most novel aspect of this new machine was that each of the individual machines sequenced simultaneously. The machine cycle was controlled by a common shaft which regulated the pace of work at all 53 work stations. Each work station had a time cycle of either four or eight minutes. Each block took 224 minutes to machine. In 1924 the first automatic transfer machines were introduced. The flywheel and gearbox lines were organised on the same principles as the block line, but instead of using hand labour to transfer the components, hydraulic mechanisms were used. These transfer mechanisms were not overly successful, and Morris was forced to rearrange these lines using the hand transfer system. Automatic transfer mechanisms were not perfected until after the Second World War in the United States.[61]

The engineers responsible for these changes paid credit to the ideas of American engineers which they were exposed to in the technical press, though neither Woollard nor Taylor had visited the United States prior to 1924. Two factors seem to explain why these experiments were attempted at Morris. The first reason was the lack of space for expansion at the Coventry site and the demand for engines which had increased from 100 per week to 2000 per week in less than five years. The second factor was that both Woollard and Taylor reacted to the problem of motivating labour differently from most other

British managers. They both argued that machine pacing was the ultimate solution to the human factor problem. Taylor's views seemed closer to Fordism than those of most British managers. He wrote, 'By this arrangement all planning is carried out by technical men, the machine units being equipped, assembled, and maintained by skilled artisans, while the actual production is automatic. Such a system eliminates the human factor to a large extent and reduces repetition production to its proper level of an automatic mechanical operation'.[62] Woollard justified machine pacing on the grounds of its moral justice. 'Mechanical movements of the work piece are possibly even more of moral than of physical value, notwithstanding the fact that it is the physical help they give that makes the moral value possible. The mechanical movement is a metronome which beats out time for the whole work. . . . It is beneficial in redressing injustices to the overworked by urging those who do less than their share.'[63]

Taylor and Woollard also agreed that rising wages were necessary for high output. Taylor argued 'So long as conditions are good and improving, the mass of the people will remain quiescent: should the general trend be stable or backward, the mass will ultimately revolt.' Woollard argued that the payment of high wages was not an altruistic act, but based 'upon the hard facts of business efficiency'.[64] Where Taylor and Morris differed was over whether wages should be paid by the piece or on day rates. Woollard strongly favoured piece-work. Taylor argued that, with the type of machine methods found in the engine factory, day-work was the better system.[65] Woollard's philosophy towards wages was adopted in the inter-war period, with Morris factories remaining on individual or, in a few cases, group piecework.[66] This may explain in part why, despite introducing a chassis assembly line in 1919, and the expansion of output from 2000 in 1920 to over 60,000 in the late 1920s, the line was not mechanised until 1934.[67]

One further aspect of Woollard's attitude towards labour relations is worth noting. In sharp contrast to Rolls Royce and many other British vehicle producers, Woollard and Morris were not enthusiastic about welfare programmes. Woollard suggested he was 'not in favour of overmuch welfare work or paternalism . . . The factory is a means of enabling them to earn a decent living and they are better citizens if they control their own activities outside the factory'.[68] Accounts of factory life at Morris suggest that the philosophy of work as a means to an end, the end being an improvement in the quality of life outside the factory, may have been carried to an extreme. Inside the factories life was most uncomfortable, and questions of health and safety seem to have received less attention than they might have done.[69]

Austin and Piece-Work as a Managerial Strategy

Austin's approach to the problem of the human factor was very different from Woollard's. Austin argued that the most important production problem was the attitude of labour and that this could be best altered through the wage payment system. In commenting on Woollard's description of the hand transfer machine, Austin argued that it was inflexible and unsuited to current production requirements. He was unable to see any of the advantages of machine pacing.[70] At a meeting of the Institute of Production Engineers, Austin commented on his recent visit to the Ford factories. The thing that impressed him the most was that 'everybody in the establishment seemed to be trying to do their best'.[71] This led him to argue that, if Britain was to improve its industrial performance relative to the United States, it needed an improved spirit amongst labour, not new machine methods. In arguing this we are suggesting that Austin's decision not to install new machine techniques until well into the inter-war period was not only determined by the shortage of capital as has been suggested by Church.[72]

C. Englebach, the works director, and P. Keene, the head of the cost department at Austin, stressed on a number of occasions that factory organisation and improvements in worker motivation were more important for improving productivity than new machine systems. Engelbach argued, 'Good organisation and an indifferent plant achieve better results than a good plant and indifferent organisation.' Keene stressed that the main objective of the Austin organisation was to convince the work-force that their interests were best served by co-operating with management. He argued, 'The obvious difficulty at the moment is lack of confidence as between employer and employed.' This difficulty was to be overcome through a novel payment system called bonus on time. The unique feature of this system was that prices were set in minutes rather than in pence. Keene argued that with 'such a basis, many economic problems become common to both employers and employed, and interests commonly flow in one direction. . . . The reason why the system of control became really efficient was that they inculcated into the whole staff a maximum idea of personal responsibility to the firm itself whereby they and the firm were likely to prosper.'[73]

Under the bonus on time payment system, each task was assigned a time value, and the workers were paid the number of hours they had earned times their base rate. The system encouraged the firm to use the lowest rated worker possible on every job. A study of the system, by the EEF, indicated that the rate fixing department was made responsible both for setting the time a job should take and for determining the grade of labour to be used. Austin was able to capture much of the gain resulting from technical change by reducing the base rate for labour. This was a regular complaint by the workers. They were allowed bonus rates as high as 100 per cent, but base rates were very low. The Federation recognised that the system was successful mainly because the unions were poorly organised at Austins. It was argued that, 'The more powerful the union becomes, the more they will be able to break down the present system because they will be in a position to force the company to follow the generally observed district rates.'[74] Not only were the unions weak at Austin, but it seems that they were less able to defend the base rate which should be paid for a specific type of labour than they were in defending the price per piece which was the normal issue under systems of payment by result.

The weakness of the unions at Austin was caused partially by Austin's antagonistic attitude towards them. His 'firmly held belief in the identity of interests between himself and his workpeople' led him to see the unions as unnecessary bodies designed to reduce output. Austin had little sympathy for works committees. The Austin works committee was not allowed to function freely, and by 1928 Keene could claim that, 'We definitely set out to manage as managers and the result is that we have no representation anywhere from the workers' side. No shop stewards, or shop committees, or anyone wanting to interfere with management.'[75]

On a number of occasions the work-force resisted the payment system, but they had little success. The first successful action took place in 1928 when the workers became dissatisfied with the company's policy of sacking highly rated workers and offering to retire them at a lower base rate. After having gone through the official channels of procedure, they tried to reach the best compromise possible in light of their weak position. These terms were wholly unsatisfactory to the workers who proceeded to occupy the factory for five days. Work was resumed only after Austin agreed to meet a joint union-worker delegation. Austin wanted to reduce time allowances because bonus levels had risen in the period 1923–7 when new production methods had been installed. At the time of the strike, 41 per cent of all workers earned more than 100 per cent bonuses. Austin wanted to cut this back to 75 per cent. The workers complained that their higher bonus levels were compensations for reductions in base rates guaranteeing a minimum of 34s per week to machinists and 24s per week to women workers.[76] In 1938, another major conflict over the payment system erupted in the Aero Works. Despite the fact that other members of the EEF felt that Austin workers had a good case, they did not expect Austin to make any concessions. Minor concessions were made to prevent the strike from spreading to the vehicle factories, but base rates at Austin continued to be 20 per cent lower than at other EEF firms.

There is no evidence that machines were being linked together to provide flow production as at Morris. Chassis continued to be assembled on the stationary principle. In 1920, there were 120 chassis assembly stations. Between 1920 and 1924, some minor changes in production methods were made. This included the introduction of a number of unmechanised assembly lines. It was not until 1924 that major changes were initiated which pushed Austin towards flow production. Prior to this date, all components were delivered to, and issued from, the central stores. This inhibited the flow of components throughout the plant on an automatic basis. After 1924, the factory was reorganised so that components would flow directly to the next work area. Parts flowed directly from the machine departments to the assembly lines. The engine and chassis assembly lines continued to be hand-powered. Mechanised assembly lines were not introduced until after 1928.[77] The Austin system depended upon the financial incentives provided by their system of payment by results to create what to management appeared to be a situation of common interests between capital and labour. The very high bonus levels meant that Austin workers had to accept the work pace as determined by management or suffer drastic reductions in their pay level. To Keene, the efficiency of the payment system was obvious: 'The remuneration the worker is able to obtain through savings is a sufficient incentive to him to make large output effective with the minimum of supervision.'[78]

A 1934 submission by Austin to the EEF made it clear that Austin's management saw their system as an alternative to Fordism. They argued,

> There are still a few employers who object to piecework on principle. Their stand-point is that an efficient management ought to be able to get the same results at an agreed rate of wage without having to pay more money to encourage the men to work harder. . . . Some form of extra wage must be paid to a man if he is expected to work harder. The only alternative is to pay a high wage similar to the Ford system and insist upon task achievement. The obtaining of results by this system could not be regarded with favour by an Employers' Federation, as the advantage would be to one particular firm only. When every other concern came into line, the *status quo* would be again obtained, and a circle of rising wage competition would begin . . . The daily task system at fixed wages may be workable in American, or even Continental factories, but the necessary . . . driving works policy, would not be acceptable either to English Labour or Management.[79]

Rover and Associated Equipment Co.: the Rejection of Day-Work
The Associated Equipment Company (AEC) were the first British vehicle producer to install an assembly line in 1917. A mechanised

moving platform, 265 feet long and designed to hold ten chassis, was set up at a total cost of £3500.[80] However, it appears that the line did not result in a major increase in management's control over the workforce. The workers were able to protect a number of customs which kept earnings high and reduced the work load.[81] Union organisation remained relatively strong and in early 1926 a shop stewards' committee was established.

During 1926, the firm set up a new factory in Southall, some twenty miles from the old factory on the other side of London. G. Rushton, who was formerly involved with the London General Omnibus Co., was given control of the new plant. Rushton was described by Bayley from the EEF as a man suffering from 'Forditis'.[82] The Southall factory had two features which are of some interest. The works was organised on flow principles, and the workers were paid fixed day rates. Component assembly lines, of which there were twelve, fed into the main L-shaped assembly line. The works were designed to produce from 80 to 100 chassis per week.[83] The most radical change, and also the one which was the most contentious in the opinion of the EEF, was the shift to day-work. The London Engineering Employers' Association argued that, 'The essential difference between his Southall scheme and schemes in operation at Walthamstow and other federated firms was a payment in anticipation of output, whereas the scheme approved by the Association were payments made after the results had been assured.'[84] The workers were to be placed into three grades. Toolmakers and a few erectors were to be paid 2s, the majority of erectors and some of the machinists were to be paid 1s 9d, and the rest were to be paid 1s 6d per hour. Management had calculated these rates based on output levels and bonus earning at the old plant. If output at the new plant was above or below what they expected, the managers reserved the right to change wages immediately. The new production process and the new wage payment system were a success. Average cost after three weeks had been reduced from £39 to £27 per chassis. By the middle of 1927, the total cost of a chassis had fallen from £267 to £168. The firm paid out an extra bonus of one-half a week's wage per worker after the first six months. During the same period, profits rose from £65,000 to £118,000. The London Engineering Employers' Association were concerned about the high day rate policy being followed by AEC. The London Association had all but decided to expel the firm when the Federation intervened to try to resolve the problem. The Federation informed Rushton that the problem with the participating bonus scheme was that it was being operated on day-work principles. The firm was told that, 'The Federation objected to the participating bonus because the company paid over the district rate without any check that the workpeople earned their money.' Rushton replied that the firm did not need a check on the workers because that was management's task. 'The workman earned the participating bonus, otherwise the workman would not be in the works.' The Federation appealed to Rushton on the grounds that it was not fair to the other members of the EEF. They argued,

> if his company was allowed to pay in this system, other members must also be allowed; that Mr. Rushton's advantage in getting, as he said he did, good men and good work by paying a high fixed wage, was dependent entirely on the fact that this high fixed wage was above that ordinarily paid in the district, and that this advantage would not exist if all members of the Federation were allowed to pay as much as they thought they could afford, the district rate would no longer exist and Mr. Rushton's advantage through paying above the district rate would disappear.

The other members of the EEF investigating the system came to an even stronger conclusion. They argued that the, 'participating bonus as practised by the company was altogether inconsistent with the existence of the Federation'. However the Federation and the London Employers' Association learned to live with the AEC system, although there was pressure against its acceptance in other engineering shops.

In 1930 a similar situation developed at the Rover Co. when the management was criticised by the Federation for being sympathetic to Fordist ideas. In that year Captain Wilks tried to introduce the Bedaux system of payment by results. Wilks argued that, after investigations by the Bedaux experts, productivity would rise and more money would be available for the workers. The workers rejected Wilks's proposals. They saw the new system as a means of increasing the work load, while keeping wages fixed at base rate plus 50 per cent. Wilks made a deal with the union officials, but the workers rejected it and struck, supported by the National Union of Vehicle Builders and the Workers' Union.[85]

Wilks proposed to resolve the strike by moving to a system of daywork at enhanced rates with complete managerial control of the work pace. The unions' reactions to this proposal have not been recorded, but the Coventry Employers' Association were not pleased. The secretary spoke to Wilks. 'He warned the company as to such a step being retrograde in the opinion of the Association and had mentioned the harmful effect which the giving of enhanced day rates would have on the industry of the district.'[86] Cole from the Federation argued that, 'Captain Wilks, to my mind, is suffering from some rather ill-digested views with regard to Capital and Labour. He is a great admirer of Mr. Ford and American methods. His idea is that everybody should receive a high day rate and then be compelled to work as hard as possible and if they do not then they are to be fired'.[87]

Rover and the unions came to an agreement without the help of the Coventry Employers' Association. The union agreed to accept Bedaux on the condition that the firm agree to pay the women, working the system, a minimum wage of £2 15s. This was well above the local average of £2. The Coventry Association criticised this agreement and demanded that the firm change the rate paid to women. The issue was defused when the firm delayed adopting the Bedaux system and remained on ordinary piece-work. Relations between the firm and the Coventry Association remained cool though, and the firm did not attend any Employers' Association meetings for five years.[88]

Conclusions

The main objective of this paper has been to study how the relationship between capital and labour influenced the choice of technique. It has argued that the weakness of the Braverman model is its failure to accept the complexity of the relationship between capital and labour. Braverman saw only one capitalist technology epitomised in Fordism, when in fact technology could follow a number of paths. During the period we have examined, Fordism was rejected by British management. It was rejected because it required a degree of managerial control which seemed incongruous with what management had been able to achieve during the war. Of equal importance was management's perception of labour. While American managers might have been influenced by their perception of an innately lazy labour force, British management perceived labour to be dissatisfied and becoming increasingly antagonistic towards capitalism. This affected British methods of production in two ways. First, it was necessary, both nationally and at the level of the firm, to convince labour that it was in their own interest to support capitalism. Second, day-work with complete managerial control was rejected and replaced by new forms of payment by results. These systems became much more than a mechanism for penalising unproductive workers. At Austin, the payment on time system was designed to reform labour's attitude towards capital.

In some cases it was actually the workers and their representatives who were the strongest advocates of Fordism. They were attracted by the belief that a Fordist managerial policy could provide both high wages and acceptable work conditions. These demands can be seen as part of a fairly broad critique by labour of managerial policies. In 1921, the TUC criticised the performance of British management.

> The British engineering industry is, with few exceptions, badly organised from one end to the other. Therefore with many American establishments, and even with the best in this country, the great majority of British engineering workshops are badly laid out, often badly lighted, inadequately equipped, and, many of them, wastefully managed'.[89]

On a number of occasions, it was clear that British labour was sympathetic towards a Fordist strategy if it could be guaranteed that high wages would result. If their enthusiasm for the system would have persisted after its introduction cannot really be answered. During the negotiations which resolved the 1922 lock-out, it was the unions which pressed for a new managerial initiative which would produce high wages. Brownlie, of the AEU, suggested that systems such as Scientific Management and Fordism must be considered as possible methods of boosting productivity. He argued, 'The individual or the organisation that stands in the way of utilising the improvements of the machine tool, or the improvements brought into being by the application of science to industry, is standing in its own light.'[90] The representatives of the National Union of Vehicle Builders went as far as to suggest that Fordism was an acceptable system to their members. South replied for the EEF, 'Do you think for one moment your men would submit themselves to the principles of Henry Ford?' The reply was, 'They do it. . . . Our people seem quite well satisfied. It is true for a period they did not take to it, but today they are quite satisfied with their employment.'[91] The union representative was of course referring to their experiences with the Fordist system at Ford's Manchester works which had introduced high day wages-high effort system in 1914.

It would be a mistake to argue that British vehicle firms did not exhibit any of the characteristics suggested by Braverman. The rise of managerial capitalism and the function of management reduced labour's control of the conception of work. What has been shown here, though, is that the extent of this process and its actual form in the British economy appears to have been unique from the American experience. The remarkable rise of worker control at the Standard factories in the early 1950s suggests that British workers retained a greater degree of control over production decisions than their fellow workers in factories run on Fordist principles.[92] The tendency towards machine pacing also seems to have been weaker. In its place was found an attempt to reduce the antagonism between capital and labour through welfarist schemes, consultative arrangements, and payment by results.

Although payment by results played a role in each of our case studies, its relative importance varied considerably. At Rolls Royce and Austin it was quite important, while at Vauxhall and Morris, payment by results was combined with a strategy of direct control and some machine pacing. We would argue that the latter two were moving in a direction outside of the main stream of British management thought.[93] The interpretation of Fordism as a disease or mental deficiency, which was revealed by the Federation's response to experiments at Rover and Associated Equipment Co., was more representative of managerial thought.[94]

The ability of Morris and Vauxhall to move against the mainstream of management policy seems in part to be explained by the ability of these firms to insulate themselves from the social and political factors which we have argued influence managerial strategy. At Vauxhall, their isolated location, and the complete rejection of their product by the market in 1921, gave them both the reason and the ability to demand radical changes from their workers. They did not move immediately to a policy of machine pacing, but, over a period of years and helped along by an infusion of American ideas in 1925, machine pacing grew in importance. It is more difficult to explain how Morris's Coventry engine plant was able to isolate itself from its recent past as the centre of the unofficial Coventry shop stewards' movement and from events in Coventry itself. There seem to be two important factors. The first was the constant and rapid growth of the firm which saw engine output increase twenty-fold in five years. In such a situation, management's suggestions to the workers that their interests were served by the firm must have been more convincing than in a stagnant or shrinking company. The second was that senior management at Hotchkiss and Morris seem to have placed an important emphasis on minimising conflict between capital and labour. Perhaps this was a result of their experiences during the war as a centre of labour conflict. This made it possible for them to push through major changes in machine methods and organisation with practically no labour resistance.

It is now possible to provide at least a tentative answer to another of our original questions, viz. will the degree of machine pacing be reduced if a means can be found of reducing the antagonism between capital and labour. The research presented here suggests that Fordism and machine pacing are viable only where the conflict between capital and labour has abated. Machine pacing is not the cause of the real subordination of labour, it is merely the manifestation that labour has already accepted a subordinate role.[95] British managers, who perceived labour antagonism to be their major post-war problem, rejected machine pacing as a means of overcoming this antagonism. This raises the question of why a passive work-force needs to be machine paced and controlled. It seems that a distinction must be made between a co-operative work-force, which we would argue is the objective of welfarism and payment by results, and a passive work-force, which while not resisting capital would not on its own increase productivity. Fordism became a means of converting a passive work-force into a productive one.

It is also necessary to place into perspective the two types of increases in labour productivity made possible by Fordism. These are its ability to increase management's control over labour and the increases in labour productivity made possible by what we shall call increases in efficiency.[96] In the early period, when existing machine methods and work methods were reorganised into flow production and assembly line production, the emphasis seems to have been over-whelmingly on the control aspect. This is not to deny, though, that once the new methods were established, a learning process set in which forced management to improve its co-ordination skills and allowed new types of machinery to be produced. Hence the lethargy for which British management has been criticised seems not to be a failure on their part, but rather the fact that they got on the wrong learning path, a path which at the time of its adoption seemed the only profitable strategy.

Notes

1. I am pleased to acknowledge the generous access to their archives provided by the Engineering Employers' Federation. I am also grateful to assistance from D. Broom, L. Hannah, T. Lawson, N. Mason, R. Moore, and N. Theocharkis.
2. H. Braverman, *Labor and Monopoly Capital* (1974).
3. See, for example, S. Wood, *The Degradation of Work? Skill, Deskilling and the Labour Process* (1982), especially T. Elger, 'Braverman, Capital Accumulation and Deskilling'.
4. Braverman (1974), pp. 56–7, 195, 150, 98–9. For an analysis which described the differences between Scientific Management and Fordism, see C. Palloix, 'The Labour Process: From Fordism to neo-Fordism', in CSE Pamphlet, No. 1, *The Labour Process and Class Strategies* (1976). For an investigation of weaknesses in using the assembly line to control productivity see B. Corriot, 'The Restructuring of the Assembly Line', *Capital and Class* (1980).
5. A.L. Friedman, *Industry and Labour* (1977).
6. B. Palmer, 'Class, Conception and Conflict: The Thrust for Efficiency. Mana-gerial Views of Labour', *Review of Radical Political Economy* (1975).
7. D. Noble, *America By Design* (1979). See also R. Edwards, *Contested Terrain* (1979), D. Nelson, *Managers and Workers* (1975), and Lazonick in this volume.
8. M. Burawoy, 'Towards a Marxist Theory of the Labour Process: Braverman and Beyond', *Politics and Society* (1978), pp. 256, 263, 268. See also M. Burawoy, *Manufacturing Consent* (1979).
9. D.F. Schloss, *Methods of Industrial Remuneration* (1892 edn), p. 57.
10. Engineering Employers' Federation (EEF), P(2)15 Section II, W.G. Bannister, Paper presented to the students of the Institute of Civil Engineers, 11 March 1904.
11. G. Brown, *Sabotage* (1977) p. 148.
12. E.J. Hobsbawm, 'Custom, Wages and Work Load' in A. Briggs and J. Saville (eds.), *Essays in Labour History* (1960).
13. Schloss (1892), p. 15. See also G.D.H. Cole, *The Payment of Wages* (1928) and C.R. Littler, 'Understanding Taylorism', *British Journal of Sociology* (1978).
14. Hobsbawm (1960).
15. Conditions covering the adoption of premium bonus systems were agreed between the EEF and the ASE executive in 1902. (EEF P(2)3, Carlisle Memorandum.) In 1913, when the members of the ASE were given a chance to vote on the memo-randum, they rejected it. (EEF A(4)7). For the spread of premium bonus in the

early motor car factories, see 'The Humber Works', *The Engineer*, 4 September 1903, and P. Martin, 'Works Organisation', *Proceedings Institute of Automobile Engineers* (1906).

16. See below. G.D.H. Cole (1928), p. xi, argued that, with the adoption of modern machine methods in mass production factories, the need to adopt incentive payment systems was reduced. The objective of this paper is to show the reverse, viz. that the reliance on new forms of incentive system by British management reduced the speed at which new machine methods were developed.

17. See Noble (1979); S. Pollard, *The Genesis of Modern Management* (1965); A. Chandler, *The Visible Hand: The Managerial Revolution in American Business* (1977); L. Hannah, 'Managerial Innovation and the Rise of the Large Scale Company in Interwar Britain', *Economic History Review* (1974); J.A. Litterer, 'Alexander Hamilton Church', *Business History Review* (1961).

18. L. Urwick and E.F.L. Brech, *The Making of Scientific Management*, vol. II (1946), p. 11.

19. I. Lloyd, *Rolls Royce: The Growth of a Firm* (1978), pp. 36–8.

20. E. Cadbury, *Experiments in Industrial Organisation* (1912), Lord Leverhulme, *The Six Hour Day* (1918).

21. For an analysis of Whitleyism see R. Charles, *The Development of Industrial Relations in Britain* (1973). M. Cowling, *The Impact of Labour* (1971) has also argued that throughout the period 1906–26, labour was gaining a new self-awareness of its ability to influence the direction of society.

22. E. Garcke, 'The Industrial Situation', *The Engineering Review* (1919).

23. Sir R. Hadfield, 'Address to the London Association of Foremen', *Managing Engineer* (May 1916), p. 189.

24. Ibid.

25. 'Applied Time Studies', *Automobile Engineer* (December 1920).

26. A.W. Reeves and C. Kimber, 'Works Organisation', *Proceedings Institute of Automobile Engineers* (1916/17), p. 375.

27. Ibid. pp. 373 and 389 and T.C. Pullinger, 'Opening Address', *Proceedings Institute of Automobile Engineers* (1917/18).

28. Sir H. Fowler, 'Some Notes on Production', *Proceedings Institute of Automobile Engineers* (October 1916), pp. 27, 29.

29. 'Discussion', *Engineering and Industrial Management* (January 1920), p. 14.

30. EEF, W(4)3, Sir A. Smith to H. Lawson 22 December 1914, and Special Conference, EEF and Various Unions, 13 January 1915.

31. See F.W. Carr, 'The Rise of Labour in Coventry, 1914–1939' (Warwick PhD, 1979).

32. J. Hinton, *The First Shop Steward Movement* (1973), pp. 213–34.

33. ASE (Cov.) 5 October 1915, 7 March 1916 and 3 April 1917.

34. DC ASE (Cov.) 5 August 1916; EEF, S(4)6, CDEEA to EEF, 14 April 1917.

35. EEF, S(4)11, CDEEA to EEF 11 December 1917.

36. EEF, S(4)12, Special Conference of EEF and Craft Unions, 7 December 1917, and Special Conference, 20 December 1917. P(5)27, Local Conference, CDEEA and CEJC, 6 March 1919. Shop Stewards and Works Committee Agreement, EEF and Various Unions, 20 May 1919.

37. On the Engineers' Charter see EEF, Special Conference, EEF and AEU, 27 October 1920, pp. 252–7.

38. EEF, Special Conference, EEF and AEU, 10 November 1921, pp. 256–90, 394.

39. EEF, Special Conference, EEF and AEU, 27 October 1920, pp. 508, 519.

40. EEF, P(5)27, Local Conference, CDEEA and CEJC, 6 March 1919 and 13 March 1919.

41. DC ASE (Cov.) 14 December 1918, 21 January 1919, 28 January 1919. EEF, P(5)27, Local Conference, 18 December 1918. CDEEA to EEF 11 February 1919, 30 March 1919. M(17)6, Fifty Per Cent Agreement, 26 June 1919.

42. Lloyd (1978), pp. 47–50, 71.

43. H. Swift, 'Efficiency', *The Managing Engineer* (October 1920), p. 114; see also A. Wormald, 'How We Solved Our Labour and Output Problem', *Works Management* (November 1919), p. 10.
44. Wormald (November 1919), p. 18.
45. Lloyd (1978), pp. 21–2. See also 'Rolls Royce Methods', *Engineering Production*, 29 December 1921.
46. A. Wormald, 'British Origins of Productions', *Engineering Production*, 5 May 1921.
47. Wormald (November 1919), p. 19. For the reply to this point from the superintendent of the Ford factory see A.T. Giebert, *Engineering Production*, 23 June 1921.
48. During the war, there were a number of conflicts between the firm and the union over use of women in the factory. EEF, D(8)3, Derby EEA and Various Unions.
49. EEF, M(15)54, RR to Local Association and EEF, 18 May 1920.
50. A. Wormald, *Works Management* (December 1919), p. 95. H Swift, 'Efficiency', *The Managing Engineer* (October 1920), p. 114.
51. 'Quality Production', *Engineering Production* (August 1923); 'The Works of Rolls Royce', *The Automobile Review* (February 1927); 'An Interesting Visit', *Engineering Production*, 4 January 1923.
52. L.H. Pomeroy, 'Automobile Engineering after the War', *Proceedings Institute of Automobile Engineers* (1914), p. 22.
53. 'The Works of Vauxhall Motors', *The Automobile Engineer* (June 1920); 'Vauxhall Motors Ltd', *Engineering Production,* 8 June 1922. EEF, D(8)2, Bedfordshire EEA to EEF, 7 December 1917.
54. EEF, Membership Files, Luton News, 6 October 1921. Vauxhall to EEF, 15 July 1921. EEF W(3)48, Vauxhall and Payment by Results.
55. *Engineering Production*, 8 June 1922, and *Automobile Engineer* (June 1920). 'The Works of Vauxhall', *Automobile Engineer* (October 1925).
56. 'The Works of Vauxhall', *Automobile Engineer* (October 1925), p. 347.
57. 'Motor Manufacturing Practice', *Machinery*, 15 March 1928. E.W. Hancock, 'The Trend of Modern Production Methods', *Institute of Production Engineers* (1928).
58. H.E. Taylor, 'The Principles and Psychology of Production', *Machinery* 1 November 1928, p. 139.
59. The EEF became concerned about the increase in real earnings at Morris and tried unsuccessfully to get the Oxford plants to join the Federation.
60. 'Production of an Automobile Power Unit', *Engineering Production* 27 July 1922 and 3 August 1922; 'Manufacturing Practice of Light Motor Car Power Unit', *Machinery*, 9 March 1922 to 7 September 1922.
61. F.G. Woollard, 'Some Notes on British Methods of Continuous Production', *Proceedings Institute of Automobile Engineers* (1924–5), pp. 423, 429, 437–8.
62. Taylor (1928), p. 137.
63. Woollard (1924/5), p. 441.
64. F.G. Woollard, *Principles of Mass and Flow Production* (1954), p. 180; H.E. Taylor, 'Production and Psychology', *Journal Institute of Production Engineers* (December 1929), p. 23.
65. Woollard (1924/5), p. 424. H.E. Taylor, 'Efficient Production', *Automobile Engineer* (December 1927), p. 499.
66. W.R. Morris, 'Policies that Built the Morris Motors Business', *System* (February 1924); H.A. Goddard, 'Profit Sharing and the Amenities of the Nuffield Factories' in F.E. Gannett, *Industrial and Labour Relations in Great Britain* (1939).
67. P.W.S. Andrews and E. Brunner, *The Life of Lord Nuffield* (1955); R. Church, 'Myths, Men and Motor Cars', *Journal of Transport History* (1977); R. Overy, *William Morris* (1976).
68. Woollard (1924/5), p. 424.
69. A. Exell, 'Morris Motors in the 1930s', *History Workshop* (1978/79).
70. Woollard (1924/5), p. 459.

71. *Proceedings Institute of Production Engineers* (1924/5), p. 7.
72. R. Church, *Herbert Austin* (1979), p. 69.
73. London School of Economics, Ward Papers, MRGI, Organisation Section, W/8/29–34/13/476, pp. 2–14.
74. Ibid.; EEF, A(1)51, G.E. Nines, Austin Payment on Times Systems.
75. P. Keene, 'Production, A Dream Come True', *Proceedings Institute of Production Engineers* (1928), p. 28, and Church (1979), pp. 31, 45.
76. EEF, S(5)9, Sit-in at Austins, Grading Strike 1929; Church (1979), pp. 150–2; ASE, *Monthly Report*, February 1929.
77. 'Making the Austin Twelve', *Automobile Engineer* (August 1931).
78. London School of Economics, Ward Papers, W/8/29–34/476, P. Keene to MRG 1, 2 December 1930.
79. EEF, W(3)129, Piecework in the Tool Room, 1 February, pp. 26–8.
80. *The Motor Trader*, 19 March 1919.
81. EEF, Membership Files, AEC, Failure to Observe Rules.
82. EEF, Membership Files, AEC, W.L. Bayley to A.C. Bayley, 18 March 1927.
83. EEF, Membership Files, Interview 21 March 1927; 'The Works of Associated Daimler Company', *Auto Engineer* (January 1928).
84. EEF, Membership Files, Failure to Observe Rules and Interviews 19/7/27.
85. EEF, P(20)5, Local Conference, 14 April 1930.
86. Coventry District Engineering Employers' Association, Executive Meeting, 31 March 1930.
87. EEF, P(20)5, Cole Memo, 10 September 1930.
88. EEF, P(20)5, Proposals regarding Bedaux strike, 11 September 1930.
89. TUC, 'Comments on the Present Economic Position of the Engineering and Allied Industries' (1921), pp. 23–4.
90. EEF, Conference, 24 July 1919, p. 29.
91. EEF, Special Conference, 1 May 1925, p. 7.
92. For a comprehensive study of the Standard situation se S. Melman, *Decision Making and Productivity* (1958).
93. By the mid-1920s a few writers were beginning to suggest that payment by results might be preventing the proper development of management. See, for example, J.E. Powell, *Payment by results* (1924).
94. Internal job ladders and high wages, which were seen as the American system, drew support from a few British spokesmen. See B. Austin and W. Francis Lloyd, *The Secret of High Wages* (1926).
95. For the distinction between the formal and real subordination of labour, see Brighton Labour Process Group, 'The Capitalist Labour Process', *Capital and Class* (1977).
96. W. Baldamus, *Efficiency and Effort* (1961), argues that all questions of efficiency are really questions of controlling human effort.

5 Technological Change and the Control of Work: The Development of Capital–Labour Relations in US Mass Production Industries[1]
William H. Lazonick

Mass Production and the Capital–Labour Relation

Between the 1880s and the 1920s, the giant enterprise arose to transform the American economy from one dominated by relatively small producers and competitive markets to one dominated by corporate control. In his outstanding book, *The Visible Hand*, Chandler provides an incisive and detailed analysis of both the strategies that the successful 'industrial imperialists' pursued in building their empires and the internal hierarchical structures that the new corporate capitalists developed in order to ensure that massive productive potential would be translated into profits.[2]

The pursuit of profits meant maintaining high product prices and cutting costs. The strategy to achieve high product prices entailed the control of horizontal competition, evolving from the price pools of the 1870s to the trusts of the 1880s, to the massive merger movement of 1898–1902. While not all-pervasive in the early twentieth century, oligopoly emerged as a dominant characteristic of the US economy. The firms that came out on top, as Chandler demonstrates, were those that were able to cut costs dramatically by a strategy of vertical integration, redesign of plant layout, standardisation of inputs, and mechanisation of heavy and skilled work. The result was mass production to supply the burgeoning mass markets of the country. As epitomised by Carnegie's steel mills, those firms that integrated, redesigned, standardised, and mechanised were able to reap enormous internal economies – not just economies of 'scale' but also, and more importantly, economies of 'through-put'. Such economies were decisive in the competitive struggle.

In order to achieve these internal economies, plant managers had to develop methods of co-ordinating the rapid flow of inputs through the various processes in the enterprise, consequently the movement towards systematic management came into being. Successful systematic management did not simply entail the standardisation, speed-up, and co-ordination of the flow of capital inputs; it also meant the standardisation, speed-up, and control of workers. The craft skill and judgement of the worker had to be as much as possible superseded as did the control of workers over the pace of work.[3]

Moreover a new type of worker had to be created – the machine operative – who came to be classified under the vague heading of 'semi-skilled'. On mass production technologies, the standardisation of workers was not achieved simply by embodying specialised skills in the machine and by transferring control over work organisation to managers. One worker did not automatically become as good – that is, as productive – a worker as another; the introduction of machine processes did not in itself create a homogeneous mass of interchangeable workers as, for example, Braverman has recently assumed.[4] Rather there was a radical transformation in types of 'skills' that really mattered in capitalist production processes: as specialised cognitive skills became less relevant on the shop floor, more general behavioural traits and attitudes became of paramount importance. With craft production methods, the capitalist was dependent on, as Marx put it, 'the strength, skill, quickness, and sureness' of workers in handling their tools.[5] With mass production methods, based on expensive capital inputs and high-speed through-puts, the capitalist was dependent on the reliability, dependability, attentiveness, and loyalty – and in many cases the judgement if not the craft skill – of the 'semi-skilled' worker. The efficacy of capitalist mass production methods required that the machine operative be disposed to take orders from above and, what is the other side of the same coin, indisposed to sabotage the rapid flow of production from below. The 'good' machine operative was made, not born. How to get work out of a worker, and hence output out of the machines, became a major managerial problem with the development of mass production methods.[6]

The problem of how to get work out of the worker was, of course, central to Karl Marx's theory of capital accumulation. Marx's distinction between labour-power (i.e. the capacity to work) and labour (i.e. the amount of work actually performed) confronted this problem directly. However, there are serious shortcomings with Marx's own analysis of how the problem of getting work out of the workers was solved under capitalism. In Marx's view, the introduction of division of labour eroded the craft control on the shop floor by dividing off various auxiliary tasks performed by, or at least under the jurisdiction of, the skilled craftsmen, reallocating these tasks to less expensive and more docile segments of the labour force. But Marx recognised that division of labour itself could not eliminate real craft skill from the work-place, nor could it undermine the craft organisation of those who possessed these skills. For Marx, it was the introduction of machinery that, by superseding the need for human strength and skill on the shop floor, did away with both craftsmen and their craft unions, including restrictive union rules concerning the organisation of the labour process. Moreover, by throwing workers out of work, machinery would augment the reserve army of the unemployed which in turn would force those who remained employed 'to submit to over-work and to subjugation under the dictates of capital'.[7]

Marx provides us with invaluable rudiments of a theoretical frame-work for analysing the nature of the capital–labour relation. But, Marx's own theoretical framework is incomplete and some of his con-clusions are empirically incorrect. Take, for example, Marx's classic case of the use of technology by capital to dominate labour: the intro-duction of the automatic ('self-acting') mule in place of the common (or hand) mule in British cotton spinning. To demonstrate the effec-tiveness of this machine technology in eliminating the craft control of the common mule spinners, Marx relied on statements made in the mid-1830s by the 'philosopher of the factory', Andrew Ure. Marx, writing some three decades after Ure, failed to separate the 'philos-opher's' ideology from industrial reality: the highly competitive character of the British cotton industry enabled mule spinners to retain rigid *craft control* in their work processes – control over the pace, organisation, and remuneration of work – despite the fact that the actual *craft* basis of this control had been substantially under-mined. This craft control permitted the self-acting mule spinners of the late nineteenth century to resist unremunerated intensification of labour at work and protect themselves from an habitual reserve army of mule spinning labour.[8].

Once he had determined that machinery solved the problem of the appropriation of labour – getting work out of workers – Marx had no need to investigate the question further. Labour disappeared as an active force in shaping the social and technical organisation of work. Moreover, having firmly rooted the subjection of labour to capital in the production process itself, Marx saw no need to look beyond the capitalist enterprise to see how the development of political and cul-tural institutions affected the attitudes and power of workers *vis-à-vis* their employers in the work-place. The impressions one gets from reading the first volume of *Capital*, are that, as nineteenth century capitalism developed, the working-class family was destroyed and schooling for working-class children had no real function other than to comply with certain clauses in the Factory Acts; and that, indeed, once the 'normal' ten-hour working day was achieved through state legislation, neither the state nor trade unions had any important institutional role to play.[9]

Braverman wholeheartedly roots his own analysis of the development of the twentieth-century capitalist labour process in Marx's analysis. Indeed he argues that the explanation of the apparent lack of concern by Marxists with the analysis of the labour process since Marx 'probably begins with the extraordinary thoroughness and prescience with which Marx performed his task'.[10] With such unquestioning acceptance of Marxian theory, Braverman's work reflects all the shortcomings of Marx's analysis of the development of capital–labour relations. He assumes that, in modern capitalist industry, the problem of getting work out of the worker is resolved by mechanisation and automation. Of paramount importance in this regard is the industrial engineer, who designs a job so as to reduce the skill and knowledge of the workers to a minimum while vesting all knowledge of the production process with management. Of little importance are the personnel managers whose 'petty manipulations' merely habituate the worker to the realities of job design. Indeed, citing an article by three industrial engineers to make his point, Braverman argues that 'job design represents *reality* while personnel administration represents only mythology'.[11]

In the introduction to his book, Braverman asserts that he will make no attempt 'to deal with the modern working class on the level of its consciousness, organization, or activities. This is a book about the working class as a class *in itself*.'[12] Yet in his statements on the relative importance of personnel management and job design in effecting (as Marx put it) the subjection of labour to capital, Braverman in fact assumes an understanding of the relation of workers' attitudes and aspirations – their 'consciousness' – to job design; an understanding that is derived by citing the pronouncements of the job designers themselves as well as a very one-sided and, as I shall argue, erroneous interpretation of the work of the originator of the system of Scientific Management, Frederick Taylor.[13]

Indeed from this perspective – one that analyses the labour process solely in terms of its technical organisation – Braverman goes so far as to deny that social processes outside of the work-place are related to the capitalist labour process at all. Specifically, as part of his argument that 'semi-skilled' workers are in fact 'unskilled' workers, Braverman attempts to show that historically 'the continuing extension of mass education for the non-professional categories of labour increasingly lost its connection with occupational requirements'. He notes, that over time, educational requirements for mass occupations have risen while job-specific skill requirements have been degraded; and he concludes that employers must be using educational attainment as a screening device in hiring. However he then goes on to argue that there is no job-relevant content to mass education, and indeed that there is a 'growing recognition among corporate managers and education researchers that the commonly made connection between education and job content is, for the mass of jobs, a false one'.[14]

Hence, in his discussion of mass schooling, even more so than in his discussion of personnel management, Braverman chooses to ignore the importance of workers' attitudes and personality traits to the levels of productivity and capital accumulation. In their analysis of the historical origins of mass schooling and the job-relevant content of the present schooling system, however, Bowles and Gintis come to a quite different conclusion. They agree with Braverman that the corporations do not rely on the mass schooling system to develop job-specific cognitive abilities. But, unlike Braverman, they do not therefore regard the content of schooling as irrelevant. Instead they argue that the mass schooling system in the United States has, over the last century, become integrally related to the capitalist labour process as an institution that inculcates and reinforces in future workers behavioural characteristics that have been and continue to be highly relevant on the job.[15] Capital accumulation on the basis of mass production technologies is dependent on the characteristics of the human products of mass schooling precisely because of its need for dependable, reliable, attentive, and loyal workers. In facing the problem of getting work out of the workers, the attitudes, norms, and personality traits – the 'consciousness' – of workers is of substantial importance to those whose goal it is to accumulate capital.

One cannot begin to understand the development of capitalist production processes without analysing the social institutions, including the capitalist enterprise itself, that shape the attitudes and outlooks of workers. In dialectical fashion, mass production technology in solving one problem in capitalist accumulation – the reliance of the capitalist on the craft skills of his workers – created, or at least heightened, another problem – the reliance of the capitalist on the willingness of the workers to work hard at jobs over which they exercised no control. The complete solution to the old problem required the destruction of old social institutions such as the craft unions while the solution to the new problem entailed the construction of new social institutions, most notably the mass schooling system and corporate bureaucracies for the management of people. The social relations of craft production disappeared; the social relations of mass production came into being. The basis of capital–labour relations, whether stable or unstable, co-operative or conflictual, had changed.

What follows is an attempt to summarise the history of the conflicts, compromises, and institutional developments that characterised this transformation of production relations. In so doing, I shall draw upon a growing body of relevant historical research in addition to selected contemporary documents. My purpose here is not so much to draw historical conclusions as to put our current understanding of the development of modern corporate production relations into a sharper theoretical perspective.

From Craft Production to Mass Production

In late nineteenth-century US manufacturing, control over production – hiring, firing, promotion, discipline, wage setting, work organisation – was generally located on the shop floor. Especially as markets expanded, capitalists as managers of the enterprise as a whole busied themselves with marketing, purchasing, and finance, leaving production decisions in the hands of those actually supervising the work. This control was usually exercised by a foreman or supervisor, either as a salaried employee or as an inside contractor.[16] Recent research has shown, however, that such control was often in the hands of highly skilled craft workers who not only had 'functional autonomy' over their own skilled work but also hierarchical control over subordinate workers and hence over auxiliary aspects of the work process. Such craft control over production was especially true in the metal and metal using industries which were to form the core of the new industrial revolution. As epitomised by the Amalgamated Association of Iron and Steel Workers, the strongest craft union in the newly-formed American Federation of Labour (AFL) of the late 1880s, skilled craft workers had considerable power not only over the organisation and pace of work but also, by means of collective bargaining, over levels of piece rates.[17]

Capitalists had neither the incentive nor possibility of ending their reliance on craft control as long as production was to order and hence small batch, and as long as the technical skills of the craftsmen were central to the manufacturing process. In the third quarter of the nineteenth century, however, and especially in the decade or so after the Civil War, the rapid development of machine technologies and mass markets transformed the production possibilities and profitable opportunities facing industrial capitalists. By the 1870s, conditions of supply and demand had emerged that promised enormous profits to those capitalists who could introduce systems of high-speed through-put into vertically integrated series of manufacturing processes.

Even as craft skills were undermined by the development of new technologies the craft unions threatened to obstruct the path to lower unit costs. The problem was not that the craft unions refused to accept the new technologies; the very supersession of their craft skills meant that the workers had little power to make such demands. The problem was that the craft unions sought to use their established collective bargaining positions to maintain jurisdiction over the new machine tending occupations and thereby maintain control over the levels of work-loads and piece rates. That the persistence of such 'craft' control in the presence of mechanisation was a possibility was to be demonstrated by British workers in the 1890s and beyond.[18] In the United States, the mobility of capital permitted new plants to be set up in non-union areas while the mobility of labour lessened the commitment of machine operatives to unions, frustrating attempts to maintain craft control. In some of the older plants in craft union centres, however, capitalists had to take more active measures to rid themselves of craft control. This was the case at Carnegie's Homestead steel mill, the site of the most famous and most important clash to abolish craft control.

In his valuable book, *Steelworkers in America*, Brody details the generally destructive effect that the Homestead defeat had on craft control in the US steel industry. The steel capitalists had won the right to run their plants as they saw fit but Brody overstates the victory for profit-making: 'Unencumbered, the steelmaster could base his labor decisions on the *objective criteria* of what minimized cost and maximized his profit. He could *with impunity* manipulate the wage rate, step up the work, and extend the twelve-hour day and seven-day week. The antiunion triumph completed economical steel manufacture.' That this triumph was not complete is recognised by Brody in the very next paragraph (thus setting out the problem to which the rest of his book – as well as this paper – is devoted):

> The (antiunion triumph), however, much widened the area of labor relations for the industry. The union, despite its drawbacks, had been the basis of a stable and viable labor system. That structure was shattered with the union organization. *Labor stability had to be built anew.* The burden, once the function of the union machinery, passed to the steel man.[19]

Brody is quite correct: labour stability had to be built anew. But the separation of labour history and economic history implicit in the two preceding passages is incorrect. To recognise that industrial relations remains an issue after such a thorough defeat of collective bargaining is to recognise that there are no objective criteria of cost minimisation and profit maximisation. The capitalist cannot manipulate wage rates and work-loads with impunity precisely because he still has to deal with a labour force, whether unionised or not. He has to get his workers to work for the company. His success in so doing in conjunction with mass production technologies, and not the latter alone, will determine 'minimum' unit costs and 'maximum' profits.

The problem facing the steel capitalists, like all other mass production capitalists freed from craft control, was how to get their machine operatives to work steadily and reliably so as to realise as fully as possible the technical potential of their mass production methods. It was this problem that from the mid-1880s led Frederick W. Taylor to develop a theoretical system of capital–labour relations that became known as Scientific Management.

Much has been written in recent years concerning Taylor and the role of his system in the development of production relations in US corporations.[20] A very widely read and influential account is that of Braverman who argues 'Modern management came into being on the basis of (Taylor's) principles.' He sums up Taylor's system in terms of three general principles:

1. Dissociation of the labour process from the skills of workers;
2. Separation of the conception of work (the preserve of management or more specifically industrial engineers) from its execution (the role of workers);
3. The use by management of this monopoly over knowledge to control each step of the labour process.[21]

Hence for Braverman, Taylorism is a process of taking craft skills away from workers and vesting the knowledge of work in management, thus enabling capitalists to control the worker.

There is no doubt that the process that Braverman describes – the increasing detailed division of labour in the production process accompanied by the increasing managerial control of technical knowledge – has been a major characteristic of US capitalist development from the late nineteenth century. But it is wrong to assume that control by capitalists over the planning of work in itself enables them to control their workers. To make this assumption is to ignore the fundamental problem that Frederick Taylor confronted.

Braverman's first error is to disregard the integral relation of the development of Taylorism to the development of mass production technologies. While he recognises that Scientific Management arose with the development of large-scale, technically advanced enterprises, Braverman argues that, 'Logically, Taylorism belongs to the chain of development of management methods and the organization of labor, and not to the development of technology, in which its role was minor.'[22] To argue that 'Taylor was not primarily concerned with the advance of technology' as does Braverman is, however, to misunderstand the problem that Taylor was trying to solve, as well as the way in which Taylor developed his system of management.

Taylor did most of his writing on shop management after the turn of the century, but the actual development of his ideas arose out of his experiences in the last two decades of the nineteenth century. His most fruitful years in this regard were those spent in the nation's most technologically advanced machine shops both at the Midvale Steel Co.

as foreman and mechanical engineer during the 1880s and at the Bethlehem Steel Co. as a consulting engineer employed to introduce a piece rate system between 1898 and 1901. During the 1880s and 1890s, Taylor was continually involved in metal-working experiments that would increase the technical potential for high-speed through–put in the machine shops. Indeed, according to one authority on the history of technological change, Taylor is 'generally considered the outstanding inventor of machine tools in the last two decades of the (nineteenth) century'.[23] His most notable achievement was the discovery of high-speed tool steel after years of experimentation. As a 'shop floor' engineer, however, Taylor understood that it was not enough to develop a technology to overcome the limitations that craft skill placed on through–put. One also had to convince those who held the purse-strings that the new technology would actually result in enough cost savings to make the introduction of the new method economically worthwhile. In order to demonstrate the economic potential of the new technology one had to get the operative to work at a pace commensurate with the technical potential of the machine. The very success of the mechanical inventor as a technological innovator (to use a Schumpeterian distinction) was dependent on the ability to exercise control over the workers.

In Taylor's system, a prelude to control of the worker was redesign of work by a 'planning department', the main purpose of such redesign being to specify narrowly defined tasks that could then be evaluated through time study in order to set standards for performance. Braverman's second, and more serious, error is to assume implicitly that scientific managers, having set these standards of performance, were then actually able, by virtue of the very redesign of work, to implement these standards on the shop floor.

In *The Principles of Scientific Management*, Taylor himself devoted much discussion to the problems that he had both at Midvale and at Bethlehem in increasing the pace of work. The crux of the problem was 'soldiering': the collective, and quite rational, resistance of workers to the speed-up of work at given piece rates. Workers knew from their experience that while they might get higher earnings in the short run, in the longer run the result of their extra effort would not be substantially higher pay but rather a cut in the rates.[24] As Taylor later described the situation at Midvale in the early 1880s:

> Almost all of the work of this shop had been done on piece work for several years. As was usual then, and in fact as is still usual in most of the shops in this country, the shop was really run by the workmen, and not by the bosses. The workmen together had carefully planned just how fast each job should be done, and they had set a pace for each machine throughout the shop, which was limited to about one-third of a good day's work.

Every new workman who came into the shop was told at once by the other men exactly how much of each kind of work he was to do, and unless he obeyed these instructions he was sure before long to be driven out of the place by the men.[25]

By his own account, it took Taylor as gang boss three years of rate busting to increase productivity ('in many cases doubled') in the machine shop, during which time the workers were continually breaking their machines to indicate to Taylor's superiors that their shop floor supervisor was running the capital equipment faster than was technically possible. In the face of such demonstrations, Taylor emphasised that his success in raising output was largely due to the unusual confidence that his own boss, Midvale president William Sellers, placed in his rate busting endeavours.[26] But despite such entrepreneurial support, Taylor recognised that, due to the hostility of the workmen who had indeed found their piece rates being cut, the productivity increases that had been achieved were in constant jeopardy.

This situation Taylor blamed on the use of the traditional rate cutting system. Hence, 'after being made foreman [in 1883] . . . he [Taylor] decided to make a determined effort to in some way change the system of management, so that the interests of the workmen and the management should become the same, instead of antagonistic'.[27] The result was the development of the principles of Scientific Management based on both job redesign and the implementation of a new piece rate incentive system by the scientific managers. In the area of job redesign, the growing importance of technical change was already making many (but by no means all) of the craft skills of the machinist obsolete and vesting key knowledge in the ranks of mechanical engineers, a 'profession' growing rapidly in prestige and practical importance in the last two decades of the nineteenth century.[28] In a period of intense market competition based on rapid technological change and high-speed through-put, technically trained men like Taylor found a new role in the capitalist enterprise to redesign not only the division of labour but also the flow of work. In this respect, Taylor's efforts were part and parcel of the much broader movement of systematic management. For Taylor, it was not job redesign *per se* but rather his piece rate incentive system that was the key to the setting of 'scientific' standards of performance and hence to the existence, never mind success (which in Taylor's view would inevitably follow), of a system of scientific management.

Yet Bravermen in his account of Scientific Management omits any discussion of the nature or the role of Taylor's piece rate incentive system – an omission quite in keeping with his view that job design represents reality while personnel administration represents mythology.[29] Taylor first made public his piece rate incentive system in a paper presented to the American Society of Mechanical Engineers (ASME) in 1895. He viewed his system as both an extension and a critique of earlier incentive systems presented to ASME by Henry Towne in 1889 and Frederick Halsey in 1891.[30] All three systems were attempts to divide out productivity gains between capitalists and workers on a stable, pre-determined basis so as to avoid the frequent rate cutting that in turn gave workers the incentive to 'soldier'.

In an era when craft control was posing a serious problem for capitalists in mass production industries, all three incentive systems represented managerial attempts to achieve a division of productivity gains that both sides would view as 'fair' without resorting to collective bargaining. The possibility that workers might assert craft control was especially threatening in the metal-using industries (with which Towne, Halsey, and Taylor were all involved), for despite the rapid pace of technological change in machine tools, the reliance on the manual skill and judgement of machinists was being only slowly superseded.

Hence in an era of intense competition and rapid technological change, the purpose of the incentive schemes was to stabilise capital–labour relations. The rapid development of technology held out great prospects for simultaneously lightening the physical strain of work and increasing productivity. But the inherent conflicts of interests between capitalist and workers over the appropriation of productivity gains and over the pace of work were constantly tending to destabilise any agreement on these issues and undermine the co-operation and trust required to realise potential productivity increases. Unbeknown perhaps to themselves (and unfortunately also to Braverman), Towne, Halsey, and Taylor were grappling with the Marxian dialectic: the interaction between the development of the material forces of production and the nature of the social relations of production!

Towne's system was a 'profit-sharing' scheme and hence rewarded workers as a group for superior performance. Halsey and Taylor by way of contrast emphasised the importance of rewarding each worker according to his individual performance. They therefore proposed differential piece rate plans so that the harder-working individual would reap higher earnings. But Taylor, the 'shop floor' engineer, viewed the systems of Towne and Halsey, both entrepreneur-engineers, as alike in one crucial respect: both simply recorded the quickest time in which a job had been actually performed, and fixed this as the standard.[31] In effect, under these systems, the workers still set the pace of work. Taylor's main addition to the 'Towne–Halsey plan' was time study, the setting of 'scientific' work standards by the 'planning department' as a prelude to the 'scientific' determination of shares in productivity gains. Hence Taylor integrated the redesign of work into a wage incentive system.

Taylor's efforts to solve 'the labor problem' were carried on by his disciples such as Gantt, Barth, Cooke, and Gilbreth. In the period between 1901 and 1917, they were able to redesign work in some fifty firms, but they had little success in winning the workers over to their 'scientific' standards.[32] Taylorism had succeeded in focusing the attention of mass production capitalists in the United States and abroad on the problem of motivating the worker, but it had by no means provided a solution. As Slichter argued in his pioneering work, *The Turnover of Factory Labor*: 'The abuse of the piece work system had caused workmen to regard all merit systems simply as speeding up devices and this prejudice is frequently difficult to overcome.'[33] Restriction of output and rate cutting persisted as an endemic problem in the largely non-unionised mass production industries of the United States.

However, at least one wage incentive scheme – Henry Ford's '$5 day' – clearly worked in this period. From 1908 to 1913, Ford had been standardising and mechanising the mass production of the Model T from the foundry to final assembly, cutting costs all the way by increasing through-put. Virtually all the processes in Ford's Highland Park plant became technically interrelated as part of a co-ordinated flow of work. Workers were put on time rates (an unusual practice in the automobile industry at that time) and supervisors sought to ensure that they kept pace with the work flow and performed their task properly. By 1913, Ford was producing almost 40 per cent of all cars sold in the United States (up from 20 per cent in 1911), but labour problems were mounting. In 1913, labour turnover at Ford was 370 per cent while absenteeism was averaging 10.5 per cent per day. The very speed with which workers were entering and leaving employment inevitably entailed a lack of discipline – and hence productivity – on the job.[34]

In 1914, Ford was about to install the mechanical assembly line itself. To ensure labour stability he decided to promise mass production workers who stayed with the company for six months at least $5 per day, about twice the prevailing rate in the industry. The $5 per day was not guaranteed; it was actually a profit-sharing plan, but Ford's position in the industry (as well as the publicity surrounding the introduction of the plan) gave workers the confidence that they weren't being set up for a wage cutting fall. Aided by a substantial increase in general employment, labour turnover fell to about 40 per cent and absenteeism to 0.4 per cent day in 1914. With the stick of a huge reserve army of workers seeking employment at Highland Park and the carrot of the $5 day, Ford apparently took firm control of his workers.

But, as far as the inherent shortcomings of wage incentive schemes are concerned, Ford's success is the exception that proves the rule. As long as he was in the process of attaining maximum productivity from his plant and equipment and as long as he was outpacing the competition, his high-wage labour policies remained in place. But by the early 1920s, when productivity increases could not longer be enticed from the workers and machines and the competition began to close in, Ford's name became, as Alfred Chandler has put it, 'synonymous with many of the most notorious labor malpractices, such as speed-up of work, the dropping of the older, higher-paid men, arbitrary discharges, and so on'.[35] The Ford Motor Co. that had been able to buy control of its workers as it brought mass production techniques to a new stage of perfection was to remain the most violently anti-union employer in the automobile industry until 1914 when it was forced to recognise the United Automobile Workers in the wake of mass unionism.

Hence wage incentive schemes that were unilaterally instituted and controlled by management did not as a rule solve the problem of getting the worker to work. In a speech delivered to the Taylor Society in 1920, William R. Leiserson, who was to become a leading figure in New Deal industrial relations in the 1930s, put forward a more democratic conception of 'scientific management':

> The workman has constantly in his mind what is a fair and honest day's work, and you can't set wages by time study or by any other scientific method that does not take into consideration the worker's judgement of fairness in this thing. You have got to measure that. This is one of the elements, and if you leave that out you haven't a proper wage; because, no matter how scientifically you measure it, he is going to give the day's work that he conceives fair and honest and he is no more dishonest than the managers are. He has his idea of justice and fair dealing in a day's work, and the managers have their ideas of justice. A really scientific method of fixing wages is one that will put together the management's idea of a fair rate and the workman's idea of a fair rate, and I don't see any other method of doing that except through collective bargaining.

Leiserson went on to argue that if employers required the services of experts in fixing wages so too did the workers and that 'The only way working people can have equal opportunities with employers in hiring expert scientific services for their side is for them to join an organization chip in and pay dues, and hire a union official who is their labor expert to deal with the employers' labor expert.'[36]

Indeed, after the First World War, many of the followers of Taylor, recognising the failure of management-dictated wage incentive systems, began to welcome the participation of labour in the quest for higher productivity. Moreover, the AFL, an organisation committed to the retention of restrictive craft control prior to the war, now sought to construct a new role for itself in the mass production industries through its ardent support of union–management co-operation in increasing productivity. The capitalists in these industries, however, having banished formal craft control from their production processes, showed no interest in voluntarily sharing power with the unions.[37]

Instead they continued to search for methods of labour management that would increase labour productivity without relinquishing unilateral control over questions of work organisation and pay. One such method that had been widely used up to the First World War was close supervision of the pace of work. This policy of increasing productivity by driving the workers was itself facilitated by the advent of mass production methods. Detailed division of labour, by isolating the worker in a single task in a single place, made the job of the foreman much easier. The worker no longer had any legitimate reason to wander here or there on the shop floor. And technological change, by rendering the manual skill and judgement of the worker less important, placed the foreman in a much better position to detect 'work' activities not absolutely necessary to the business at hand. Technological change even relieved the foreman of the responsibility of setting the pace of work; his new role was to supervise the pace determined by a more centralized co-ordinating authority, a pace manifested in the flow of work and the speed of machines. The ratio of foremen to operatives in US manufacturing increased by 15 per cent between 1900 and 1910 and by another 35 per cent in the following decade.[38]

However the success of close supervision was seriously limited not so much by craft control but more by the mobility of semi-skilled and unskilled labour. For the greater the possibility for labour mobility in the economy, the less compelled was the worker to submit to the authority of the foreman. And the development of mass production methods served only to increase labour mobility. Technological change, by diminishing the importance of job-specific skills, made it easier for workers to move in and out of jobs. In addition, the destruction of formal craft control over mass production industries (a process that by no means occurred in Britain for example) meant that there were no organisational barriers to entry in mass production jobs and and occupations.

Clearly, the foreman was more constrained in getting work out of the worker in prosperity than in recession. Here is a speech by John R.

Commons to the National Association of Employment Managers in December 1919:

> What about restrictions of output? Everybody knows that in good times working people 'lay down' on the job, no matter whether organised workers or not. People do not work as hard in good times as they do in hard times. We have the curious paradox that in good times, when we ought to increase the output, labor restricts the output; and in hard times, when we don't want people to work so hard and increase the supply of production, then they work the hardest. A business man does not conduct his business in that way. In good times, when prices are going up, he tries to increase his output – he does not buy more than he can sell. In other words, labor works just the opposite of business.[39]

Close supervision could not solve this problem. Mass production required reliable, dependable, attentive, and loyal workers. Over-bearing foremen created 'just the opposite' at precisely the times when those qualities were needed most. Moreover, in the context of mass production with its expensive capital equipment and interconnected work flow, the threat to profit-making went far beyond the craft workers' notion of 'soldiering'. During the first two decades of this century, the Industrial Workers of the World were openly advocating 'sabotage' and obstruction as a means for workers to combat the power of capital.[40]

One response of management during these two decades was to demonstrate to workers that they really cared. As Nelson has shown, the managerial strategy of 'welfare work' was adopted by many large mass production firms between 1900 and the First World War, a strategy based on the notion that 'voluntary efforts by employers to improve the lot of the workman encouraged individual self-better-ment, loyalty and cooperation – that they inspired the employee to become a better worker and better person'.[41] Some efforts were limited to brightening up the work environment, but more extensive programmes attempted to influence the home lives of workers as well and the latter could easily be transformed from mere 'fringe benefits' into forms of social control. The US Steel Corporation, for example, was in the forefront of the welfare work movement in this period. In 1919, some months before the great steel strike, its president, Judge Gary, warned his top executives that there was 'only one way of combatting and overcoming the wave of unrest'.

> Above everything else, as we have been talking this morning, satisfy your men if you can that your treatment is fair and reasonable and generous. Make the Steel Corporation a good place for them to work and live. Don't let the families go hungry or cold; give them playgrounds and parks and schools and churches, pure water to drink, and recreation, drawing the line so that you are just and generous and yet at the same time keeping your

position and permitting others to keep theirs, retaining the control and management of your affairs, keeping the whole thing in your own hands.[42]

Welfare work did not get the workers to work. In a land that promised ample occupational and social mobility through the 'free market system' and the freedom from autocratic rule that such mobility was supposed to entail, workers responded to fair dealing and to opportunity, not to paternalism. Workers wanted remedies to their shop floor grievances and they wanted to see their work today as a route to something better tomorrow. They wanted to be dealt with not as 'appendages to the machine' but as human beings. High turnover, absenteeism, restriction of output, and the growth of radical unionism were manifestations that these basic human needs were not being met.

It was the First World War, with its dramatic effect on the curtailment of labour supply relative to demand, that compelled employers to take note. Even before United States entry into the war, net migration had dropped precipitously (from 815,000 in 1913 to 19,000 in 1916). The subsequent military enlistments as well as the spread of the eight hour day exacerbated the labour shortage. By the end of the war, labour turnover was double its 1914 level as the unemployment rate had dropped to 1.4 per cent. Work stoppages multiplied and union membership flourished. 'Under these conditions', wrote Slichter from the perspective of the late 1920s, 'the old drive policies . . . simply drove men to quit and strike. Consequently employers suddenly became interested in gaining labor's good will.'[43]

One way for the corporations to win the loyalty and effort of the worker was to hold out the promise of mobility within the firm. Even before the war, companies such as Ford and US Steel had developed the practice of promoting from within along what have come to be known as 'internal job ladders'. In 1919, Slichter claimed: 'The knowledge that there is a future for good workmen in the plant has exerted a strong influence upon the stability of the force.' He went on to argue the importance of the institution of systematic promotion policies based on merit and that 'a cardinal principle in every plant (would be) that no job should be without an outlet'.

It is frequently possible to establish systematic lines of promotion so deserving workers are advanced through a definite sequence of positions. In many instances, however, definite lines of promotion are not practical because there are many operations which are substantially an equally good preparation for a large number of more exacting positions. In such cases the positions are divided into several grades and promotions made regardless of the specific operation from class to class.[44]

There exists virtually no firm-specific historical research on the actual development of internal job ladders in this period, much less on their effects on productivity, absenteeism, labour turnover, and unit costs. But Slichter's advice to employers does support the recent contention by Stone that the structure of internal job ladders and the related differential wage structures in the steel industry were *not* based on the need for on-the-job technical training.[45] The basis for promotion along these job ladders, it can be argued, was not so much the acquisition of cognitive skills but rather, or at least more importantly, the demonstration by the worker that he or she was dependable at work and loyal to the firm. Research on promotion policies in contemporary corporate work-places supports the view that the 'good' worker is defined in terms of such behavioural characteristics. But as for the technologically-dynamic era of the early twentieth century, the documentation of the evolution of internal job ladders and the relative importance of cognitive skills and behavioural characteristics for promotion along them awaits further research.

The development of systematic promotion policies and internal job ladders in large integrated enterprises meant that authority over hiring, promotion, and firing could no longer be left to the foreman on the shop floor. Like the co-ordination of the technically integrated workflow so the co-ordination of staffing of the various processes involved went far beyond the foreman's domain. Shop floor conflicts could no longer be settled there in a manner consistent with the overall flow of work or employment policy.[46] Moreover, since foremen were party to the conflicts (even if not always the perpetrators), it was unlikely that workers would view the solution to the conflicts as fair. Indeed, the foremen's solutions often exacerbated the problems of turnover and restriction of output. In the absence of an institutional structure for dealing with grievances, the foreman tended either to discharge workers who questioned his authority when replacements were easily available or, in the presence of tight labour markets, to assert his authority on the shop floor, thus inciting the workers to sabotage, to join unions, or to introduce an individualistic form of shop floor democracy by voting with their feet.[47]

As both turnover and strike activity mounted during the war, employers began to see that grievance settlement as well as employment decisions should be taken off the shop floor. Under government sponsorship, employment management courses were set up around the country. The employment management movement continued after the war, and by 1920 about 400 corporations had installed employment departments.[48] Although some of these were disbanded in the next two years as labour markets slackened and although some foremen regained some of their traditional functions, personnel management had come to stay, particularly in the larger mass production enterprises.[49] A bureaucratic form of industrial relations had begun to develop in the manufacturing corporation.

Developing alongside these personnel or industrial relations departments, and also emerging out of the labour difficulties of the First World War and its aftermath, were employee representations plans and works councils, more generally known as 'company unions'. The idea was once again to get conflicts off the shop floor by developing a defined bureaucratic structure through which workers could air their grievances. Like wage incentive schemes, welfare work, and internal job ladders, company unions represented an effort to keep workers satisfied so as to raise their productivity without giving them any authority or power over the issues of work and pay. Company unions gave workers neither the funds nor the right to strike. In fact, a prime motivating factor in the development of company unions was the desire by management to co-opt the AFL unions that were, in the 1920s, demanding a more profound form of industrial democracy than was inherent in the 'like it or leave it' democracy of the 'free market'.[50]

Company unions, then, were part of a broader managerial attempt in the 1920s to increase productivity by eliminating the underlying cause of labour turnover and restriction of output – that is, by getting workers to like their work rather than leave it, or worse yet, undermine it. There is certainly no evidence that the personnel management of the 1920s succeeded in convincing workers to like their uncreative, repetitive, and enervating mass production work for its own sake. Indeed, the 'human relations' school of management that developed out of Elton Mayo's experiments at Western Electric in the late 1920s (but which became a 'movement' only from the late 1940s) was based on the finding that workers were 'dissatisfied' with the content of their work.[51] However, by listening to workers' grievances, by developing a structure of industrial relations through which concessions could be made when necessary, by eliminating indiscriminate discharge, lay-offs, and wage cutting, and by rewarding the worker with stable and somewhat better employment in return for his or her good work, the corporations undoubtedly increased their ability to get their workers to work dependably and attentively in the 1920s.

Rising real wages in the 1920s aided in stabilising capital–labour relations, but cannot be accorded a decisive role. Between 1919 and 1929, average real weekly earnings of US manufacturing workers rose at a rate of 1.5 per cent per year after having risen at a rate of 1.9 per cent in the previous decade. However in the late 1920s, corporate management, with its eye on the problem of labour mobility, took advantage of the new stability in production relations to encourage workers to invest their savings in company stocks, pensions, and insurance schemes as well as in homes – all of which were supposed to render it more costly for the worker to leave the firm.[52]

In so far as these new personnel policies were successful (and we require much more research on the extent, forms, and effects of these policies), 'like it or leave it' was reduced as a realistic option for the individual worker. The available evidence indicates that despite relative prosperity from 1923 through 1929, labour turnover fell substantially in the last half of the 1920s. So too did union membership – in the metal and metal using industries it declined by 75 per cent between 1920 and 1924, and failed to recover until after the depths of the Depression.[53]

In the 1920s, after four decades of stormy conflict, a measure of stability in the relation between capital and labour was achieved. It was not permanent stability (as the 1930s were to show) for it had as its fragile basis the one-sided power of capital over labour to control the conditions of work and pay. Nevertheless, the 1920s represent an important transition in the development of corporate power. In subsequent decades the labour movement (with the help of the state) would rise again to compel the corporations to share power with the workers in the determination of pay. But industrial unions in the United States have not been able to compel the corporations to share power in the determination of work. In the 1980s workers in the United States continue to suffer the consequences of the corporate defeat of the labour movement over the issue of the control of work in the early decades of this century.

Capital–Labour Relations and Institutional Structure

During the 1920s output per worker-hour in manufacturing rose at a rate of 6.3 per cent per year compared to annual rates of 0.8 per cent, 1.6 per cent, and 2.0 per cent in the 1890s, 1900s and 1910s respectively.[54] To what extent the new structure of capital–labour relations contributed to this tremendous increase in labour productivity we cannot yet say. But it is clear that the whole question of changes in productivity and the diffusion of technology needs to be analysed in the context of the development of particular institutional structures.

In exploring this question, historians will derive little direction from conventional economic theory – at least not from the neo-classical role of thought that dominates today. There the theoretical focus is on making optimal choices subject to given constraints, when what we want to know is how the constraints developed and what choices remained. Moreover, the entire theoretical structure of neo-classical theory is based on the premise that economic organisation is equivalent to organisation of the economy through the operation of markets. It is debatable whether that premise is valid even for analysing the nature of nineteenth-century competitive capitalism. It is clearly an inadequate starting-point for analysing the nature of twentieth-century capitalism.

In *The Visible Hand*, Chandler has shown how, from the last decades of the nineteenth century, the heads of large capitalist enterprises in the United States have striven to assert power over the destinies of their companies by the elimination of horizontal competition and by the integration of vertically interrelated processes from raw materials to the sale of finished products. The result has been the rise of the giant corporation – a social institution that has been able to render itself independent of the free play of those markets in capital inputs and outputs that are key to its success. Similarly, if one accepts the analysis of the capital–labour relation that I have presented here, the industrial relations strategies of the giant corporation can be viewed as aiming and tending to the same result: to render it independent of those markets in labour that are key to capital accumulation.

For the issues of the role of industrial organisation in economic development with which he is concerned, Chandler draws upon the theoretical insights of Joseph Schumpeter, who, it should be noted, was profoundly influenced by Marx.[55] For the issues of the role of industrial relations in economic development that have been the focus of this paper, the insights of John Commons and Sumner Slichter are invaluable. They too, like Schumpeter disagreed with Marx's ideology and with many of his conclusions, but nevertheless took the Marxian perspective on capitalist development very seriously.[56]

In my view, the contemporary relevance of Marx's economics lies in both his understanding of the fundamental conflicts inherent in the capital–labour relation and his search for the implications of these conflicts for economic development and social change. But by assuming as he did that division of labour and mechanisation permitted capitalists to win complete control of the work process, Marx failed, as I argued at the outset, to explore the problems for the control of work and capital accumulation that technological change created. Braverman's faithfulness to Marx in this regard leads him, as we have seen, not only to misrepresent Taylor's Scientific Management, but also to assert that industrial engineering – technical division of labour and mechanisation – is the only relevant aspect of the capitalist management of work. As a result, he ignores the conflicts that the introduction of mass production methods generated as well as the institutional structures that arose within the capitalist enterprise to resolve these conflicts.

A more perceptive Marxian analysis of these issues can be found in Edward's recent book *Contested Terrain*. Edwards argues that, in order to get work out of workers, capitalists have combined bureau-cratic control with technical control, and that indeed bureaucracy has surpassed technology as a form of control in the modern corporation. In Edward's view, bureaucratic control developed during the post-Second World War period and was first applied to white-collar workers. 'The defining feature of bureaucratic control', says Edwards,

> is the institutionalization of hierarchical power. 'Rule of law' – the firm's law – replaces 'rule by supervisor command' in the direction of work, the procedures for evaluating workers' performance, and the exercise of the firm's sanctions and rewards; supervisors and workers alike become subject to the dictates of 'company policy'. Work becomes highly strati-fied; each job is given its distinct title and description; and impersonal rules govern promotion. 'Stick with the corporation,' the worker is told, 'and you can ascend up the ladder.' The company promises the workers a *career*.[57]

This constitutes a more sophisticated extension of the modes of personnel management – internal job ladders, promotion by merit, defined grievance procedures, bureaucratic hiring and firing – that began to be developed in mass production industries in the 1920s as a strategy for getting work out of the production workers. In fact, Edwards provides us with excellent discussions of some of these managerial strategies, including the uses of company unions and the changing role of the foreman in mass production industries.[58] But in these pre-Depression decades, he argues, it was 'technical control' – specifically the development of mass production work-flows – that solved the problem of getting work out of the workers. As Edwards puts it (with my emphasis)

> The line now determined the pace [of work] and the foreman had *merely* to get workers to follow that pace. The actual power to control work is thus vested in the line itself, rather than in the person of the foreman. Instead of control appearing to flow from boss to workers control emerges from the much more impersonal 'technology'.[59]

There is no evidence, however, that workers in the pre-Depression decades were under the illusion that the speed of the line emerged from impersonal 'technology' or that they simply accepted that speed as the pace at which they had to work. Indeed the evidence from this period that I have cited in this paper, as well as much of Edwards's own discussion of work-place conflicts, indicate the contrary. Workers' acceptance of 'the legitimacy of the line' depended not on their rela-tion to technology, but rather on their relation to their superiors. Technological change, as I have argued in this paper, certainly under-mined the technical bases of craft control and created the possibility for the development of mass production methods. But the introduction of these methods created new problems that, far from being solved by the new technological structures, were exacerbated by them. On the basis of available evidence it seems warranted to argue that it was only when a new structure of capital–labour relations emerged in the 1920s – a structure that recognised that the attitudes and aspirations of workers were crucial determinants of productivity – that the conflicts created by mass production methods *began* to be resolved.

This having been said, however, we cannot then assume that it was the new managerial strategies and structures alone that account for the stability of capital–labour relations in the 1920s. Indeed it may even be valid to argue that the success of personnel administration was determined almost entirely by developments that occurred outside the capitalist enterprise. For the capitalist enterprise did not operate in a political and cultural vacuum. If we recognise that the key issue in capital–labour relations was the 'consciousness' of the worker, we must also recognise that the stability of those relations cannot be understood in abstraction from the wider social system in which the worker develops culturally and participates politically. During the first decades of this century radical transformations occurred in the spheres of culture and politics that were clearly conducive to the stabilisation of capital–labour relations. Alongside the mass production corporations arose a vertically integrated mass schooling system that offered a route to economic opportunity for all – a route that quickly became replete with testing, tracking, and 'Americanising' for the purpose of turning out 'productive' citizens. At the lower levels, 'vocational education' – the preparation of workers for their future work roles – emerged as a public purpose of schooling while at the higher levels the schooling system was transformed to provide the managerial and technical personnel to fill the corporate bureaucracies.[60] In the political sphere a new corporate liberalism emerged, one that stood ready to accommodate working-class movements that respected existing property relations and to eradicate those that did not. On the one hand, from the turn of the century, many leaders from the community of big business sought out the leaders of the conservative labour movement in attempts to work out class differences, not in their corporate enterprises, but rather through the medium of the state. On the other hand, during the First World War and its aftermath, state repression of both the radical labour movement and the socialist party helped to narrow dramatically the political choices open to Americans.[61]

Hence, it can be argued that not only the institutional transformation of the capitalist enterprise but also, and perhaps more fundamentally, the institutional transformation of the larger society was required to stabilise capital–labour relations in the mass production industries. By the 1920s, American life had become profoundly influenced not only by the mass of corporate outputs (and the development of a dominant culture of consumerism)[62] but also by the corporate input requirements – masses of obedient, co-operative, loyal human beings. Technological change had been central to the rise of corporate capitalism from the 1880s, and particularly to its ultimate ability to 'deliver the goods'. But technology did not dictate the political and cultural content of the institutions that emerged. The driving force in the shaping of these institutions, including the capitalist enterprise itself, was, I would argue, the attempt by corporate capitalists to secure the co-operation of masses of working individuals in 'producing the goods' while denying them the right to control their working lives. By the 1920s, corporate capitalists had achieved a large measure of success in this endeavour. In the process, however, autocratic organisation dependent on the co-operation of rightless individuals became and remains a central characteristic – and a central contradiction – of corporate capitalism in the United States.

Notes

1. This paper is based upon research supported by the National Science Foundation under Grant No. SES 78–25671.
2. A.D. Chandler, *The Visible Hand: The Managerial Revolution in American Business* (1977); see also A.D. Chandler, *Strategy and Structure: Chapters in the History of the American Industrial Enterprise* (1962).
3. L.H. Jenks, 'Early Phases of the Management Movement', *Administrative Science Quarterly* (1960); J.A. Litterer, 'Systematic Management: The Search for Order and Integration', *Business History Review* (1960); J.A. Litterer, 'Systematic Management: Design for Organisational Recoupling in American Manufacturing Firms', *Business History Review* (1963).
4. H. Braverman, *Labor and Monopoly Capital* (1974), chapter 20.
5. K. Marx, *Capital*, vol. I, (International Publishers edn 1967), p. 338
6. This problem had confronted capitalists in the textile industries of the first industrial revolution. Indeed, Marglin argues that a major reason for the rise and success of the factory was that it enabled capitalists to control the duration and pace of work. S.A. Marglin, 'What Do Bosses Do?: The Origins and Functions of Hierarchy in Capitalist Production', *Review of Radical Political Economics* (1974)
7. K. Marx, *Capital*, vol. I, parts III–V, esp. pp. 338, 367 and 636
8. W. Lazonick, 'Industrial Relations and Technical Change: the Case of the Self-Acting Mule', *Cambridge Journal of Economics* (1979). See also Lazonick, 'Production Relations, Labor Productivity, and Choice of Technique: British and U.S. Cotton Spinning', *Journal of Economic History* (1981), for a comparison of the development of British and US mule spinning.
9. For a critique of such a view of British capitalist development in the first three-quarters of the nineteenth century, see W. Lazonick, 'The Subjection of Labor to Capital: The Rise of the Capitalist System', *Review of Radical Political Economics* (1978).
10. Braverman (1974), p. 9
11. Ibid. p. 146n (emphasis in original).
12. Ibid. pp. 26–7.

13. Braverman has the bad habit of relying on 'authorities' from the pro-capitalist camp rather than on historical analysis to establish his argument, much in the manner of Marx's use of the pronoucements of Andrew Ure. See, for example, his uses of the view of Drucker on pages 85-8 of his book. In particular, he relies on the views of industrial engineers to belittle the role of personnel management. See Braverman (1974), pp. 140n, 146n

14. Ibid. pp. 439 and 440

15. S. Bowles and H. Gintis, *Schooling in Capitalist America: Educational Reforms and the Contradictions of Economic Life* (1976).

16. J. Buttrick, 'The Inside Contract System', *Journal of Economic History* (1952); D. Nelson, *Managers and Workers: Origins of the New Factory System in the United States 1880-1920* (1975) chapter 3.

17. D. Montgomery, *Workers' Control in America* (1979), chapter 1; D. Brody, *Steelworkers in America* (1960), chapter 2; K. Stone, 'The Origins of Job Structures in the Steel Industry', *Review of Radical Political Economics* (1974); B. Elbaum and F. Wilkinson, 'Industrial Relations and Uneven Development: A Comparative Study of the American and British Steel Industries', *Cambridge Journal of Economics* (1979).

18. Elbaum and Wilkinson (1979); J. Holt, 'Trade Unionism in the British and U.S. Steel Industries, 1888-1912: A Comparative Study', *Labor History* (1977); Lazonick (1981); W. Mass, 'The Adoption of the Automatic Loom', photocopy, Harvard University (1980).

19. Brody (1960), pp. 78-9, my emphasis.

20. See especially D. Nelson, *Frederick W. Taylor and the Rise of Scientific Management* (1980); C.D. Wrege and A.G. Perroni, 'Taylor's Pig-Tale: A Historical Analysis of Frederick W. Taylor's Pig-Iron Experiments', *Academy of Management Journal* (1974); M.J. Nadworny, *Scientific Management and the Unions 1900-1932* (1955); H.G.J. Aitken, *Taylorism at Watertown Arsenal: Scientific Management in Action 1908-1915* (1960); D.F. Noble, *America by Design: Science, Technology and the Rise of Corporate Capitalism* (1977), chapter 10; Braverman (1974), part I.

21. Braverman (1974), pp. 112-20.

22. Ibid. p. 85

23. W.P. Strassman, *Risk and Technological Innovation: American Manufacturing Methods During the Nineteenth Century* (1959), p. 42.

24. There is a large literature on restriction of output in US industry since the late nineteenth century. See especially Montgomery (1979), chapter 1; Stone (1974); J.S. Peterson, 'Auto Workers and Their Work, 1900-1933', *Labor History* (1981), pp. 227-34; US Commission of Labor, *Eleventh Annual Report*, 'Regulation and Restriction of Output' (1904); D.A. McCabe, *The Standard Rate in American Trade Unions* (1912); S.B. Mathewson, *Restriction of Output among Unorganised Workers* (1931); V.D. Kennedy, *Union Policy and Incentive Wage Methods* (1945), chapter IV; W.F. Whyte, *Money and Motivation* (1955); J. Seidman and J. London, 'The Slowdown as a Union Tactic', *Journal of Political Economy* (1957); M. Burawoy, *Manufacturing Consent* (1979).

25. F.W. Taylor, *The Principles of Scientific Management* (originally published in 1911), reprinted in F.W. Taylor, *Scientific Management* (1947).

26. Ibid. p. 51.

27. Ibid. pp. 52-3; Nelson (1980), p. 39

28. M.A. Calvert, *The Mechanical Engineer in America* (1967); Noble (1977), chapter 3; E.T. Layton, *The Revolt of the Engineers* (1971), chapter 2.

29. Braverman (1974), p. 146n.

30. F.W. Taylor, 'A Piece Rate System', *American Society of Mechanical Engineers, Transactions* (1895); H.R. Towne, 'Gain-Sharing', *ASME Transactions* (1889); F.A. Halsey, 'The Premium Plan for Paying for Labor', *ASME Transactions* (1891).

31. F.W. Taylor 'Shop Management' (originally published in 1903), reprinted in F.W. Taylor, 'Scientific Management' (1947), pp. 38-9.
32. Nelson (1975), chapter 4.
33. S.H. Slichter, *The Turnover of Factory Labor* (1921), p. 350.
34. See. A. Nevins, *Ford: The Times, The Man, The Company* (1954), chapters XVIII, XX; A.D. Chandler, *Giant Enterprise: Ford, General Motors and the Automobile Industry* (1964), pp. 3-5; Slichter (1921), pp. 34, 266; J. Russell, 'The Coming of the Line: The Ford Highland Park Plant, 1910-1914', *Radical America* (1978); D. Gartman, 'Origins of the Assembly Line and Capitalist Control of Work at Ford' in A. Zimbalist (ed.), *Case Studies on the Labor Process* (1979); F. Maltese, 'Notes for a Study of the Automobile Industry' in R.C. Edwards, M. Reich and D. Gordon (eds.) *Labor Market Segmentation* (1973).
35. Chandler (1964), pp. 194-5.
36. W.R. Leiserson, 'The Worker's Reaction to Scientific Management' in E.E. Hunt (ed.) *Scientific Management since Taylor* (1924), p. 224.
37. J.T. McKelvey, *AFL Attitudes toward Production 1900-1932* (1952); Nadworny (1955), chapters 7-8; D. Stark, 'Class Struggle and the Transformation of the Labor Process', *Theory and Society* (1980), pp. 102-6. For the definitive work on the actual implementation of union—management co-operation in the United States along the lines envisaged by Leiserson and others, see S.H. Slichter, *Union Policies and Industrial Management* (1941).
38. US Department of Commerce, Bureau of the Census, *Historical Statistics of the United States, Colonial Times to 1970* (1975), pp. 142-3. Between 1920 and 1930 this ratio declined by 4 per cent.
39. J.R. Commons, 'Introduction', in Commons (ed.), *Trade Unionism and Labor Problems* (1921, 2nd edn), pp. 6-7.
40. G. Brown, *Sabotage* (1977), p. v. See also M. Davis, 'The Stop Watch and the Wooden Shoe: Scientific Management and the Industrial Workers of the World', *Radical America* (1975).
41. Nelson (1975), p. 101. Also R.C. Edwards, *Contested Terrain: The Transformation of the Workplace in the Twentieth Century* (1979), pp. 91-7; R. Ozanne, *A Century of Labor—Management Relations at McCormick and International Harvester* (1967), chapters 2, 11.
42. Quoted in Brody (1960), p. 228.
43. S.H. Slichter, 'The Current Labor Policies of American Industries', *Quarterly Journal of Economics* (1929), p. 395. See also P.F. Brissenden and B. Frankel, *Labor Turnover in Industry* (1922).
44. Slichter (1921), pp. 290-1, 352.
45. Stone (1974), p. 136.
46. See P.H. Douglas, 'Plant Administration of Labor', *Journal of Political Economy*, esp. p. 548; see also Edwards (1979), chapter 7.
47. Slichter (1921), chapter XII; F.H. Colvin, *Labor Turnover, Loyalty and Output* (1919), chapter VII; B. Emmet, 'Labor Turnover and Employment Policies of a Large Motor Vehicle Manufacturing Establishment', *Monthly Labor Review* (1918).
48. H. Eilbirt, 'The Development of Personnel Management in the United States', *Business History Review* (1959), p. 359.
49. Slichter (1929); W.R. Leiserson, 'Contributions of Personnel Management to Improved Labor Relations' in *Wertheim Lectures on Industrial Relations 1928* (1929); W.J. Donald and E.K. Donald, 'Trends in Personnel Administration', *Harvard Business Review* (1929); H.S. Dennison, 'Management', in vol. II of National Bureau of Economic Research, *Recent Economic Changes in the United States* (1929); R. Bendix, *Work and Authority in Industry* (1956), pp. 287-307; Montgomery (1979), chapter 2.
50. Edwards (1979), pp. 105-9; Ozanne (1967), chapter 7; National Industrial Conference Board, *Collective Bargaining Through Employee Representation* (1933);

Slichter (1929); McKelvey (1952), chapters V, VI; Stark (1980), pp. 111–13.

51. E. Mayo, *The Human Problems of an Industrial Civilization* (1960 originally published in 1933); L. Baritz, *The Servants of Power: A History of the Use of Social Science in American Industry* (1960), chapters 5–6, 9.
52. US Department of Commerce (1975), pp. 164, 170; Slichter (1929), pp. 403–11.
53. US Department of Commerce (1975), pp. 135, 178, 182.
54. Ibid. p. 162.
55. Chandler (1962), chapter 6; J. Schumpeter, *Capitalism, Socialism and Democracy* (1950 3rd edn), part I.
56. S.H. Slichter, *Economic Growth in the United States* (1961), chapter 1; J.R. Commons, *Institutional Economics* (1959), chapters VIII and XI. On the evasion of the basic insights of institutional economics by modern neo-classical economists, see A.J. Field, 'On the Explanation of Rules Using Rational Choice Models', *Journal of Economic Issues* (1979).
57. Edwards (1979), p. 21.
58. Ibid. chapters 6–7.
59. Ibid. pp. 117–20.
60. Bowles and Gintis (1976), part III; J.H. Spring, *Education and the Rise of the Corporate State* (1972); M. Lazerson and W. Norton Grubb (eds.), *American Education and Vocationalism* (1974); Noble (1977).
61. J. Weinstein, *The Corporate Ideal and the Liberal State* (1968); J. Weinstein, *The Decline of Socialism in America 1912-1925* (1967); W. Preston, *Aliens and Dissenters: Federal Suppression of Radicals, 1903-1933* (1966).
62. See S. Ewen, *Captains of Consciousness* (1976).

6 Scientific Management and Personnel Policy in the Modern German Enterprise 1918–1939: The Case of Siemens[1]
Heidrun Homburg

Introduction

The existing literature has analysed the development of bureaucratic patterns in German industrial management.[2] Given the absolutist tradition in Germany, bureaucratic structures and processes were pre-industrial and the civil and military bureaucratic administrations acted as important models for the developing factory system. However, much of this analysis is confined to senior and middle management and has little to say about labour management and work processes. In order to investigate the area of labour management it is necessary to move beyond a broad, Weberian notion of bureaucracy[3] and make use of some conception of Taylorism.

Contemporary manuals on personnel management stress the impact of F.W. Taylor's concept of Scientific Management on the development of labour management.[4] In German manuals this general statement is, however, not accompanied by any empirical analysis of how and when Taylor's principles were adopted by German employers and how they impinged on the existing labour policies. This absence of empirical data might be due to a lack of interest, but it also reflects the fact that there has been little research into the techniques of management. Consequently, detailed case studies are necessary as a first step to illuminate the interrelationship between Taylorist concepts and the establishment of personnel management as a specific structure and a specific strategy of employers' labour policies.

Frederick W. Taylor (1865–1915) is generally seen as one of the first and possibly the most influential to develop a coherent view of the objectives and the means of personnel management. Emphasising labour as a factor of production, Taylor defined the allocation, co-ordination, and monitoring of labour as an important task of management and subsumed it under a general theory of scientific management. The objective consisted in providing the most efficient input of labour for which Taylor systematically elaborated technical and organisational means. These were a centralised personnel administration and research, an internal labour market policy (concerned with allocation, remuneration, training), a centralised administration of the work, production process and the working conditions in so far as they influenced directly the work performance or indirectly the workers' motivation, and exact 'scientific' methods of fixing, calculating and controlling labour's performance. Taylor defined the proposed system of direct managerial control as the precondition for 'efficiency engineering'. At the same time Taylor realised that the proposed system of managerial control could only be successfully applied if it was supplemented by a special legitimation which made the loss of autonomy and the increased intensity of work deriving from it acceptable to the workers. The legitimation offered by Taylor consisted in the different nature of control, which was to change from a personal to a functional one, and in a different relationship between management and labour, which was no longer to be based on personal authority and arbitrary decisions but on general, 'objective' principles of functional authority and economic rationality. The primary rationale for labour to co-operate under the proposed system of managerial control was defined by Taylor in terms of labour's economic self-interest in objective procedures of assigning the task and of fixing wage rates as well as in predictable wage increases correlated to increased performance and in a stable wage income. The primary rationale for management to adopt his system was seen by Taylor in terms of the economic and social advantages, for the proposed system of efficiency engineering served not only to reduce the overall cost of labour but also the need for social engineering; optimal efficiency engineering was simultaneously a means of optimal social engineering.[5]

Taylor's systematic approach to the problems of efficiency engineering, as well as his proposals of an economic pay-off in order to legitimate the new system of managerial control can be understood as a paradigm for the structure and strategy of labour control during a period of transition to more capital-intensive techniques of mass production. This approach regards Taylor's concept as an ideal model and stresses the economically calculated input of labour and thereby the restructuring of the relationship between management and labour according to the principles of economic rationality. This approach seems to me historically justified because of the attention the German interested public (employers, trade unions, and politicians alike) paid to Taylor's writings, especially after Germany's defeat in 1918.[6] It is also heuristically useful for a comparative analysis as it allows the identification of structural and strategic aspects of personnel management as elements of a coherent system and thereby allows the specification of the mode and characteristic qualities of German rationalisation.

In view of the limited historical research it is difficult, if not impossible, to give a general outline of the transition to a managerial system of labour control in German industry. Therefore this paper is a case study of German's leading electrical manufacturing firm – the Siemens Co. in Berlin. It deals with the development of personnel management in this company, its structure and strategy mainly during the inter-war period, 1918–39. For the purpose of this study personnel management is defined as a system of managerial control for the allocation, co-ordination and monitoring of labour which partially substitutes a bureaucratic system for the 'invisible hand' of the market.[7]

The enterprise studied, the Siemens Co., was the largest German electrical engineering firm and in terms of the nominal worth of its share capital in 1907 and 1927 belonged to the top group of ten German enterprises whose capital amounted to a hundred or more million marks. Siemens adopted comparatively early such strategies and administrative structures which Alfred Chandler defined in his research as a pre-condition for, and feature of, the economically successful large enterprise. Already before the First World War Siemens was among the group of highly diversified and functionally integrated enterprises and it also developed a decentralised multi-divisional structure.[8] In terms of its strategies of growth and its administrative system Siemens realised or even anticipated trends which – albeit some decades later – were to become general features of the large, highly diversified enterprises. This suggests that Siemens can be seen as a trend setter with respect to the product diversification and integration of other basic economic functions. Did Siemens play a comparable role in the field of labour management? With reservation as to the results of further research, I would argue that there is good reason to suppose that this was the case. Firstly, Siemens, as well as the other large German electrical engineering firms, were heavily engaged in the technical rationalisation of their production process after the First World War. All of them played a prominent role in the different organisations which were founded after the war in order to promote the ideas and the techniques of Scientific Management and of rationalisation, such as the National Efficiency Board, the National Committee for Time Studies, and the National Board for Industrial Standards. Efficiency engineering as well as the transition to more capital-intensive mass production processes and their further expansion required, however, a system of managerial labour control. Secondly, the structure of the local labour market also influenced the structure and strategy of the company's labour policies and probably accelerated the development of personnel management. Thirdly, Siemens never totally relied on the employers' organisation as a collective means of labour control. It regarded 'delegated multi-employer control' as a functional supplement to, but never as a substitute for, internal company means of labour control.[9]

In what follows I will first outline the economic and labour market conditions Siemens saw itself confronted with after the First World War and ask whether they represented a stimulus to rationalisation. I will then turn to the structure of the company's personnel administration, and finally I will analyse the strategy of the company's personnel management. In the conclusion I will discuss the similarities and dissimilarities between Taylor's concept and the system of labour control which Siemens developed and analyse the reasons for the deviating mode of the company's personnel policy.

The Economic and Social Setting

Siemens & Halske, founded in Berlin in 1847, was the oldest German electrical engineering firm and also the first in the world. The same considerations which had led Werner Siemens and Johann G. Halske to choose Berlin as location for their telegraph construction firm later attracted other entrepreneurs in the electrical field to follow their example: the proximity of their most important customers, the state and the municipal authorities; the existing and further expanding industrial and private local market; the favourable transport and communication conditions in Berlin, its geographical situation as well as the availability of a skilled labour force and a variety of middle and higher educational institutions. In the last quarter of the nineteenth century, when the electrical industry, the light and especially the heavy current branch, achieved major break-throughs, a series of new firms were founded in Berlin, and Siemens lost its former quasi-monopolistic position. Due to the expanding market for electrical goods, the newcomers, especially Edison Gesellschaft (founded in 1883, and re-founded in 1887 as Allgemeine Elektricitäts-Gesellschaft, otherwise known as AEG) prospered and soon developed into serious competitors for market shares and labour. In 1895, 1907 and 1925 about 50 per cent of all those employed in the German electrical industry were working in Berlin firms. Even by 1939 the figure was 44 per cent. These percentages are very constant if compared to the total growth of those employed in the industry (with the exception of the depression year 1933) from 18,704 in 1895 to 539,735 in 1939, and underline the dominant position of Berlin as the centre of the German electrical industry. The local concentration of the electrical engineering industry in Berlin corresponded with its rank as one of the largest employers in the city. In 1925 it employed almost one-fifth

(186,302) of Berlin's industrial labour force and ranked slightly below the clothing industry (204,495 employees), Berlin's largest industrial employer.[10]

During the period of rapid growth of the industry at the turn of the century the predominant position of Siemens in terms of the number of employed persons, capital, turnover, variety of products, technical knowledge, and a world-wide distribution and customers' network did not stay uncontested. For almost two decades between 1890 and 1910 AEG took the lead. And although Siemens managed to catch up with AEG and even to overtake it by 1914, the competition between the two giants played a decisive role in the structural development of the German electrical industry. Siemens and AEG (their German subsidiaries outside Berlin included) employed in 1907 about two-thirds, and in 1939 about 40 per cent of the total work-force in the German electrical industry. In 1929 it was estimated that Siemens was producing more than 30 per cent and AEG more than 20 per cent of the total production of electrical goods in Germany. Due to the fact that most of the production facilities of both enterprises were situated in Berlin, the competition for market shares was not limited to the product market but also included the labour market.

Both the conditions in national and international product markets and the structure of the labour market underwent important changes after the 1890s and these were accelerated by the First World War and its aftermath. On the one hand the American electrical industry entered into competition with the Germany industry, first on the world market and after the war even in the German market itself. The German share of the world production of electrical goods sank from 34.9 per cent in 1913 to 23.3 per cent in 1925 whereas the American share increased from 28.5 per cent in 1913 to 48.1 per cent in 1925. And the German electrical industry, which in 1913 had still dominated the world export trade (46.4 per cent), no longer did so after the First World War. Its share had by 1925 declined to 25.8 per cent and was now only slightly higher than that of the American and British competitors. Although the German industry was successful in its efforts to regain its former leading position in the export trade, with a share of 34.9 per cent in 1932 (United States 19.7 per cent, Britain 14.0 per cent), it was, however, not able to restore its predominant position of the pre-war period. The rise of new competitors in the international market meant a special challenge for the two German giants, Siemens and AEG, whose expansion in the pre-war period had been heavily export-led and whose export ratio was markedly higher (about 30 per cent and more) than the overall average of the German electrical industry (about 20 per cent).[11] After the First World War the trade regulations in the Treaty of Versailles and the ensuing protective trade policies of the United States, Great Britain, France and other European countries further restricted export and growth potential. In the German market the transition from the war to the peace economy and the restoration of competitive market conditions increased the pressure for competitive prices and cost reduction.

As far as the labour market was concerned the structural changes were closely linked with the growth and increasing strength of the trade unions since the 1890s. They not only challenged the autocratic position of the employer, but their fight for collective wage agreements and their success in enforcing them – even if it was quite limited until 1916 – challenged the employer's autonomy of fixing the wage level and the wage system and of reducing the wage cost at his own will. The social and labour legislation after the war continued the wartime development towards the institutionalisation of collective bargaining and secured the trade unions' participation in such newly created national institutions as arbitration committees, unemployment relief, and labour exchanges. Industrial sectors which were either labour intensive or whose wage costs were rather high due to their dependence on highly skilled labour saw themselves especially confronted with the impact of the social and legal developments on their cost of production and competitiveness. The cost structure in the electrical industry varied considerably not only between the light and heavy current branches, but also from product to product. For the heavy current division, Siemens estimated in 1927 that in the important branch of transformers, dynamo generators and the like the portion of wage cost amounted to 30–45 per cent, whereas it was said to be in general still higher in the light current division.[12]

After the re-emergence of the socialist trade unions, which had been legally suppressed from 1878 to 1890, Berlin soon developed as one of their strongholds. And the Berlin metal workers were one of the best-unionised and most radical branches. By 1906 more than two-thirds of the Berlin metal workers who were eligible for membership had joined the union. In 1919 it organised approximately 60 per cent of all Berlin metal workers, a percentage which rapidly declined after the stabilisation of the currency to about one-fifth at the end of 1925, but then increased again and amounted to almost 50 per cent in 1933. Although the German metal workers' union was founded as an industrial union in 1891, it was the skilled workers who were – with the exception of the immediate post-war period – its backbone till its forced dissolution in 1933. This was also the case in Berlin: about two-thirds of the skilled workers were between 1927 and 1931 organised in the socialist union.[13]

Before the war Siemens tried to curtail the trade union's rising influence at the work-place by an openly anti-union strategy when it decided to promote a company union and tried to use it as a means of labour control by perverting the idea of a closed shop into an employer instrument. Although the chosen organisational means, the 'yellow' union, was doomed to failure due to political and social developments during and after the war it represented a first, and for some years quite successful, attempt by the Siemens management to develop a system of internal organisational means to control the labour force and to preserve the firm's relative autonomy with regard to the labour market and to any form of external regulation of the cost of labour.[14].

On the eve of the German Empire's collapse in 1918 and in view of the impending revolutionary upheaval Siemens drastically changed its former policy. Carl Friedrich von Siemens, the youngest son of the founder, Werner von Siemens, who at this time held the position of the general manager of the heavy current division and was to become the head of the company after his brother's death in October 1919, belonged to the initiators and supporters of employer negotiations with the trade union leaders and the associated idea of a permanent social partnership as a means to handle the economic and social problems in the turbulent transition from war to peace. The new co-operative spirit found its general codification in the famous Stinnes-Legien Agreement in 1918 which established a *Zentralarbeitsgemeinschaft* as an administrative body on the basis of parity between labour and management and led to the general recognition of the trade unions and to the acceptance of collective bargaining.[15] Thus the Siemens management played an important role in bringing about the first collective agreements for the blue and white collar workers of the Berlin metal-working industry in 1919 by means of its influential position in the employers' organisation and its participation in the negotiations. Although the Siemens management observed the new rules of social partnership and adhered to the collective agreements, it did, however, not refrain from a massive critique of the trade unions' wage and social policies, nor from attempts to reduce the impact of the collective agreements and to curtail the trade union's influence at the work-place. In the last analysis the former commitment to social partnership did not prevent the Siemens management from silently accepting the trade unions' dissolution after Hitler's seizure of power.[16]

The transition to collective bargaining after the war definitely changed the functions of both the employers' organisation and of Siemen's labour policies. The company joined the employers' organisation of the Berlin metal working firms only in December 1904, fourteen years after its foundation, in a period of rising social tension and open industrial conflicts. This was a belated commitment by Siemens to the employers' collective action in order to defend managerial prerogatives and to curtail trade union activities in the labour market and in the work-place. However, the post-war central role of the employers' organisation in bargaining for wages and work conditions induced the Siemens management to engage more intensively in its policies and Siemens used its position as the largest local metal working firm to influence and direct the organisation's decision making process according to its interests. The representation of the company's interests required, however, exact knowledge of personnel matters and an organisational structure of personnel administration which could provide it. Indeed the first collective agreements in 1919 required intensive preparatory work, and, after they were finally accepted, extensive administrative work by the company's management because the multitude of wage rates for individual workers and professions had to be standardised and grouped into five categories on the basis of the agreed-upon job evaluation. Although the extent of this supplementary work to the wage agreements was subsequently less onerous, it was nevertheless considerable.

The new collective agreements affected the restructuring and functional transition of the company's labour policies to a system of personnel management in many other direct and indirect ways. The standardisation of the wage rates covering the entire Greater Berlin metal working industry levelled down the differences between individual firms and subsequently rendered job changes for the workers less risky, whereas employers had to reckon with higher rates of labour turnover. The increased cost awareness as well as the shortage of skilled labour, especially in boom periods, constituted a problem for the company's means of labour control. The numerical reduction of the labour force and the change of its composition as a means to shake off the bonds of the collective wage agreements came to be more important than ever before and accounted for the primary role of efficiency engineering as a function of personnel management. And it was in fact after the First World War, when the German electrical industry tried to regain its lost international markets and when the relative autonomy of the employer to fix and alter the wage level and to determine the wage system was at least questioned, if not actually reduced, that Siemens reorganised its personnel administration and widened its range of activities.

The Structure of Personnel Management

The Pre-War Development

Siemens began the first step towards an institutionalisation and centralisation of its personnel policy in 1904. The 'works committee'

(*BetriebsausschuB*) was formed shortly after the company joined the employers' organisation covering the Greater Berlin metal working industries and during a period of rising tension and widespread industrial conflict. Its task was to co-ordinate and unify labour policy within Siemens and to define its policy towards the employers' organisation. In this context, it is important to note that Siemens comprised the Siemens & Halske Co., the light current division, and the Siemens–Schuckert Co., the heavy current division, which were relatively autonomously operated.[17] The centralisation of the personnel policy covered the company as a whole and it hence defined the personnel administration as a strategic factor whose control and monitoring was subject to central administration. The members of the works committee included five plant managers, four deputy plant managers and two workshop managers. Four of the plant managers were at the same time members of the board of directors. The works committee was designed as an advisory staff for the board of directors and as a line authority towards the single plants.

The second step towards centralisation of personnel management occurred in 1906 when Siemens decided to promote a company union. A new committee was set up, the 'committee for social affairs', which was a sub-committee of the respective boards of directors of the two Siemens firms. Arnold and Wilhelm von Siemens, then the heads of the company and the representatives of the supervisory board, presided over its sessions. The creation of this committee hence introduced a centralised collective decision process at the highest administrative level with regard to the fundamental questions of the company's personnel policy. The committee for social affairs was supplemented by the lower-ranking works committee which continued its work on a reduced and changed scale. It was limited to dealing with the administration of the plant personnel (blue and lower-ranking white collar workers). It had to decide on the demands for wage and salary increases, to discuss the development of the wage level and of wage and salary differentials and it dealt with questions of work motivation and work discipline and eligibility to the company's social benefits such as vacations, bonuses, pension plan in case of a worker's participation in strikes. However, its main task consisted in administering the pay of the plant personnel and this meant that it had first to collect information about the existing plant by plant practice and was only then able to develop general guide-lines.

In relation to the previously wider functions of the works committee there was a new staff office installed in 1911, the 'office for economic affairs', which was renamed in 1917 the 'economic department'. This new office served as an advisory board for top management in relation to the basic problems of the company's personnel policy and for the overall development of social and economic policies, and commercial relations. In addition it prepared the company's contacts with political authorities and pressure groups and often served as its external representative in these matters.[18]

Almost immediately after the outbreak of war Siemens, AEG and the other metal working firms in Berlin were confronted with the problem of labour shortages which developed into a crucial problem during the war. By the summer of 1914 already 30 per cent of the Siemens labour force (blue and white collar) were drafted and this percentage was to rise to almost 50 per cent, while at the same time the war orders increased.[19] The Siemens management reacted immediately and decided to establish a new central agency, the 'central personnel department under conditions of mobilisation', which was to deal with all personnel reports and requests, to handle the problems of labour supply and to organise an internal labour exchange for blue and white collar workers. But in spite of this quick reaction and further expansion of the Siemens personnel administration into the field of allocation, it does not seem as if the wartime difficulties and changes in the supply of labour, the shortage of skilled labour, the rising percentage of female workers, the demands for higher wages, and finally the new form of arbitration and workers' and employees' committees induced a fundamental reorganisation of the company's personnel administration. Such a reorganisation did, however, take place almost one year after the war.

The Development after the War
Personnel management was by this time recognised as an important function of management. The post-war reorganisation introduced a centralised, hierarchically structured administration and institutionalised an integrated system of direct managerial control on three different levels. Top management's prerogative in personnel policies was established, whilst the previous extensive autonomy of plant managers in personnel affairs was heavily reduced. Plant and workplace labour management itself was systematically centralised and the former system of delegated control was superseded by a system of direct managerial control, whilst, thirdly, the previous extensive autonomy of foremen in work-place labour management was heavily cut back or even abolished and replaced by a new intermediate managerial hierarchy of production engineers.

On the top level Carl F. von Siemens created in March 1919 the new position of a 'common board adviser in personnel policy' (*Personalreferent im Vorstand*) whose special position and authority derived from the fact that he had an intermediary position between the head of the company and the boards of directors of the two Siemens firms and that he was exclusively subordinate to Carl F. von Siemens. The adviser's task was to supervise and co-ordinate the company's personnel policy, to see that the most important decisions on personnel affairs were reserved to the board of directors, to draw up general guidelines, to prepare an efficient centralised decision process and to control the implementation of these decisions. In September 1920 the adviser proceeded to install four 'management committees' (*Direktionsausschüsse*), one for the personnel administration in general, the second exclusively for office workers, the third exclusively for the blue collar workers, and finally the fourth for problems arising in connection with the white collar collective wage agreements, the first of which had been concluded for the Berlin metal working industries in September 1919. These committees superseded the 1904 works committee. They were formed by the members of the board of directors, the plant, and the department managers of the two Siemens firms. They served as discussion and advisory boards for the board adviser and introduced an element of collective leadership into the company's personnel administration. In addition to the new position of a board adviser and his general function of policy formation and co-ordination, Carl F. von Siemens allocated to a member of the board of directors the company-wide responsibility for all questions concerning the blue collar work-force.

The second hierarchical level established by the reorganisation in September 1919 was the 'department for social politics' (*Sozialpolitische Abteilung*) which was subordinate to the board adviser. It was part of the company's general office and was conceived as a staff line office, as it had not only an advisory function but also line authority. It served as advisory staff in all questions of social and labour legislation. It represented the company in all cases of legally enforced or voluntary negotiations between management and labour as well as in cases of labour unrest or claims and complaints. Finally, its function consisted in the centralised administration of social benefits and welfare schemes as well as of collective wage agreements. In the beginning the department of social politics was subdivided into four offices: the office for general questions of social legislation and social policies, personnel statistics, and social benefits; for staff and the internal transfer of staff; for workers and the internal allocation of workers; and finally the general registration and information office. The subdivision was subsequently further refined in accordance with the expansion and diversification of the company's personnel management.[20]

Thirdly, it was at the level of the plant and work-place labour management that the personnel administration was reorganised. In 1919 each plant manager was asked to install a 'work office'

(*Arbeitsbüro*) which by then had only existed in two plants. Its establishment reduced the foremen's functions and abolished their previous autonomy in work-place labour management. The work office centralised the hiring of workers, job assignment, rate fixing, and wage calculation on the level of the single plant and was the organisational means for the introduction of direct managerial control on the shop floor.[21]

Personnel Management Strategy
So far I have examined changes in the *structure* of labour management at Siemens but these changes were a precondition for, and marked the beginning of, a centralised and planned personnel *strategy*. What policies were developed and what objectives did they serve?

Unfortunately the source material is less plentiful and precise at lower management levels and concerning working conditions. It might be possible to date exactly the introduction of different measures, but it is far more difficult to obtain a detailed idea of the gradual changes in the scope and the way of their application as well as of their impact. In spite of the fact that the available source material reduces the choice of possible approaches, it is, however, one possible approach to study the underlying intentions of personnel management by the measures which were developed.

The development of the instruments of personnel management seems to have proceeded in three subsequent waves over the inter-war period: in 1919–22, 1925–8, and 1935–7. A functional regrouping of the methods allows us to differentiate between five categories: (a) productivity increases; (b) work motivation; (c) job training and education; (d) integration/company spirit; and (e) commitment to the company. A comprehensive survey using these categories shows that the introduction of such policies which belonged to the first category coincided in general with the introduction or further extension of policies belonging to the other categories.

According to the organisational and technical means which were introduced at the workshop level in order to increase the productivity of labour, these waves corresponded with three distinct efforts of rationalisation: the adoption of Taylorist principles in 1919–22; the first and rather limited introduction of Fordist techniques of standardised mass production in 1925–8; and finally an extension of standardised mass production associated with a higher level of mechanisation in 1935–7.

The transition from 'the older empirical way to the systematic, scientifically based and analytic method of management' – as a former Siemens manager retrospectively described the development – which took place after 1919 had already started in 1913/14.[22] But it was only after the war that these methods were systematically adapted and realised on a company-wide level. The first and most important organisational innovation was the general introduction of the 'work office' whose task was defined as 'to bring about scientific management'. In 1919 it began to calculate the performance of each available machine tool, and started systematically to carry out time, motion, and fatigue studies, and to develop programmes for aptitude tests. One of the first groups of workers who in 1919–20 were confronted with these tests were the female coil winders. Due to the aptitude tests at the beginning and the subsequent performance screening it was possible to reduce the job training time from 8–10 weeks to 5–6 weeks. This success, the increased awareness of training as a cost element, and the efforts to reduce the increased training cost because of the high rates of labour turnover very soon led to the introduction of a 'psychological section' in each plant. And the aptitude tests were then extended to every newly hired unskilled worker.[23]

Improved methods of time study and progress in their extension, and finally the rapid inflation which made the adjustment of the piece-based wage calculation time both labour consuming and absurd, led to the introduction of time wages instead of piece-based wage incentive systems in 1921. This transition reflects both the advancing implementation of direct labour control and its interdependence on the economic context.

In the second phase, 1925–8, the pivot of the rationalisation effort was no longer the notion of Scientific Management but the notion of the flow of production. The first step towards such a reorganisation consisted in gathering information. Koettgen, the general manager of the heavy current division, visited several American enterprises, including the Ford Co. in the autumn of 1923 in order to study American production techniques. His trip was, however, only the first of a great number: almost every Siemens plant manager subsequently visited the United States in the 1920s. After preliminary informal contacts in 1922 Siemens and Westinghouse (the second largest American electrical firm) institutionalised these contacts in 1924. Both companies concluded an agreement to exchange patents, progress in research and development, and production process specifications for a period of ten years.[24] The second step of adapting the production facilities, the working process, and the administration to the new principle of flow production and to Fordist techniques of standardised mass production soon followed. In 1925 the first assembly lines were installed in the workshops of such plants where the quantity and the uniformity of the goods produced made it economically reasonable to do so. Subsequently the conveyor belt was extended to some metal working departments and finally to the casting departments in

1927–8. The introduction of the conveyor belt into a few production units was, however, only the most salient of the changes which included the further subdivision of work and the general change-over from the driving belt to the separate drive. Thus the working speed of the machine tool as well as the work intensity increased 50 to 100 per cent.[25]

The forced rearmament after 1933 rapidly changed the formerly depressed market conditions, and it was especially the electrical and metal working industries, and Berlin as one of the main centres which participated very early in this boom. The best production year for the Siemens heavy current division had been 1928/9. If turnover for that year equals 100, then it had diminished to 28.2 in 1932/3; it was augmented by almost two-thirds in 1933/4 and amounted to 47.1 per cent of the former maximum. Of this expanded production 50 per cent or more was caused by direct or indirect armaments orders. Great numbers of unemployed skilled and semi-skilled workers in Berlin were reintegrated into the production process by the end of 1934, and already by 1935 Siemens and the other metal working and electrical firms in Berlin were faced with a scarcity of skilled and even semi-skilled workers.[26]

Siemens reacted to the changes in demand and to the drastically changed situation on the labour market with a further increased rationalisation. In 1935–6 Siemens systematically extended the methods of standardised mass production both quantitatively and qualitatively. The most advanced highly capital-intensive techniques were now introduced and further developed with integrated machine tools and special devices for their easy operation.

With respect to office work it is more difficult to discern distinct phases of reorganisation and work intensification. However, there are some indicators of such changes which can be found. From 1919 the top management repeatedly complained about lack of work discipline and low performance of the employees and pointed to the increased division of responsibility and the specialisation and mechanisation of office work as possible causes. Although mechanical typewriters had been introduced before the war, it was only after the war that Siemens forced their introduction and that there were special training programmes developed for the touch system in 1919–20. The change-over to electrical typewriters in the late 1920s continued the trend towards mechanisation and further increased the intensity of work. The increased proportion of female office workers (more than 20 per cent in January 1919), which was never again reduced to its pre-war level of about 5 per cent, underlines this development.[27] The daily control and reporting sheets for employees, identity cards and the yearly performance rating which were introduced in 1922 can be seen as indicators of the organisational changes in the offices and of their impact on the relationship between management and the rank and file employees. Further indicators are the three anti-waste campaigns which were subsequently launched in 1923-4, 1926 and 1929-30 in order to increase the efficiency of office work. In the instructions for the second campaign the 'personnel department' recommended the extension of the piece-work system to white collar workers as far as their duties were more or less standardised or recurrent and also urged the reorganisation of office work according to the principles of a flow administration.

Policies which aimed at productivity increases by means of technical and organisational rationalisation (i.e. by means of direct control), were in general accompanied by policies which belonged to the categories of work motivation, training, integration, and commitment to the company. This chronological coincidence indicates management's combined effort of efficiency *and* social engineering. The Siemens personnel management followed this double strategy, both to increase the productivity of labour and to counteract the impact of the increased degradation of work on work motivation, on interest in vocational education, on labour turnover, on identification with the company, and finally on the differentiation between blue and white collar workers as a means of social control. The increase in job training had, however, not only a compensating, but also a supplementary function to the measures of technical rationalisation.

During the first wave of rationalisation in 1919-22 the following measures of social engineering were introduced: with respect to training – scholarships for highly qualified apprentices to study at technical colleges, systematic and company-wide unified vocational training programmes, the training of commercial apprentices; with respect to integration – the monthly publishing of a company journal which was mailed to every blue and white collar worker, the opening of a sanatorium for workers (another one for salaried employees had existed since before the war); with respect to commitment to the company–the construction of company dwellings, the introduction of a further internal differentiation of status for middle and higher salaried employees, and diverse social benefits.

During the second wave of rationalisation in 1925-8 management launched a formal selection procedure for suggestions of improvements and announced money rewards for the best suggestions in order to increase work motivation and to promote active co-operation of the workers. Management further engaged in internal company training programmes by opening courses for time clerks, and running courses and lectures on technical, commercial, economic, and social topics for most staff. The increased importance management attributed to internal company training found its most salient expression in the setting up of a central staff office and associated committees for commercial and technical training programmes and the administration of internal company careers. The extended promotion of company-sponsored social activities after work (Siemens clubs covered almost every possible leisure time occupation from sports to stamp collecting) represented integration policies. Finally, the introduction of service bonuses, the extension of company housing and several extensions of the welfare programme aimed at the individual's commitment to the company and at the promotion of a company spirit.

During the third wave of rationalisation in 1935–7 the company training programmes were heavily extended both in number and scope. More trainees than ever before were employed and new programmes were developed for retraining of skilled workers from non-metal trades, for vocational rehabilitation of previously long-term unemployed metal workers and commercial employees, for crash courses for instructing unskilled workers, and for on the job training of male and female commercial and technical lower ranking employees. Thus, due to rationalisation and in view of the scarcity of skilled labour and the regulation and restriction of inter-firm and inter-local movement of labour by the Nazi state authorities, training and allocation of labour developed into a primary function of management and were more than ever before incorporated within the firm's administrative system. During this period there was also a further extension of company housing and the introduction of Christmas bonuses – all of which served to promote integration and commitment to the company.[28]

The overall expenditures for this 'social programme' were considerable, both in absolute and relative terms, and it was an element of the company's social engineering policy that they were made known to the employees by means of the company journal and to the public by means of the annual reports. Siemens was the first Berlin firm to publish 'social balances', and began to do so in 1929/30; AEG did so much later, in 1937/8. In the business year 1918/19 the expenditures amounted to 13.3 per cent of Siemen's total wage and salary cost; in 1919/20 – the first 'normal' business year without war subsidies – to 3.3 per cent. Between 1924/5 and 1928/9 the average percentage per business year slightly increased as compared to 1919/20; it amounted to approximately 4.2 per cent of the annual total wage and salary cost. During the Depression (business years 1929/30 to 1932/3) it was markedly increased to 9.5 per cent (in the average of the four years), mainly because of anticipated pensioning of salaried employees, and paid lay-offs for this group. Although the percentage decreased in the ensuing boom period, nevertheless in the business years from 1933/4 to 1938/9 it reached a higher level than during the previous boom. The overall cost of the 'social programme' amounted in this period to a yearly average of approximately 8 per cent of the respective total wage and salary cost. The latter percentage was relatively high, if compared to the 2–3 per cent which the German Labour Front stated as the average of a non-specified group of German firms, but it only surpassed the 'social endeavour' of AEG, the most serious rival to Siemens in the local labour market, by a small percentage: the overall cost of the AEG 'social programme' amounted in the business years 1933/4 to 1938/9 to a yearly average of 6.7 per cent of wage and salary costs.[29]

Probably the most important Siemens social engineering policy, however, was that of internal status differentiation and the internal company careers created by means of it. Whereas the differention between blue and white collar status (resulting in the blue collar workers' common striving for promotion into a white collar position, and conversely the white collar workers' perception of themselves as socially superior and their fears of social degradation) served these ends in general, the Siemens management did not confine itself to exploiting this differentiation but further pursued a policy of status differentiation among the white collar labour force. The most peculiar measure (and to my mind the most revealing with respect to the company's strategy for social control) was, however, the reintroduction of a staff status (that of *Beamter*) for white collar workers in 1921 – a status which had been rendered obsolete by the first collective agreement on salaries and working conditions in September 1919. This led to an internal differentiation among the rank and file employees who were subject to the collective salary agreements, in respect of the company's social benefits and pension plan and to relative job security. The reintroduction of the *Beamter* status as a means of differentiation relating to the mass of white collar workers was supplemented by the creation of different ranks for senior employees in the same year. The internal differentiation of the white collar workers therefore seems to have been one of the primary objectives of the Siemens personnel policy. During the period of the gradual degradation of office work as a general phenomenon, only a few of the lower ranking employees were in fact marginalised, whereas others were at least socially or symbolically privileged by their appointment to the subcategory of *Beamter*.[30]

Conclusion
The comparison of Siemens's personnel management style and Taylor's concept of personnel policy shows that Siemens's personnel

administration corresponded to it in many respects. Siemens both created the structural pre-conditions for a centralised, planned and calculated factor input, and adopted organisational and technical means to increase the productivity of labour. The reduction of labour to an administered cost was advanced. Taylor's concept as an integral whole consisted in the postulated congruity of efficiency and social engineering: Scientific Management as a technique of 'objectively' fixing the adequate wage for the adequate performance was simultaneously the means as well for the recruitment, the integration, and the motivation of the worker. It is a decisive and consistent constituent of the Taylorist model that the worker himself can dispose of the additional income which results from his increased performance. The strategies of Siemens's personnel management suggest, however, that there were different underlying aims to its wage and personnel policy. Siemens managers did not rely on the actual wage level and so-called objective techniques of fixing adequate wages, nor was policy restricted to that wage which was actually paid to the worker. Rather, the Siemens management relied, even in its Taylorist phase immediately after the war, on such measures of additional payments which management disposed of and which were intended to promote both blue and white collar worker commitment to the company. The social benefits which were promised to every employee regardless of status, but were awarded by management according to the aims of the company's personnel policy, contradicted Taylor's concept of substituting functional authority and economic rationality for the previous system of personal dependence and arbitrary management decisions. The Siemens personnel management combined efficiency and social engineering, but in a quite different way from that which was inherent in Taylor's model.

Despite the special post-war conditions, the cyclical developments, and the traditions of the Siemens Co. as a family-owned enterprise, it seems as if the collective wage and salary agreements which were for the first time agreed upon after the war in 1919 had some impact on the strategies of Siemens's personnel management. The policies of integration, commitment to the company and promotion of a company spirit had the additional advantage that they also constituted a means to intervene in the workers' social life (associations, clubs, educational establishments) which in the Weimar period – especially in the 'red capital' Berlin – was mainly organised by the trade unions. 'The battle for the worker's soul' was, however, one of the battlefields into which Siemens re-entered immediately after the war and revolution in order to reduce the trade unions' influence on the worker, to undermine their strength, and to curtail their influence in politics, in the labour market, and at the work-place. And it was on this battlefield that its personnel policy was seen and consciously used as a weapon.[31]

The political and social conditions in post-war Germany, the strength of the trade unions, and the legal enforcement of collective bargaining were definitely different from the American context which underlay Taylor's concept of personnel management. In spite of these restrictive conditions the Siemens personnel policy approximated to one aspect of Taylor's prophecy: personnel management was successfully developed as a means to reduce the impact of non-economic and company external factors on the wage policy and on the relationship between management and labour. The combination of strategies to achieve the latter goal was different from that which Taylor had proposed. On the contrary, it was in the phase of Taylorist efficiency engineering that Siemens's management developed a special additional set of social engineering strategies and the basic characteristics of its personnel policy for the years to come.

The scattered evidence that exists suggests so far that the development of labour market and industrial relations at Siemens was fairly typical of large industrial enterprises in Germany during the inter-war years, but detailed studies are still lacking and a firm conclusion must await further research.[32]

Notes

1. This paper is primarily based on unpublished sources of the Siemens archives, the Werner-von-Siemens Institut für Geschichte des Hauses Siemens, in Munich. I wish to thank Dr Sigfrid von Weiher who kindly allowed me the access to the archive and Mr Teichmann who was very helpful in supplying the files. I have limited the references to direct quotes and to calculations of my own based on the Siemens files. Siemens records are introduced by the following abbreviation: Siemens Archiv Akte = SAA, plus the archival record number.
2. See especially J. Kocka, 'Family and Bureaucracy in German Industrial Management, 1850–1914: Siemens in Comparative Perspective', *Business History Review*, (1971); J. Kocka, 'The Rise of the Modern Industrial Enterprise in Germany' in A.D. Chandler and H. Daems (eds.), *Managerial Hierarchies* (1980).
3. M. Weber, *Wirtschaft und Gesellschaft* (1964).
4. H. Hartmann and P. Meyer, *Soziologie der Personalarbeit* (1980); E. Potthoff, *Betriebliches Personalwesen* (1974); C.C. Ling, *The Management of Personnel Relations* (1965).
5. F.W. Taylor, *Scientific Management* (1947); H. Homburg, 'Anfange des Taylorsystems in Deutschland vor dem Ersten Weltkrieg' in *Geschichte und Gesellschaft* (1978).
6. L. Borchardt, 'Technischer Fortschritt und sozialer Wandel. Das Beispiel der Taylorismus Rezeption' in W. Treue (ed.) *Deutsche Technikgeschichte* (1977), pp. 52–98; Homburg (1978).
7. P.B. Doeringer and M.J. Piore, *Internal Labor Markets and Manpower Analysis* (1971); A.D. Chandler, *The Visible Hand. The Managerial Revolution in American Business* (1977).
8. Kocka (1980); J. Kocka and H. Siegrist, 'Die hundert agrossten deutschen Industrieunternehmen im späten 19. und fruhen 20. Jahrhundert', in N. Horn and J.

Kocka (eds.), *Recht und Entwicklung der Gross unternehmen im 19. und fruhen 20* (1979), pp. 55–122; H. Siegrist, 'Deutsche Gross unternehmen vom späten 19. Jahrhundert bis zur Weimarer Republik' in *Geschichte und Gesellschaft* (1980).

9. See Gospel chapter in this volume.
10. P. Czada, *Die Berliner Elektroindustrie in der Weimarer Zeit* (1969).
11. Ibid.; J. Kocka, 'Siemens und der aufhaltsame Aufstieg der AEG' in *Tradition* (1972),
12. Czada (1969), p. 203.
13. D. Fricke, *Die Deutsche Arbeiterbewegung 1869–1914* (1976), pp. 730–2; H.H. Hartwich, *Arbeitsmarkt verbände und Staat 1918–33* (1967), pp. 65–70, 410–13.
14. H. Homburg, 'Externer und Interner Arbeitsmarkt: zur Entstehung und Funktion des Siemens-Werkvereins 1906–1918', in T. Pierenkemper and R. Tilly (eds.), *Historische Arbeitsmarktforschung* (1981).
15. G.D. Feldman, *Army, Industry and Labour in German 1914–1918* (1966); G.D. Feldman, 'German Business between War and Revolution: The Origins of the Stinnes–Legien Agreement', in G.A. Ritter, (ed.), *Entstehung und Wandel der modernen Gesellschaft, Festschrift fur H. Rosenberg*; G.D. Feldman, 'The Origins of the Stinnes–Legien Agreement. A Documentation', in *Internat. Wissenschaftliche Korrespondez zur Geschichte der deutschen Arbeiterbewegung* (1973).
16. SAA 47/Lg 768.
17. This structure was the result of the economic down-turn of 1900–2 which had hit the German electric industry hard and resulted in a general merger movement. Siemens took over the struggling Schuckert Co. and formed an independent firm, Siemens-Schuckertwerke GmbH (SSW), in 1903 which specialised in power current products. Siemens & Halske served as the holding company for SSW. See Kocka (1971).
18. J. Kocka, *Unternehmensverwaltung und Angestelltenschaft am Beispel Siemens 1847–1914* (1969a), pp. 350–63, 442–9; Homburg (1981).
19. SAA Chronik, p. 81, 47/Lg 768.
20. SAA 33/Li 278; 47/Lg 768.
21. SAA 11/Lf 444 (Köttgen Chronik), pp. 167 ff.
22. SAA Chronik, pp. 66, 163 ff., 202.
23. SAA Chronik, p. 167.
24. The agreement also consisted of market share arrangements and paralleled an agreement which AEG had concluded with the American General Electric Co. SAA 47/Lg 768; M/Lf 384 (Köttgen).
25. SAA Chronik, pp. 169–74; 11/Lg 713 (Franke).
26. SAA Chronik, pp. 291–3, 250, 283.
27. SAA 11/Lf 495 (Köttgen); 32/Lg 605; 11/Lf 103 (Köttgen); 29/Lt 500.
28. SAA 33/Li 278; 15/Li 779; 47/Lg 768. Circulars of the social and personnel department.
29. Deutsche Arbeitsfront, Arbeitswissenschaftliches Instit (DAF AW1) 1958 I, p. 112; SAA 11/Lc 594 (Graupe); 29/LS 774; 29/Li 430; AEG annual reports.
30. SAA circulars of the social and personnel department.
31. F. Fricke, *Sie suchen die Seele, Berlin, Verlagsgesellschaft des Allgemeinen Deutschen Gewerkschaftsbundes* (1927); SAA, 15/Lc 774 (1919/20).
32. See W. Fischer, 'Labor–Management and Industrial Relations in Germany 1870–1930' in K. Nakagawa (ed.), *Labor and Management* (1979).

7 Japanese Employer Labour Policy: The Heavy Engineering Industry in 1900–1930
Reiko Okayama

Introduction

Since Abegglen's *The Japanese Factory*, published in 1958, the Japanese system of industrial relations has been studied by students of various disciplines as well as by managers and business consultants. Nevertheless, in spite of the subject's popularity in terms of the peculiar characteristics of Japanese employment, few business historians have focused on this area of management. The efforts of business historians in general have been directed towards financial, commercial or organisational aspects of management. This paper will shift the focus to the employer side of Japanese industrial relations, and make clear the aspects of direct labour management developed in large heavy engineering firms from the turn of the century to the 1930s. The material is drawn mainly from existing company documents and the literature of labour history.

During the 1930s large firms in various industries tended to adopt more sophisticated techniques of labour management and to formalise labour management relations, centrally and on the local level. The development of this process varied between industries, but during this period, which was one of rapid industrialisation, heavy engineering represented one important pattern of rationalisation in labour management.

Traditional Forms of Labour Management

Heavy engineering was one of the most important industries in the Meiji Government's strategy for making Japan self-sufficient in munitions production. The Government fostered and promoted the industry, not only running its own arsenals and factories but also encouraging large private firms by furnishing them with subsidies.

The character of this industry, imported by the Government at an early stage in industrialisation in order to achieve its political objectives, was also reflected in its peculiar structure. By the end of the nineteenth century there had been erected, on the one hand, a small number of large-scale government factories devoted mostly to military purposes, and, on the other hand, a large number of small and medium-scale engineering businesses, many of which had hardly developed beyond the cottage industry stage. Nevertheless there were a few large shipyards in the private sector, general heavy engineering enterprises which built not only ships but also steam engines, boilers, railcoaches, heavy electric equipment, etc. During the periods of industrial expansion which followed the wars against China (1894–5) and Russia (1904–5) the private sector reached large-scale proportions and by 1914 quite a large number of engineering firms had been established. Many of today's big businesses in Japan have grown from these firms. It was in the decade before the First World War that the large firms in the heavy industry sector started to abandon indirect labour management practices.

The meaning of 'indirect labour management' here is not strictly synonymous with a subcontract system, although both may have coincided with each other. In the late-nineteenth century, it was usual for a work group called a 'kumi' (a team or gang) to be allocated by the management to do a certain kind of work. Usually this group was divided along trade lines and was under the direction and supervision of an 'oyakata'.[1] The position of the oyakata in the work-place seems to have been similar to a foreman since all the workers, not only the oyakatas but also their kumi men, were employed directly by the firm.

However, when the oyakatas were invited by the management to submit tenders for a certain amount of work, the picture tended to become complicated. When one of the oyakatas made a successful bid, he would carry out the work with his kumi and receive the difference between the bid and the sum total of the wages paid to the men. Even if the wage rates of kumi members had been fixed by the managements, the oyakatas could use their discretion firstly in selecting the workers who would be asked to work as kumi members and secondly in how much of the premium which resulted from the contracted work was to be distributed among the men.[2] The main bulk of the work in shipyards was performed under the bidding system, unlike other areas of engineering.

Yet there were sub-contractors, too, who were independent craftsment and were also called oyakata, and they existed in both traditional and 'modern' trades. They provided their apprentices with board and lodging and brought them as their helpers to the work-place where they were doing contracted work.[3] A subcontract system seems to have been ubiquitous in small or medium sized businesses in the industry, particularly in some traditional trades such as wooden ship construction.[4] Shipwrights, as a contemporary reporter noted in 1897, would make a lump sum contract with shipyard owners or managers, and when the work was finished they would keep most of the money for themselves and give only pocket money to the apprentices who were dependent on them. The subcontracting oyakatas' often had gangs consisting of several dozen workers.[5] In consequence the assertion that a subcontract system in which labour was employed by the subcontractor was widespread in the engineering and metal working industries overlooks the broad picture and the complexities of labour management at this time.[6]

It is important to note that subcontractors or company foremen could exist side by side in the same plant.[7] Most of them had risen from similar origins as workmen and their positions stemmed in large part from their experience with the trade. It has been suggested that a considerable number of them, with the exception of traditional craftsmen, would have gained their trade knowledge while working under the instruction of foreign engineers or craftsmen at the government-operated factories during the period of the transfer of Western technology to Japan in the early Meiji era.[8]

The oyakata had by around the 1890s come to enjoy a wide range of authority in labour as well as production management. They fulfilled the production functions of planning, allocation and speed of work, and working methods, and also performed the personnel functions of recruiting, training, promoting, demoting and payment as well as handling discipline and dealing with grievances, both in the shop and in private life – although some advanced companies laid down regulations for hiring and firing and for discipline.[9] Until the late nineteenth century it was in general the usual practice for even large firms in the private sector to rely on the oyakata for his authority over labour and for production management.[10] Therefore the employers gave their oyakata workers favourable conditions of employment in order to retain them.

However, employers were confronted with gradually increasing difficulties in relying on the oyakata system. In the work-place there often arose quarrels and strife over the oyakata's arbitrary and coercive control, in particular over shares in the premium or in the allocation of work.[11] Bribery of the oyakata in order to win his favour was rampant among the workers.[12] Increasingly, in the face of rising discontent and conflict at the work-place, employers tended to adopt the alternative strategy of direct control in the labour process.

There is no doubt that the oyakata system had great advantages for employers at this time when a large part of the work at shipyards or engineering plants was dependent on the manual dexterity of skilled workers. It was particularly important because most company first-line supervisors did not have a knowledge of the trade: they could not assess the degree of skill of a worker applying for a job, or allot him to the work most appropriate for him.[13] Even more, under the bidding system, the employer could expect the oyakata to extract the maximum efficiency out of his men. Moreover, the system had the additional advantage that the employers could avoid over-staffing when they suffered from a depressed product market.[14] In fact, until well into the Sino-Japanese War of 1894–5, the product market of this industry was a narrow and limited one, and the industry was very vulnerable to fluctuations and uncertainty.

The strategy of direct management of labour by the employer meant that he had to take over the functions hitherto performed by the oyakata in the field of labour management: that is recruiting, training and motivation of workers, as well as paying wages and maintaining better employer–employee relations. However, this switch-over to direct management did not necessarily proceed at a uniform pace throughout the industry. A large firm such as the Shibaura Engineering Works dismissed a great number of its oyakata workers in 1900, during the time of the depression, and then abolished the oyakata system.[15] But this was unusual; among even some of the large firms it was not until the period after the Russo-Japanese War of 1904–5 that the abolition of the system was carried out. In fact, the oyakata system lingered on among engineering firms, in large as well as small sized firms, until the 1920s.[16] After they abolished this system, some firms introduced an incentive wage system. The Mitsubishi Nagasaki Shipyard, for instance, in 1908, in the midst of the depression, abolished the oyakata bidding system in the hull construction department and instead adopted an incentive wage system which they called 'the increase time system'. They themselves wanted to estimate the cost of labour in the department instead of entrusting the task to their senior workers, in order to rationalise their production costs.[17] Here can be seen, as will be pointed out later, another motive for the employers to try to abandon the oyakata system. In 1913, the shipyard made up twelve price lists for each machinists' job at the conclusion of which the chief engineer of the department consulted with the principal workers and obtained the approval of the factory manager.[18] It is important to note that the introduction of incentive wage systems meant that management became increasingly able to assess a fair day's work to be assigned to the workmen and pay them for their results, and gained increased expertise in the division of labour within the production processes. In such ways employers in large heavy engineering firms gradually obtained complete control over the labour process, although the allocation of jobs to each man and the direction of their work was still dependent on the principal workers, who were sometimes still called 'kumi-cho' (group boss), but who now were incorporated into the lowest stratum of management organisation in the workshop. In the same way, these principal workers maintained a strong voice over hiring and firing as well as over wage rates, for they, *de facto*, carried out the search for new recruits, although under the direction and approval of the department manager, and assessed the skills of the applicants.[19]

It was natural that this development in direct management involved increased numbers of white collar foremen and discipline of the labour process. The trend was reflected in the increased ratio of white collar employees to blue collar during the decade before the First World War. For instance, in the Mitsubishi Nagasaki Shipyard, the ratio was 1:23 in 1902, whereas, after the abolition of the oyakata system, the ratio rose to 1:9 in 1910.[20] In the same way, when the Shibaura Engineering Works abolished their oyakata system in 1900, the white collar ratio went from 1:8 in 1898 to 1:3 in 1911.[21] Of course, the increase in labour management staff was not entirely responsible for this trend to bureaucratisation. The rationalisation of labour management at this time was mainly at the level of the plant, and so it would be safer to say that the development of bureaucratisation in this period was rather due to a considerable increase in the number of engineers as well as staff in other managerial areas, such as accounting. It is important, however, to note that in the Mitsubishi Nagasaki Shipyard the rationalisation of labour management had been introduced by the employers partly to rationalise their cost accounting: 'For to become the final winner in a competitive market you have to cut your production costs. For this reason it is essential to study and control each cost, both in labour and materials.'[22] We can assume that Mitsubishi were not the only firm to make this decision, although they were one of the most advanced. Meanwhile, however, this development in direct control led to the centralisation of the functions of labour management, and a considerable number of large firms in the industry established a special department of labour management, centrally and locally, during the period between the First World War and the mid-1920s. Why did they need such departments at this particular time? What problems did they have to cope with and what labour strategies did they have? I will take up these questions next.

Industrial Relations and the Bureaucratisation of Management
After an initial year of economic turmoil, the First World War triggered off a boom in the economy and resulted in an enormous expansion in industry, especially heavy engineering. The larger firms

consolidated their position, expanded in size and were able to install advanced mechanical equipment, and this resulted in increased specialisation in products. The 'zaibatsu' turned their attention towards heavy industry and there emerged a certain number of large corporations.[23] To take one or two examples: the Nagasaki Ship-building Co. had 15,631 employees in 1918 compared to 6371 in 1910; the Shibaura Engineering Works, the largest engineering firm at that time and the predecessor of the present Toshiba Co., employed in all 4005 people in 1917 as against 1297 in 1911.[24] The increase in the size of firms and plants during this period is indicated by the fact that in 1909 35.9 per cent of engineering workers were employed in factories with 500 or more employees, whereas by 1919 this proportion had shot up to 55.5 per cent.[25] At the same time, the number of workers in the private sector continued to increase more rapidly than in the public sector. The number of workers in private firms first exceeded those in the public sector in 1900, when there were 30,000 in private firms as against 28,500 in the public sector. In 1914 the figures were 102,300 and 77,300, and reached 261,300 as against 111,800 by 1919.[26]

Meanwhile, as the rapid growth in industry involved an increasing demand for labour, it gave rise to an acute labour shortage of, in particular, skilled men. Labour mobility increased and the employers had to cope with a very high rate of labour turnover. Wage rates went up but prices rose even higher and this caused a lot of discontent and disputes at the work-place. In 1914, the number of strikes was 50 with 7,904 men involved, whereas in 1917 the number of strikes went up to 398 with 57,309 involved.[27] Furthermore, before long, the employers in heavy industry found themselves being threatened by organised labour with regard to their managerial prerogatives. It could be argued that labour militancy, to a large extent, led the employers to the bureaucratisation of labour management during the 1920s. Therefore it would be useful to look briefly at the development of Japanese trade unions.[28]

Trade unionism in Japan started in 1897 under the influence of a number of Christian intellectuals. In heavy industry, they tried to organise workers in almost all trades, except for unskilled labour, and soon succeeded in setting up their branches in large firms. This success in increasing membership was largely due to the participation of oyakata workers, with their subordinates following their example. Union organisers aimed at improving the social status of members, encouraging them with the idea of the dignity of workers, but nevertheless maintained co-operative attitudes towards employers. Despite this the employers and the Government refused to accept the existence of unions. The enactment of the Public Peace Police Act in 1900 played an important role in repressing the fragile union movement.[29] The dismissal of activists, the intervention of the police in union activities and the unions' inability to maintain the solidarity of members, all helped during the early days to bring trade unionism to a standstill. In 1912 the Yuaikai, the Friendship Society, was established under the leadership of a Christian, Suzuki Bunji, who was moved by the poor and pitiful conditions of workmen in the larger firms. The society tried to rebuild trade unions by persuading workers to unite in order to improve their lives, and gradually gained members in engineering establishments. In 1916 membership reached 10,000 and before long the society's strategy revealed itself as it began to drop the guise of a friendly society and demand collective bargaining and the right of unions to exist. In 1919 71 new unions were set up and labour began to demand not only recognition for unions but also the repeal of section 17 of the Public Peace Police Act, which hampered unions' activities, an eight hour working day and universal suffrage. These demands were helped greatly by Taisho democracy reflecting the spirit of the time[30] and internationally favourable conditions towards labour and socialism in other countries which influenced Japanese government officials. In 1921 the Yuaikai finally changed itself into Dainihon-Rodo-Sodomei, the Japanese General Federation of Labour, and this heralded a new start for industrial unionism in Japan. In the depression after the war the labour market turned in favour of employers. Nevertheless, severe labour strife continued in the larger firms, supported by the unions which demanded collective bargaining and pay for redundant employees. It was this labour unrest and militancy which was responsible for employers adopting labour management strategies to strengthen and fortify their right to manage.

The employers' initial response to the workers' demand for collective bargaining was to reject it. But eventually they came to realise that it would be advantageous to have regular contact with their workers and to consult their opinions concerning working conditions. Thus, in the end, they chose to set up works committees with the employees' representatives, partly affected by the government policy of establishing one labour union for each plant. Many industrialists did not necessarily support the idea of co-operation between management and workers.[31] This idea was inspired by the Kyochokai, a society of promoting co-operation between employers and employees, a semi-independent research organisation established in 1919 under the Government's auspices. But industrialists were no longer able to make use of their favourite theme that 'Japanese customs' were different from those of the West and they could not continue indefinitely the master–servant relationship which had existed up to that time.

During the early 1920s works committees rapidly spread in large heavy engineering firms, following severe conflicts between employers and men. As workers' demands for collective bargaining were not always tied to pay demands, many workers in the plants remained non-unionised, and as ideological differences between union leaders hampered union activities, the intention of employers to absorb their workers' grievances and tie them closely to the firms through works committees was gradually achieved. Furthermore some firms set up subsidiary groups of works committees at shop levels, in order to promote more frequent communication. At the same time, industrial conflicts, especially because of the post-war recession, generally resulted in defeat for the workers, which usually meant that the leaders of the disputes were dismissed. Thus as time went on the influence of previous activists seems to have died out in larger firms.

The period we are concerned with here (the 1920s) saw larger firms in heavy industry set up their own training schools for young prospective employees, in order to produce their own 'key workers' for the future. During the First World War employers had suffered from a shortage of skilled men, and the horizontal mobility in the labour market at that time had been such that employers were afraid of losing the workers' company loyalty, a fear which was heightened when they were confronted by the organised power of labour. All these factors contributed to their establishment of training schools within their premises. Prospective applicants were limited to those between 14 and 17 years old, and they were only admitted in April each year.[32] During this period some firms which had hitherto relied on vocational schools to train their prospective employees converted to the 'enterprise school' system. These schools seem to have put considerable emphasis both on inculcating company culture into young workers and producing skilled workers who fitted in with the labour requirements of each company. Furthermore, in this period employers adopted various types of supplementary payment, *irrespective of job*, largely based on the duration of employment.[33] The employers' intention of tying their workers to the firm through the measures mentioned so far was well realised in the contracted labour market during the depression in the 1920s. The number of male workers in firms employing more than 500 operatives decreased to 111,000 in 1928 from 210,000 in 1920.[34] Severe competition for job security among workers became more intense with the annual increase of 200,000 in the male working population and there is no doubt that employees in larger firms tended to hang on to their positions and rise up the ladder of promotion inside the company. In much the same way as these adult workers, most young prospective employees remained at the firm where they

acquired their skill and followed careers as 'key workers'.[35] In consequence, employers adopted a 'permanent employment system' for
their key workers, who were continuously employed by the firm unless
very severe economic down-turns occurred, though it should be
remembered that a few advanced firms had already adopted this
system at the beginning of the century.[36] However, in order to function successfully this employment system required different categories
of workers, namely temporary and casual workers. The former were
hired by employers for a limited duration, and the latter recruited by
labour agents. Employers could use them as required at times of high
demand in the market. Only key workers enjoyed employment conditions similar to those of 'shokuin', that is, office employees. With the
development of this permanent employment system employers introduced a retirement system for these key workers, too, usually at the
age of 50 to 55.

Thus under the fear of having their power threatened, the
employers developed these measures of direct labour management in
order to foster and maintain their key workers, for which a special
labour management organisation had to be established. In consequence, the period immediately after the First World War and the first
half of the 1920s saw a considerable number of large heavy engineering firms set up special departments of labour management. For
example, Kawasaki Shipbuilding, Uraga Dock, Sumitomo Steel and
Yawata Iron and Steel, established their labour management organisations in 1919, followed by Mitsubishi Shipbuilding, Osaka Steel,
Kawasaki Steel, as well as the Army and Navy arsenals. They screened
job applicants carefully and shut union activists or agitators out of
their gates.[37] And, at the same time, they also centralised the practice
of recruitment, deployment and dismissal, as well as the remuneration
of workers in the hands of management.

However, it would be misleading if we looked at the development
of direct labour management by employers only in terms of their
response to the heightened labour movement at that time. There was
also the necessity for employers to centralise labour management
because of the increased size of plants. They had to adjust the practices of labour management through all their shops from the stand-
point of the plant as a whole, especially in multi-plant organisations.[38]
Employers were obliged to co-ordinate the employment conditions of
their workers, throughout the plants.

Furthermore it should be remembered that employers in large heavy
engineering firms undertook responsibility for labour management in
order to increase the efficiency of workers and diminish the cost of
production. Thus, one of the most advanced firms, the Mitsubishi

Kobe Shipbuilding Co. put their mechanical engineers into various shops in the early 1920s to supervise production process. And as these engineers also determined the wage rates where an incentive wage system was in operation, the authority of master workers was completely undermined. Oyakata workers were incorporated in the lowest stratum of the management hierarchy in plants and the functions which they had hitherto enjoyed in labour as well as production management were transferred into the hands of specialised staff.

Eventually the employers maintained their managerial prerogatives and unilateral decision making powers over employment conditions in order to increase workers' efforts at will and decrease output costs. Such intentions on the part of employers were expressed in a remark by a distinguished industrialist: 'trade unions will hamper the improvement of production, because unions determine working hours and a 'fair' day's work. Wage rates are also determined by collective bargaining. All these will prevent industry from advanced mechanisation.[39] This attitude on the part of employers explains why employers obstinately resisted the introduction of a trade union bill at that time, and the prospects for the passage of the bill came to end in 1931.[40]

Rather than accept trade unions and collective bargaining, or institute general social security measures for all workers, Japanese employers chose the path of paternalism, giving their key workers welfare provisions not as rights but as benevolent gifts. This paternalism was underpinned by their favourite theme, 'a company is like a family': the employer was the head of this corporate family and the employees his family members, so that everyone could work in harmony. Thus the permanent employment system became linked to this familial ideology applied to labour–management relations.[41]

Conclusion

We have considered so far the development of Japanese employers' labour policy in large heavy engineering firms mainly from the turn of the century to the 1920s. It was around the turn of the century that employers in the advanced companies in heavy industry began to cease relying on indirect labour management and instituted a system of direct management. They increasingly found the oyakata system ineffectual and incompatible with increased competitive pressures and technological change. This transition was accelerated by the First World War, and resulted from the expanded market in heavy industry and also high labour turnover. After the war period, with the heightened labour movement, sophisticated direct labour management practices were gradually institutionalised in these large firms. These management practices were characterised firstly by the exclusion of trade or industrial unionism from each firm, and where need be, the setting up of works committees or enterprise unions with only blue collar workers as members. Secondly, management developed special treatment for their key workers which was seniority-based promotion and permanent employment, a strategy which had already been applied to white collar workers.

Because of this labour strategy, the employment conditions of the key workers went on improving even during the depression in the 1920s, and also resulted in significant wage differentials between large and small and medium sized companies. It should be remembered that, however, employers maintained their unilateral powers over the employment conditions of workers, although they advocated paternalism and did not refuse regular consultation with their workers.

The development of the labour management techniques described above should be seen against the background of a number of major trends: the rapid development of Japanese heavy industrialisation; the utilisation of advanced technology borrowed from the West such that there was little continuity of workers' skills with those of pre-industrial society and little time afforded the workers to cultivate a solidarity based on working in the same trade; the heavy influx of labour, mostly untrained and mainly from villages, with traditional rural values; intensified international competition after the First World War; and the concentration of capital in larger firms. Thus, having been pushed by competitive pressures, and with a drive toward increasing efficiency and cutting costs, the employers were induced to rationalise labour management.

These practices of labour management established at that time in large heavy engineering firms have been termed by labour historians and sociologists as the 'Japanese seniority system' or the 'familyism of business'.[42] However it would be misleading to think that employers completely succeeded in achieving their intention of fostering efficient, disciplined and loyal workers. For through the boom in the latter half of the 1930s, associated with the war economy, labour mobility began to increase again. And with the advent of the Second World War the seniority-based wage system was undermined due to the increased dilution of skilled workers and the increased cost of living.

How the 'Japanese system of employment' established in the 1920s has affected industrial relations in the post-war period is still a matter of debate. Some commentators trace the origin of post-war Japanese employment practices back to the experiences of the 1920s while others insist on the discontinuity of the system between the pre- and post-Second World War periods because of drastic changes in the post-war socio-economic conditions, especially those brought about by the labour policy of the Occupation forces or because of the influences coming from the Sampo movement during the war economy.[43] But whatever one's assessment of the developmental influences, it is clear that the Japanese heavy engineering industry in the inter-war years was characterised by the spread of institutionalised paternalism and resistance to trade unionism.

Notes

1. *Mitsubishi Jukogyo Kabushiki Gaishashi* [The Company History of the Mitsubishi Heavy Industries Limited] (1956), pp. 202–3; *Nihon Sangyo Kunren Kyokai, Nihon Sangyo Kunren Hyakunenshi* [A Hundred Years of Japanese Industrial Training] (1971), p. 105.
2. Noshomusho, *Shokko Jijo* [Workmen's Situations] (1903), p. 144.
3. *Tokyo Kogyo Kyoiku Gakko, Kogyo Shisetsu Shiryo* [Some Aspects of Industrial Training] (1896); *Shokko Jijo*, vol. 2, pp. 36–7; M. Sumiya, *Nihon Chinrodo no Shiteki Kenkyu* [A Historical Survey of Japanese Labour] (1976), pp. 78–84; K. Ohkochi and H. Matsuo, *Nihon Rodokumiai Monogatari* [The Story of Japanese Trade Unionism, the Taisho period] (1965), p. 3.
4. S. Ushiyama, 'Kojo Junshi-ki' [Visiting Factories], *Jiji Shinpo*, 21 October 1897, quoted in T. Hyodo, *Nihon ni okeru Roshikankei no Kenkyu* [A Study of Industrial Relations in Japan] (1971), p. 83.
5. *Shokko Jijo*, vol. 3, pp. 168–9.
6. Contrast S.B. Levine, 'Labor Market and Collective Bargaining in Japan' in W.W. Lockwood (ed.), *The State and Economic Enterprise in Japan* (1965).
7. H. Hazama, *Nihon Romu Kanrishi Kenkyu* [Studies in the History of Labour Management in Japan] (1964), pp. 443–5.
8. *Nihon Sangyo Kunren Kyokai* (1971), p. 105. The Meiji period lasted from 1868–1912.
9. C.R. Littler, *The Development of the Labour Process in Capitalist Societies* (1982).
10. *Noshomusho, Kojo oyobi Shokko ni kansuru Tsuhei Ippan* [The Circumstances of Factories and Workmen] (1897), p. 5.
11. G. Yokoyama, *Nihon no Kaso-shakai* [The Lower Class in Japan] (1898), pp. 57, 221, 234; *Nihon Sangyo Kunren Kyokai* (1971), p. 129.
12. Anonymous, 'Shokko Seikatsu 20nen no kokuhaku' [A confession of a worker about his twenty years of working life] in *Yuai Shinbun*, 15 June 1914.
13. G. Yokoyama (1898), p. 234; Sangyo Kunren Kyokai (1971), p. 129.
14. Cf. A.L. Stinchcombe, 'Bureaucratic and Craft Administration of Production', *Adminstrative Science Quarterly* (1959).
15. Y. Kimura (ed.), *Shibaura-Seisakusho 65-nenshi* (The 65 Years of the Shibaura Engineering Works Limited) (1940) pp. 38 and 39.
16. Sangyo Kunren Kyokai (1971), p. 131.
17. *Mitsubishi Nagasaki Zosen-jo, Chingin oyobi Teate-Hen* [Mitsubishi Nagasaki Shipbuilding Company, Wages and Supplementary Payment] (1928), p. 38; Mitsubishi Nagasaki Jukogyo Shashi, p. 209.
18. *Mitsubishi Goshi-Gaisha, Shokko Toraitsukai ni Kansuru Chosa-Hokoku-sho* [Mitsubishi Partnership Limited, A Report on the Dealing with Workmen] (1914), vol. 1, pp. 41–3.
19. Ibid. p. 2.
20. Mitsubishi Nagasaki Shipbuilding Co., *The Company History* (1951); Hazama (1964), p. 437.

21. Kimura (1940), p. 169.
22. Hyodo (1971), pp. 247–8.
23. 'Zaibatsu' literally means a financial clique. Essentially they were a group of selected families, based on commercial banks who used their financial muscle to build up organisational conglomerates stretching across several industries. See K. Yamamura, 'Zaibatsu Pre-war and Zaibatsu Post-war' in *Journal of Asian Studies* (1964); Littler (1982), and Littler in this volume.
24. Mitsubishi Nagasaki Shipbuilding Co. (1951); Kimura (1940), pp. 160, 169.
25. Ministry of International Trade and Industry, *The Fifty Year History of Industrial Statistics* (1962), pp. 180–97.
26. Hyodo (1971), p. 323.
27. *Nihon Rodo Undo Shiryo* [Documents on the Labour Movement in Japan], vol. 10, pp. 440–1.
28. M. Sumiya, *Nihon Rodo Undo-shi* [A History of Japanese Labour Movement] (1966), chapters 3 and 4; Hyodo (1971), chapter 3; T. Matsuo, *Taisho Demokurashii Kenkyu* [A Study of the Taisho Democracy] (1964).
29. The Public Peace Police Act controlled all outdoor and indoor assemblies and virtually prohibited strikes.
30. The Taisho era lasted from 1912 to 1926. It was a relatively liberal period in Japanese history.
31. *Nihon Kogyo Kurabu 25-nenshi* [The 25 years of the Club of Japanese Industrialists] (1943), pp. 134–8.
32. Sangyo Kunren Kyokai (1971); Hazama (1964), pp. 511–3.
33. Hazama (1964), pp. 528–8.
34. Noshomusho, Shokosho, *Kojo Tokei Hyo* [Factory Statistics] 1919–1930.
35. For example, in the Mitsubishi Nagasaki Shipbuilding Co., the proportion of 'enterprise school' leavers to the total employees in the company went up from 73 per cent in 1925 to 96 per cent in 1926. Cf. Hyodo (1971), p. 419.
36. The Mitsubishi Shipbuilding Co. had already introduced a 'permanent employment' system for their key workers in 1908.
37. *Kawasaki Jukogyo Kabushiki Gaisha, Rodo-shi* [Kawasaki Heavy Industries Limited, A History of Labour], p. 18.
38. There was only a limited number of multi-plant firms in engineering at that time in contrast with the cotton industry.
39. Shoda, 'Rodo-Mondai ni tsuite' [On Labour Problems], in *Tokyo Keizai zasshi*, 25 April 1907.
40. Y. Miwa, 'Rodokumiai-ho Seitei-Mondai no Rekishi teki Ichi' [A Historical Study on the Labour Union Bill], in Y. Ando (ed.), *Ryo-Taisenkanki no Nihon-Shihon-shogi* [Japanese Capitalism in the Inter-war Period], (1979). There were various attempts in the 1920s to enact a trade union law in order to make trade unions legal. The last attempt was in 1929–31 when the Government declared its support for such a law. The proposals were fiercely opposed by Japan's leading industrialists and financiers. At a government-sponsored meeting in December 1930 between trade unionists and employers, the employers' spokesman declared that the unionists did not really represent the mass of factory workers but only a tiny minority: further-more all unions were either communist or pro-communist and were therefore a serious threat to society. This implacable opposition meant that trade unions were not legalised until after the Second World War.
41. Hazama (1964).
42. E.g. K. Ohkochi, *Roshi-Kankei-Ron no Shitei Hatten* [Development of Industrial Relations] (1972); M. Sumiya, *Nihon no Rodo-Mondai* [Labour Problems in Japan] (1967); Hazama (1964).
43. Cf. M. Tsuda, *Nihon-teki-Keiei Kento no Kadai* [An Examination of the Japanese System of Business], paper presented to the National Conference of Business History Society of Japan in 1981. For recent research into the 'Sampo' movement

see K. Ohkochi, 'Sangyo-hokoku-kai no mae to ato to' [Before and after the Sangyo-hokoku-kai] in Sumitani and Cho (eds.), *Kindai Nihon Keizai Shi-so-shi* [Modern Economic Thought in Japan] (1966); Ujihara and Ogiwara, 'Sangyo-Hokoku-Undo no Haikei' [The Socio-economic Background of the Sampo Movement] in *The Fascist State and Society*, edited by the Institute of Social Sciences, Tokyo University (1979). The Sampo movement ('Sangyo hokoku undo' – the patriotic movement for service to the state through hard work on the job) started in 1938 under the guidance and control of the Government. It was designed to promote co-operation between management and labour and prevent industrial conflict. It attracted three million recruits and resulted in the dissolution of the trade unions.

8 A Comparative Analysis of Managerial Structures and Strategies
Craig R. Littler

The preceding chapters by Lazonick, Homburg and Okayama share many features. First, all three authors see the crystallisation of new managerial strategies as linked to the development of large corporations and monopoly capitalism. Second, the historically emergent structure of work organisation seems remarkably similar in all three societies: it is bureaucratic and based on internal promotion systems. Moreover, by means of company unions (United States), welfarism (Germany) or paternalism and works committees (Japan), managerial strategy was to counter or exclude trade union influence. In many ways, as the chapters by Zeitlin and Lewchuck show, the British case stands out as an exception. The British case will be discussed more fully later, but I propose to take the common characteristics of the American, German and Japanese experiences as a starting-point.

In the rest of this chapter I will outline a theory of work organisation and labour relations under monopoly capitalism and construct an ideal type. Then I will consider the applicability of these ideas to the four countries – Britain, Japan, United States and Germany – with which we are primarily concerned and conclude by examining the sources of deviation from the theoretical model. In this way it is hoped to draw out similarities and contrasts between the four societies which are theoretically significant. As Marsh and Mannari point out, there is a continual temptation in comparative analysis to confuse what is most *distinctive* about a society or economy with what is most important in a causal sense.[1] Only by an attention to theory can one avoid the bull fighting and castanets syndrome: namely an emphasis on contingent or trivial factors.

Monopoly Capitalism
Common to both Marxian theory and the new business history of Alfred Chandler[2] is the notion of stages of capitalism. Competitive capitalism is marked by many small, family or entrepreneur-based

firms selling to limited markets and often self-financed. Monopoly capitalism in contrast is characterised by high concentrations of capital and large corporations which have a predominant hold over particular product markets. Modern corporations, especially in electrical engineering and chemicals, have developed by incorporating science and systematic research and development. The incorporation of science shifted the balance of economic power between small and large firms decisively in favour of the latter.

However, it is not just control over technology and the forces of production which is the key factor in modern capitalism. For Chandler the key process was the 'velocity of throughput', which accelerated as modern forms of transport and communication provided fast, reliable links between production and distribution units. Mass production called for mass distribution, and it was marketing organisation which became the major barrier to entry for potential rival firms.

Chandler's contribution has also been to trace out the correlates of corporate capitalism in terms of managerial strategy – diversification across product markets and vertical integration. Modern corporations are characterised by vertical integration, forwards to take control of the market and backwards to maintain supplies of raw materials and inputs. In addition, though Chandler accepts that different organisational forms result from different types of growth, nevertheless his strategy/structure model assumes that monopoly capitalism is linked with a definable corporate structure of formal managerial hierarchy, professionalisation of management and a multi-divisional organisation. Despite the detail and value of Chandler's new business history, specific areas have remained at the level of vague generalities or unspoken assumptions. In particular, the discussion of strategy has been very much focused on product markets and inter-capitalist competition, leaving on one side the linkages between labour problems, labour relations and the development of corporate capitalism. It is this area which is central to this book and to which I now turn.

Monopoly Capitalism and Types of Skill Formation
This section considers the relation between monopoly capitalism and recent hypotheses about long-term changes in skills, as a crucial factor in the production process and employment relationships. The theorist who has been most influential in analysing monopoly capitalism in relation to the labour process is Braverman. His ideas have been discussed in earlier chapters, but essentially he selectively developed certain ideas from Marx on the detailed division of labour and mechanisation in order to identify a dynamic of deskilling as the underlying

force governing all forms of work in capitalism. During the phase of monopoly capitalism, this dynamic is based on Taylorism and automation and these processes lead to the decisive transition from formal to real subordination of labour (i.e. a qualitative shift in capitalist control) which did not occur within earlier phases of capitalism.[3]

Five years after Braverman, Edwards attempted to develop a broader perspective by bringing together the sociological literature and the recent work of labour economists such as Doeringer and Piore. Despite Edwards's indebtedness to Braverman, there are clear inconsistencies between the interpretation of monopoly capitalism in Edwards's *Contested Terrain* and Braverman's analysis. Firstly, Taylorism is primary to Braverman's argument because of its role in undermining craft control. But for Edwards, Taylorism and systematic management have a secondary significance. Instead the lessons of Taylorism are incorporated within a model of work organisation which Edwards terms 'bureaucratic control'. Braverman insists on rejecting the concept of bureaucratisation for fear of losing sight of Marxist fundamentals and of class antagonisms by making use of Weberian concepts.[4] Associated with this fundamental difference in relation to managerial strategy are conflicting views in relation to skill trends. For Braverman there is an overall trend of deskilling based on the logic of Taylorism and the implicit design principles embedded within modern machinery and automation. In contrast, Edwards points to a complex process in relation to skill levels and argues that bureaucratic control is not necessarily associated with a mass of unskilled labour:

> It seems clear that deskilling has occurred in the traditional craft trades, including the machinists' tradition out of which Braverman himself came. It also seems correct to emphasise the tendency for capitalists to replace high-skill (or more precisely high-wage) labor with low-skill (low-wage) labor whenever possible. Nonetheless, the development of both the forces and relations of production continually throw up new products, new technologies and a demand for re-skilled, especially educated labor as well as deskilled labor. Thus accumulation must be seen as simultaneously deskilling and re-skilling the labor force. Rather than the simple, one-way process that Braverman describes, we must recognize this more complicated, two-way movement.[5]

The problematic nature of the deskilling thesis is neatly illustrated by the contrast between the two major contributions to neo-Marxist theory in the mid-1970s. Mandel's *Late Capitalism* and Braverman's *Labor and Monopoly Capital* arrive at conflicting conclusions in relation to skill trends. Mandel argues that the development of the productive forces towards automation tends to *raise* the skill level of the working class, creating 'a new and highly-skilled, polyvalent work force'. Ironically, both Mandel and Braverman cite the work of James Bright on technology in support of their contradictory conclusions.[6]

Recognising this complexity of skill trends, I will attempt to define different types of skill formation. The conventional dichotomy is between skilled and unskilled work, but this rudimentary distinction tells us nothing about the processes of skill acquisition, whereas the way in which skills are acquired has a significant influence on market position. Taking into account skill formation, it is possible to define four broad types (see Table 8.1.)

Table 8.1   Types of skill formation[7]

		Linked to external labour market I		Linked to internal labour market II
Broad task range	A	Craft work based on apprenticeship system	C	Multi-valent skills based on internal promotion system
Narrow task range	B	Unskilled work	D	Semi-skilled work with on-the-job training

Type A, the craft worker or professional worker, necessitates a lengthy training period, after which there is the possession of transferable skills and knowledge such that dependency on any one organisation is limited. Even the unskilled worker, Type B, may offer readily transferable labour power for simple manual tasks with frequent job changes. Both Types A and B represent non-internalised careers. On the other hand, Types C and D consist of untransferable skills learnt on the job, or with short intra-firm training courses, such that an individual is locked into the organisational career system. Future status becomes entirely dependent on the organisation. With Type C there is a long job ladder with the accumulation of many skills and a wide task range, whereas with Type D, the semi-skilled worker, skill increases quickly over a relatively short period.

It is clear that recent theorists, such as Edwards and Piore (along with Lazonick, Homburg and Okayama in this volume), want to argue that there has been a major shift during the development of capitalism from the processes of skill formation associated with column I in Table 8.1 to those associated with column II. But none of the above writers are willing to identify or label this transition one of 'deskilling', rightly so, because the overall pattern of skills associated with internal labour markets cannot be predicted theoretically. Whilst it is clear that the development of job structures within large monopolistic corporations entails employer control over training, this does not necessarily result in an overall reduction in skill levels.

Thus, the development of monopoly capitalism cannot be identified with a unilinear deskilling dynamic and a consequent mass of unskilled or low-skilled workers. Nevertheless, the outcome of the deskilling debate does suggest that monopoly capitalism can be linked to a change in types of skill formation and, with this in mind, the next section examines the recent labour market arguments.

Monopoly Capitalism and Internal Labour Markets
The concept of internal labour markets (ILMs) has received wide discussion in the recent literature.[8] Essentially the idea is that during the monopolistic phase of capitalism relatively stable markets and certainty of demand mean that firms can adopt long-term planning horizons which give them the option of employing workers on a long-term basis as well. Such long-term employment results in training and job advancement systems being incorporated within the body of the enterprise such that an internal labour market is formed. Thus most jobs in an organisation, especially the higher and better-paid jobs, are shielded from the direct influence of competitive forces in the external labour market. Instead, positions are filled by the promotion and transfer of workers who have already gained entry to the firm. The internal labour market connects to the external market by certain job positions which constitute ports of entry into the organisation.

The suggestion that the logic of monopoly capitalism may entail the widespread development of internal career systems is not new: it was suggested by the Webbs in 1898! They called it 'regulated progression' and argued that there were good reasons for expecting regulated progression to become widely prevalent in British industry as it was characteristic of large scale modern business. Having discussed the career structures in the British Civil Service and the railways, they go on to say:

> The union of competing firms into great capitalist corporations or syndicates, such as those already prevailing in the salt, alkali and cotton thread trades, and the growth of colossal commercial undertakings under single management, appears likely to bring with it, as a mere matter of convenience and discipline, the creation of a similarly graded service in each monopolised industry.[9]

Though the Webbs were amazingly far-sighted, the phrase 'mere matter of convenience' begs the basic question of this section: what are the linkages between monopoly capitalism and the development of internal career structures?

Piore has pointed out that one fundamental impulse behind internal labour markets and the associated job security is the desire to avoid the impact of economic fluctuations. The structuring of the labour market is in response to the contradiction between the inherent instabilities of capitalist economic activity and the social and political pressures for economic security.[10] Whilst this may be true, it nevertheless assumes a particular origin of internal labour markets: namely that they are a structural response to trade union and working-class pressure. Such an assumption only examines the supply side of the labour market (i.e. the preferences and characteristics of the workers), and says nothing about the demand side. However, as ILMs represent an employer labour market strategy, it is necessary to understand why large employers should be willing to adopt the strategy of internal labour markets.

One answer, the answer favoured by Lazonick and Edwards, is the control function argument. Given the relations between capital and labour there is a central indeterminacy of labour potential which necessitates some degree of motivation and commitment for getting the work out. However, the earlier and alternative labour control strategies proved to be failures or to have severe limitations. In contrast, the motivational implications of ILMs – the potential to call forth organisational commitment via a career consciousness – proved decisive for technologically based, large corporations.

But this is not a conclusive answer to the theoretical problem. If labour control is an unresolvable conflict, then there will be a continual process whereby workers react to managerial tactics, and strategies recede in importance, decay and blend with new principles of labour management. In other words, internal promotion systems may prove to be a contingent and transient phenomenon with no discernible association with the phase of monopoly capitalism. Indeed, Goldberg has recently argued that the success of an internal labour market strategy is highly contingent on the firm's rate of growth.[11] The reasons for this are straightforward: secure jobs convert the wage bill from a variable to a fixed cost. Moreover, any kind of seniority-based career structure or seniority wage system within a static or slow-moving company results in accelerating wage costs, because there is a high percentage of older and more expensive workers. In contrast, rapid expansion means that there is a frequent intake of new workers at the bottom of the wage and career scales so that overall costs are kept down. Given these economic implications of ILMs, Goldberg is reduced to explaining their American diffusion in terms of managerial 'systematic error' which the market is slow to penalise'.[12]

The control argument leaves out of account the notion that there has been a shift in types of skill formation, and it is this transition which is definitive. In the neo-classical model of the labour market it is assumed that employment, can change daily at no cost: in other words the costs of hiring and training are minimal. On this basis employers seek to recruit the most productive and cheapest labour and workers flow into and out of jobs freely acccording to marginal differences in wages. However, in the early years of the twentieth century many large corporations discovered that replacement costs for labour could be extremely high. For example, the head of Ford's employment department in 1913 cited a figure of $38 to train up a new worker; a small amount, but with an annual turnover of more than 50,000 workers (i.e. 400 per cent) the total cost was two million dollars.[13] In addition the development of new technology and products, especially in such industries as chemicals and electrical engineering, meant that many skills became firm-specific such that employers' training costs increased. Thus the employer rationale for internal labour markets is the need to stabilise quit rates and protect investments in specific training and on-the-job experience.

In essence, this shift in skill formation argument parallels the Chandlerian argument concerning the internalisation of market transactions. According to Chandler, such an internalisation by enlarged enterprises reduces information and transaction costs via increased administrative co-ordination.[14] Similarly, the internalisation of labour markets reduces transfer costs and increases the control potential via the administration of careers.

If we turn our attention to the Goldberg problem discussed above, then this partly reflects confusions concerning the level of analysis. In dual labour market theory it is frequently unclear whether the theory refers to dualism between industries or within industries or within a firm's job structure. Some of the confusion arises from the fact that writers such as Edwards and Piore tend to assume that an organisation operates in only *one* labour market, whereas large corporations straddle different labour markets. The labour market can exist both inside and outside the firm. Given this, it is more useful to think in terms of a segmented job structure based on several characteristics. Loveridge and Mok have suggested a model with a vertical dimension that distinguishes between jobs in terms of rewards, working conditions, responsibility and job security: in other words the conventional primary/secondary distinction. This is combined with a distinction between openness or closure to the external labour market to give a four-part model, consisting of a primary internal segment corresponding to the hard core of jobs within an internal labour market, a primary external segment, a secondary internal segment and a secondary external segment, the latter containing the worst jobs on the market which are typically filled by the urban poor, immigrants and casual labourers.[15] One striking feature about this conceptualisation of the range of employment conditions is the similarity to many Japanese discussions. (see Table 8.1). Loveridge and Mok believe that the personnel and labour policies of firms are often caught in an economic dilemma and solve this within the constraints of financial and investment strategy and existing technologies by a mix of jobs from different segments. If we accept this analysis, then we arrive at a more complex model of work organisation and labour strategies under monopoly capitalism: one in which internal labour markets are a key feature but are combined *within a single firm* by segments of casualised temporary or low-ceiling semi-skilled work. This core/ periphery distinction with an intra-enterprise pattern of disparity among both workers and jobs is one which was underlined by Friedman. As he points out, applying different labour management strategies to different groups of workers constitutes a major means whereby flexibility is gained in relation to economic fluctuations.[16]

So far, we can conclude that a deskilling dynamic, with its implication of a single direction for technological development, cannot be seen as an inherent feature of a monopoly capitalism model of the labour process. On the other hand, a survey of the literature suggests that segmented and internal labour markets, based on a shift in types of skill formation and on employer efforts to control the labour market, can be put forward as intrinsic characteristics.

Monopoly Capitalism and Industrial Relations
The starting point for looking at the links between monopoly capitalism and patterns of industrial relations is the assumption that the nature of unionism is largely determined by the labour market conditions and managerial strategies against which workers react *at the point of union formation.* Many Western unions developed in reaction to the labour markets of early, competitive capitalism, which was characterised by unbridled employer power to hire and fire for the purposes of labour cheapening plus consistent employer efforts to intensify labour by extending the working day. This market context resulted in the major objects of union regulation being the standardisation of wages plus the length of the working day. For example, in Britain a large part of trade union administration was created in order to deal with piece-work and standard price lists for work tasks. Equally, the demand for the nine hour day was often a rallying point around which many unions were first established or enlarged beyond local groups.[17]

Obviously the above is only part of the historical picture. The early craft unions were equally concerned with training, apprenticeship rules and job control. In addition there was a minority of unions such as the Associated Society of Locomotive Engineers and Firemen (ASLEF) and the steel unions who can be described as 'promotion unions' concerned to regulate career ladders and promotion practices *across firms*.

Employer recognition is necessary for the continuation if not the existence, of trade unions. In the formative stages of union organisation, workers have faced frequent employer hostility. But once recognition has occurred, many employers under the conditions of competitive capitalism discovered definite advantages in standardising the price of labour and so placing limits on price competition. As Phelps-Brown points out 'collective bargaining only meant that they were paying the same price as their competitors for one factor of production, just as they did when they bought a raw material in the same market'.[18] Phelps-Brown is referring to the British cotton industry, and if, alternatively, employers in other industries or economies wished to maintain a strategy of resisting unionism, then the nature of competitive capitalism meant that individual employers had limited resources for long struggles. As a consequence, successful employer resistance depended on state action and oppression or on concerted action by employers' federations.[19]

In contrast to the conditions of early capitalism, under monopoly capitalism with bureaucratic work organisation and internal career structures, the nature of the labour market is markedly different. Wages are no longer the price of labour as a factor of production in a neo-classical sense but become relatively inflexible; work hours are regulated both by law and bureaucratic rules and job security in some degree underpins the career structure. Under these circumstances any labour unions which are formed will centre their regulations on job security and dismissal procedures, promotions and job transfers. Dismissals and redundancies are on extremely important object of regulation because it is difficult to move to another firm and the costs of doing so in terms of lower wages, poorer working conditions, lost promotion and pension rights is very high.

During the phase of monopoly capitalism, employers may be just as resistant to union recognition as during the earlier phase, but clearly employers' resources are much greater to pursue a range of strategies. For example Boulwarism, the industrial relations strategy named after Lemuel Boulware the vice-president of labour relations at General Electric in the late 1940s, is not possible without professionalised personnel management and considerable financial resources. This is because Boulwarism consisted of refusing to collectively bargain and shouting over the heads of existing unions by means of massive publicity campaigns, including mass mailing, designed to appeal to individual workers and their local communities.[20] Similarly, industrial paternalism can entail considerable expenditure on welfare, housing and extra bonuses.

In surveying the existing literature, it is clear that there is a lack of systematic analysis relating industrial relations to phases of capitalism. Though it is necessary to avoid substituting determinist models for complex processes involving historical particularities, nevertheless industrial relations as a subject would be advanced by such theorising.[21]

Accepting that competitive and monopoly capitalism are only analytic types, the implications of the different labour market and employer contexts of union formation are sketched out in Table 8.2.[22] This table tries to trace out the structural correlates of competitive versus monopoly capitalism in terms of labour market conditions, employer strategies, and patterns of industrial relations. As with all ideal types, Table 8.2 is an attempt to encapsulate the core features of complex realities. Nevertheless the evidence advanced by Lazonick, Homburg, Okayama (plus much of the Japanese literature) and labour economists like Edwards suggests that monopoly capitalism as an analytic type can be linked to bureaucratic work organisation, internal promotion systems and industrial relations more focused on job security issues which are often enterprise-specific. In the following sections I will examine the applicability of this theoretical model of production relations to Japan, the United States, Germany and Britain.

Monopoly Capitalism in Comparative Perspective

This chapter began with the simplest, most abstract conceptualisation of monopoly capitalism. In this and the next section I want to move to the more concrete level of analysis and examine the historical dynamics of the four societies considered in this book. For all four societies there was a common historical thread, namely the transition from a period of small family-based enterprises within highly competitive product markets to one of large, bureaucratised corporations with varying degrees of monopoly power. However, this transition process started from different cultural bases and occurred under different economic and ideological conditions. The consequent variations within capitalism which have been reflected in the earlier chapters of this book are summarised in Table 8.3.

Essentially the table identifies variations within capitalism round about 1930, on the assumption that it was the period 1880 to the 1930s which was the crucial change period from one phase of capitalism to

Table 8.2   Labour Markets, employer strategies and types of trade union

Phase of capitalism	Labour market conditions	Objects of regulation by Unions	Methods of union	Type of union
Competitive capitalism	Neo-classical labour market conditions. Employer strategies characterised by labour cheapening, wage cuts and attempts to lengthen the working day	(a) Wage levels (b) Length of the working day (c) Job control Unions often adapt to the labour market by becoming informal labour exchanges	(a) Collective bargaining at national (or regional) level covering all firms in the same industry (b) Control of apprenticeship system	Unskilled unions plus national craft unions. The unions attempt to unite all those who have similar skills or level of skill to sell in the national labour market
Monopoly capitalism	Characterised by a multi-segmented labour market with many firm-specific internal labour markets	(a) Dismissals (b) Promotions (c) Job-assignments Unions are primarily conerned with job security within the firm.	Collective bargaining at the enterprise level	Enterprise or company unions. National unions approximate more to federations of enterprise-based groups

Table 8.3   Variations within capitalism c. 1930

	Extent of monopolisation	Employer ideology	Sources of labour rationalisation	Predominant labour strategies	Industrial relations pattern
Britain	Persistence of family-controlled and entrepreneurial capitalism. Many mergers had taken place within a holding company framework which permitted continual family influence.	Capitalist; *laissez-faire*	Indigenous, based on the armaments industry pre-1914. Based on neo-Taylorism in the 1930s	Traditional forms of labour management. Taylorism was slow to develop. Paternalism was very limited	Collective and work group bargaining
Japan	Highly diversified zaibatsu groups dominated large areas of the economy. But they were still family-controlled.	Highly nationalistic, originally based on fear of being colonized. Widespread paternalism	Limited influence of Taylorism which was not clearly understood. In the 1930s the German Rationalizierung movement was influential	Widespread development of internal labour markets (the nenko system) and paternalism	Consultative work committees. Some weak enterprise unions. Trade unions not legalised.
USA	Entrenched oligopolies. Early diversification and vertical integration.	Capitalist; *laissez-faire*; widespread efficiency movement	Taylorism and the wider efficiency movement	Taylorite with some development of internal labour markets and paternalistic practices	Collective and work group bargaining. Some company unions
Germany	Entrenched oligopolies. Early diversification and vertical integration	Nationalistic; authoritarian paternalism	Indigenous rationalisation movement. Some influence of Taylorism	Significant development of internal labour markets and paternalistic practices in large corporations	Legal establishment of works councils in all enterprises with 20 + workers

another. The factors highlighted in Table 8.3 are the market structure in terms of the extent of monopolisation, employer ideologies as a critical mediating factor in the crystallisation of labour strategy and three aspects of labour strategies themselves.

By the 1930s the development of monopoly capitalism was most advanced in the United States. Large corporations and bureaucratic forms of control appeared first as a mechanism for administering the new forms of transport and communications, namely railways and the telegraph system. By the turn of the century, the giant manufacturing firms had emerged using the railways as an organisational model and a source of managerial skills.[23] These large industrial enterprises were clustered in a few types of industry, primarily those whose output could not be efficiently distributed by existing market channels. Generally growth occurred in two ways. One way was by internal expansion which typically involved integrating forwards to unite mass production with mass distribution and backwards to ensure supplies of raw materials and semi-processed goods. Alternatively other firms grew large by mergers 'creating combinations of small firms that placed control of production in a central administrative office and then integrated forward and backward'. As Chandler points out, 'By the time the United States entered World War I, management decisions had replaced coordination by market forces in many of the most critical sectors of the economy.'[24]

Both Germany and Japan, as their industrial economies developed, faced the situation that the existing distribution networks and marketing arrangements were grossly inadequate for large-scale modern production. In particular, Japanese producers were ignorant of overseas customers and their needs and throughout the nineteenth century relied on foreign merchants, especially British ones, to handle both the import and export trade. The outcome was that at an early stage German and Japanese firms had to evolve organisational solutions to the problems of marketing. In Germany this resulted in many fully integrated enterprises controlling their own distribution networks. In Japan it resulted in the 'sogo shosha', the large general trading companies which were part of the zaibatsu combines. However, not only did the sogo shosha handle the distribution of products of manufacturing companies within the zaibatsu group, but they also penetrated into the small-scale sector of industry providing family concerns with finance and technical advice as well as marketing their goods.

The Japanese zaibatsu are a form of economic structure and power which in terms of Chandler's four-fold dimension of integrated corporation, holding company, cartel and market approximate most closely to that of 'holding company'.[25] They entailed centralised control by one family which extended its power through strategically arranged marriages and personal patronage relationships. Secondly they were based on their own commercial banks which were used as the leverage to extend control across several industries. In other words they were 'monopolies of capital' rather than market monopolies. Usually they were organised around holding companies and controlled the affiliated firms by means of interlocking directorships and mutual stockholdings. With government protection and support the zaibatsu groups grew through the First World War boom and even the recession of the 1920s. Thus by 1933 the Mitsui empire consisted of 150 firms, and Mitsubishi controlled nearly 200 companies.[26] The reason that the zaibatsu became highly diversified conglomerates was that, unlike the United States, the Japanese domestic market was very limited and during the early period of industrialisation it was difficult for Japanese manufacturers to compete internationally. Thus, rather than stand still, they spread *across* industries.[27]

In Britain the link between family and enterprise proved to be a tenacious one. Though the Joint Stock Company's Acts of 1856 and 1862 created the legal foundations for a corporate economy, industrialists were *not* active supporters of the legislation. Even by the 1880s limited liability companies constituted a tiny minority of industrial organisations, and the preferred legal form was the private company. According to Payne, 'entrepreneurs operated within organisations which show little alteration from those of their pioneering forebears. Certainly there was little movement towards the divorce of management from ownership, towards the elongation of organisational hierarchies.'[28] This pattern of control continued well into the twentieth century. Certainly compared to the United States and Germany, large organisations in early twentieth-century Britain were distinguished by this persistent dominance of proprietorial and familial management.

The continued familial framework of many British industries meant that the development of new organisational forms was impeded. The problems which this set up were very evident in the organisations created by the turn of the century merger wave. Many of these mergers involved the coming together of large numbers of small firms and they often encountered severe managerial problems. Lacking a theory of organisation or management these multi-firm amalgamations resembled confederations of family firms. Thus the Calico Printers' Association, formed in 1899 from 46 separate companies, had a board of 128 directors including 8 managing directors in its early years.[29] In many of these early combines there was often little attempt to create a centralised administration, with an integrated production and marketing policy, nor to unify operations by standard costing systems. Thus by the first World War there had been little significant dilution of proprietorial control. Despite this, the interwar years was a period of the rapid development of corporate capitalism in Britain, such that by 1939, on paper at least, Britain had as high a concentration of capital as any other Western society. Nevertheless, neither the bureaucratisation of management nor the professionalisation of management had proceeded very far, with one or two oft-quoted exceptions, such as ICI and Unilever. Instead, there were two common organisational forms. In many small and medium sized firms owners still managed, whilst other firms had grown large enough to develop a stratum of salaried and middle managers, but the owners still made the key, strategic decisions. The second, common structure was loose organisational conglomerations nestling under a holding company umbrella, often permeated by the continued influence of the founding families or the owner-entrepreneurs, and invariably operating by means of informal practices and procedures. Such confederations were typically held apart by a desire to preserve circles of autonomy and continued distrust. Thus, as Chandler points out, the British economy long remained an example of family capitalism.[30]

Labour Strategies in Comparative Perspective

In looking at management labour strategies the chapters by Melling, Zeitlin and Lewchuk in this volume provide us with a picture of developments in Britain up to the 1930s. Melling's chapter underlines that there was a thrust towards welfarism and paternalistic strategies in some British industries during the early decades of the century but that it failed to become an important long-term strategy because of the opposition of labour, especially that of skilled workers and even of foremen. Not only did employer welfarism cut across any socialist impetus to state welfare benefits, it also was in conflict with the Samuel Smiles tradition of self-help which in practice meant a cocoon of co-op, building society, Friendly Society and adult education institute.[31]

But apart from trade union hostility to welfare measures and company unionism, welfarism in Britain had a restricted coverage because of the small firm structure of engineering, coal and many other industries. Systematic welfare measures could be expensive, and the slow development of large corporations and monopoly capitalism in Britain limited such a strategy to a few firms in a strong monopoly position.[32]

Zeitlin also underlines the fragmented, small-firm nature of the British engineering industry which persisted through the First World War and the 1920s. Becaue of the slow rate of growth of product markets, except in armaments, employers' investment decisions were guided by short or medium-term profitability. Thus, despite the Engineering Employers' Federation victories in 1897/8 and 1922 disputes there was no wholesale transformation of the division of labour parallel to that in the United States and Germany. In particular, the impact of Taylorism and the American model of management was limited up to the 1920s. British engineering employers rejected a high-wage strategy which formed a central component of Taylorism, preferring to pursue a traditional policy of low wages and labour cheapening. This policy cut across any hopes of incorporating the engineering union leaders and, perhaps, of moving towards more paternalistic strategies.

The chapters by Melling, Zeitlin and Lewchuk all point to the persistence of traditional forms of labour management in British industry in the first two decades of the twentieth century. This indicates a failure by British management to evolve coherent labour strategies in line with the development of technology, market possibilities, and organisational possibilities. But in some ways Britain is not a discrepant case in terms of a monopoly capitalism model. If we accept that managerial strategies are linked to the timing and formation of monopoly capitalism, then the persistence of family-controlled and entrepreneurial capitalism in Britain, the slow development of managerial hierarchies and professional managers partly explains the slow, piecemeal emergence of Taylorism, Fordism and flow-production methods. During the 1930s, after the absorption of the 1920s merger wave and under the blows of economic crisis, the historical picture changes somewhat and there was the diffusion of neo-Taylorite schemes such as the Bedaux system.[33] But the slow dissemination of neo-Taylorite labour strategies was not overlain, as it was in some large US corporations, by the processes of bureaucratic control involving well-developed internal promotion systems.[34] As Lewchuk notes, though there were a few British spokesmen for what was seen as the 'American model' involving internal job ladders and high wages, these were isolated voices in a mainstream which consisted of a strategy of 'cheap, manual labour'.[35]

Unlike Britain, the basic characteristics of Japanese corporations' labour strategies in the 1920s and 1930s were the 'nenko' (or seniority-based) system, lifetime commitment for key workers and paternalism. Starting with Ujihara in Japan in 1953 and Abegglen in the West in 1958 this type of strategy has been conceptualised as traditional, as a semi-feudal remnant destined to be destroyed under the impact of new technology and management practices.[36] However later research has shown that the assumption of historical continuity is false,[37] and that Japanese large firm employment practices were *introduced* from 1910 to the 1930s during the period of the formation of monopoly capitalism in Japan.[38] Indeed, though *ideologically* based on traditional values and concepts, in practice the new paternalism adopted a good deal from American and European welfare measures. Suggestion schemes were set up, influenced by the example of the National Cash Register Corporation; works councils were introduced in Sumitomo modelled on the shop committee system of International Harvester, and welfare facilities were patterned on those of Cadbury and Lever Brothers in Britain and Krupp in Germany.[39] In general, though in Japan paternalism spread later than the limited examples in Britain, when it was introduced, it spread quickly and definitively.

The diffusion of institutionalised paternalism in large Japanese corporations coincided with the international impact of the Scientific Management movement.[40] The ideas of Frederick Taylor spread to Japan as early as 1911 and gained adherents amongst intellectuals and journalists but had a limited effect in industry itself where the ideas were not clearly understood. Interestingly, given the significance of the railroads in the United States as an institutional base for systematic management, much of the initial work on scientific management was carried out by the Japanese National Railways. However, despite the early (First World War) enthusiasm of the railway engineers in the repair workshops, they delayed adopting time and motion studies until 1929. Rather, they relied upon work group discussions and group problem solving. Moreover, many Japanese industries (engineering, steel, chemicals) largely ignored foreign scientific management ideas during the first twenty-five years of this century, though one area of industry affected was cotton textiles. This development was linked to the decline of competitive capitalism.

In 1897 there were seventy-four cotton spinning companies in Japan. But from the 1890s through the First World War plant sizes and capital requirements increased rapidly and after passing through a cartel phase (the 1906 export cartel) five huge firms dominated the cotton industry at the end of the First World War. The Japanese industry largely depended on imported (mainly British) textile machines and the high cost of foreign imports led to an emphasis on full utilisation of capital based on continuous running and twelve hour shifts. The 1916 Factory Law enforced eight hour shifts, and this change in work practices, combined with the development of large corporations, stimulated an interest in Taylorism. Management sought more direct control over work standards and 'stretch-outs' (increasing the ratio of machines per worker) were common. Additionally, job analysis, standardised procedures, and time and motion studies were applied to the young girl textile workers. What this implies is that in an industry where the work was seen as simple and requiring little skill and in which there was a high turnover of workers, with a consequent low attachment to the employing organisation, Taylorite techniques were seen as a potential strategy and were used in Japan. However this is still only half the picture and in order to complete the story we need to turn to the second wave of labour rationalisation in Japan.

The second wave of rationalisation in Japan, from the mid-1920s to the end of the 1930s. was associated with a serious recession and the main ideas stemmed from the German Rationalitzierung movement. The main innovations at this time included more automatic machinery, assembly line production, and the standardisation of products. In cotton textiles the movement resulted in the establishment of standardised job classifications, promotion hierarchies, and systematic training which became linked to the widespread development of welfare measures such as improved work conditions, health care, housing, better education facilities and so on in order to stabilise the labour force. In other words, even in cotton textiles, with a labour force consisting of 90 per cent young females, high turnover rates, a low educational level of recruits and low skills, labour rationalisation and efficiency engineering were linked to paternalism. But this linkage was not simply a matter of ideas and ideology. There had been efforts towards cutting down labour turnover and increasing commitment based on paternalistic measures in cotton textiles before the First World War, but they were short-lived and foundered in the face of the wartime economic boom which resulted in intense competition for labour, especially older female workers. It was not until the 1920s and the active encouragement and regulation of the Government that the competitive barriers to setting up welfarism, which involved initial increased labour costs for *long-term* benefits, were broken. Overall, Japanese industry did absorb some Taylorite ideas, but Taylorism was adapted and diluted to fit in with existing work practices and values and with the increased diffusion of paternalism and internal labour markets as an employer strategy.[41]

Writers such as Hazama conceive the fundamental features of the Japanese employment system in terms of paternal employer/employee relationships,[42] whereas in terms of our model of monopoly capitalism it is segmented and internal labour markets which are fundamental. In this context it is important to note that the main trend in Japanese industry throughout the inter-war years was in the direction of industrial dualism with the large zaibatsu combines surrounded by a sea of small/medium enterprises. Many of the zaibatsu firms used their monopoly power to bring labour markets under their own control, especially given the fears of widespread labour/capital conflicts. The main implements of this were a systematic ranking of factory positions in terms of status associated with internal promotion systems and a seniority wage system. The nenko or seniority system entailed an implicit guarantee of secure employment for key manual and white collar workers and the welfare benefits and familial ideology were the top-dressings to this employment relationship. But in the mass of small and medium enterprises, as Sumiya points out, working and business conditions were poor, 'the authoritarian family pattern (e.g. master–servant relations) prevailed and neither paternalistic industrial relations nor the lifetime employment nor length of service systems existed'.[43] It is this set of economic relations – monopoly power, industrial dualism, and internal labour markets – which seem to be distinctive to modern, capitalistic production.

The view that ILMs are more fundamental than paternalistic practices is given added weight by the United States experience. There was a thrust towards welfare capitalism associated with the emergence of large corporations in the early years of the twentieth century. The proliferation of welfare plans amongst such companies as International Harvester, NCR and US Steel has been detailed by Brody, Brandes and Ozanne.[44] But there was a swift and nearly complete demise of welfarism in the United States with the depression of the early 1930s. Partly this was the result of worker antagonism as in Britain, ('employees . . . reasoned that money spent on welfare work was money that could have fattened their pay envelopes'[45]) and partly the result of government hostility during the New Deal years. The National Recovery Administration (NRA) code for the cotton textile industry asserted that:

> there is something feudal and repugnant to American principle in the practice of employer-ownership of employee homes . . . It is hoped that, with the creation of real industrial self-government and improvement in the minimum wage, an impetus will be given by employers to independent home ownership eventually looking toward home ownership by employees and the conversion of the differential into a wage equivalent.[46]

If this is the reaction of the NRA to company housing, then the factory dormitories and dormitory supervisors (who recognised no principle of privacy) in the cotton mills of Japan would have been cultural anathema indeed.[47] Similarly, the 1935 Wagner Act and the National Labor Relations Board systematically opposed company unions and anything that smacked of employer support for such unions.

Nevertheless, despite the demise of welfarism in the United States of the 1930s, internal promotion systems still spread in the heavy industry firms and many large corporations in other industries. The origins of this development are still in debate. For Lazonick, the 1920s decade was crucial: he argues that between 1923 and 1929 bureaucratic control consisting of job ladders, centralised managerial control and personnel management succeeded in stabilising labour/capital relationships. Other economists, such as Piore, consider that the 1930s decade had more long-term significance and that ILMs evolved primarily in response to an upsurge in labour militancy. According to this interpretation, the crucial period in the United States was the massive wave of strikes and labour unrest in 1936/7, when there was a wave of sit-down strikes in the mass production industries of automobiles, steel, textiles, rubber, oil, and shipbuilding, with the automobile industry as the storm centre. The outcome of this surge of militancy was the formation of industrial unions which brought together all the workers in a plant cutting across the craft lines of the old American Federation of Labour. Given the context of large, bureaucratic corporations and the economic depression, the newly formed unions made job security a central bargaining issue. This resulted in a series of locally negotiated agreements at enterprise level dealing with job transfers, lay-offs and promotions.[48]

In many ways the 1930s created a system of internal promotion in large US corporations which was more rigid than that in Japan. In practice the Japanese 'permanent employment system' meant that determined efforts would be made to prevent lay-offs in economic down-turns, but when this failed, management had complete freedom concerning who was to be laid off and offered no guarantee of re-employment. In the USA, the rules concerning lay-offs were (and are) based on seniority with rights of re-employment also based on seniority. Moreover, there is a linkage of the rules governing lay-offs to the system of internal job distribution: 'As a result every layoff typically involves a considerable redistribution of the remaining jobs in the establishment',[49] again according to a seniority principle. Such rules significantly narrow the discretion of management.

Thus, despite the much-debated and evident decline of paternalistic practices in the United States in the 1930s, there was the significant development of a segmented labour market, internal labour markets in large corporations and new unions primarily concerned with job security issues.

The labour management strategies in Germany of large, oligopolistic corporations like Siemens have been described in the chapter by Homburg. Essentially, Homburg takes Taylorism as a model and compares the labour strategies of Siemens in relation to this. She concludes that there were waves of rationalisation in Germany and that Taylorism was influential, particularly during the 1919–22 period. However, as in Japan, employers were concerned with the non-work life of employees in order to counter the influence of trade unions in the community and the labour market. This, combined with the strong traditions of industrial paternalism (similar to Japan) resulted in the welding together of Taylorism and welfarism.

Germany, like Japan, was marked by industrial dualism: a cleavage between the large, monopolistic organisations and an ocean of small workshops and factories. The origins of this dualism were also similar; in Germany of the 1870s, a formative historical period, there was the notion of 'infant industry protection' represented by the Verein für Sozialpolitik which resulted in import barriers and distorted capital flows.[50] Even by 1907, 95 per cent of the enterprises in industry and mining employed ten people or less, yet more than 40 per cent of the labour force worked in enterprises with more than fifty employees.[51] It was in the large, German corporations, like Krupp and Siemens, that bureaucratic patterns of management and internal labour markets developed.[52]

However, we should be cautious about generalising from the heavy electrical engineering industry to the *national* experience, because this was one industry which rapidly became internationalised. For example, before the First World War, General Electric, Westinghouse and Siemens had entered the Japanese market and established production facilities.[53] And just as the American Westinghouse Co. concluded a technical exchange agreement with Siemens in 1924 leading to the influence of Westinghouse management methods in German factories,[54] so Mitsubishi Electric had a similar agreement with Westinghouse in the 1920s. Kato Takeo of Mitsubishi went to the United States and studied Westinghouse techniques and became a strong advocate of Taylorite time and motion studies. In other words, in studying Siemens and Mitsubishi Electric in the inter-war years we are looking partly at the world-wide diffusion of Westinghouse management practices, even though such practices had to be adapted to the labour markets, economic conditions and culture of the receiving society.[55]

Conclusions

In this chapter I have argued that in order to compare the managerial strategies of Britain, Japan, the United States and Germany it is necessary to do so in terms of a theoretical model. Therefore, an ideal type of monopoly capitalism in terms of labour market conditions, employer strategies and type of trade union was formulated (see Table 8.2). In particular, it was argued that internal labour markets within an overall segmented market was fundamental and that paternalism and welfare schemes were more contingent.[56]

Given this model of the labour process and labour relations under monopoly capitalism, we looked at the evidence on employer strategies. Some of the evidence is summarised in Table 8.3. Broadly, Japan provides the best 'fit' to the model, followed by Germany, which shared a very similar pattern of industrialisation. The United

States presents a more mixed picture: in general the population of firms has experienced successive waves of development towards internal labour markets. In the 1910–20s period this tendency was combined with welfarism, only to be aborted by the 1929 depression, whilst in the late 1930s the changes occurred in response to widespread labour militancy and took place without welfare practices and paternalistic ideology because of the philosophy of the New Deal. Now, in the 1980s, there is a fresh momentum of industrial change arising from the need to increase worker efficiency and worker commitment in response to Japanese competition. Once again workers and unions (such as the United Autoworkers' Union) are being offered job security, 'a guaranteed stream of earnings', and profit-sharing in the context of the worst recession for half a century. The outcome of the present American wave of 'Japanization' has yet to be determined.[57]

The economy most removed from the monopoly capitalism model of employment and labour relations is that of Britain. The causes of deviation are complex. Partly they relate to the timing and formation of corporate capitalism in Britain. As was pointed out, there was a persistence of family-controlled and entrepreneurial capitalism in Britain associated with a slow development of flow line production and modern technologies. However, as the century wears on the differences in the extent of monopolisation and the slow diffusion of mass production technologies are not adequate explanations of the British case. What is required is some notion of uneven development: not all social institutions change as rapidly as do the processes of production. In other words organisations once formed tend to perpetuate themselves, even across modes of capital accumulation. In Britain the early unions were concerned with the wage relationship over a short time period and their members expected unemployment tomorrow or next week, or with the preservation of apprenticeship type skill formation, and these types of unions became the dominant labour institutions. As a result, within the early unions there was hostility towards promotion according to seniority and towards any development of enterprise-based career structures and job rights. For example the Webbs point out that 'The very conception of seniority as constituting a claim to advancement, is foreign to Trade Unionism', and assert that even in the case of the steel industry, with its entrenched shop floor hierarchies, the employer is free to choose from amongst the Third Hands in order to fill vacancies from Second Hands without regard to seniority.[58]

More crucially, there was a widespread union hostility towards any development of internal labour markets. In cotton textiles workers frequently resented the introduction of spinners from other mills when there were piecers who had worked long and hard for the firm.

But such rank and file feelings were never supported by the cotton unions on the basis that such 'local protectionism' is incompatible with trade unionism. Similarly, at the Blochairn steel works in Glasgow in the 1890s, the steel smelters objected to vacancies amongst the Third, Second and First Hands being filled by outsiders of those grades. They demanded that the workers at the plant have preferential rights for any vacant jobs. The Webbs describe the outcome of the dispute:

> Any such substitution of a vertical for a horizontal cleavage of the trade would . . . be inconsistent with the regulated progression enforced by the British Steel Smelters Amalgamated Association, and would have seriously hampered the employers' choice of operatives. The unions accordingly refused to recognize the claim of the Blochairn helpers, and they were eventually excluded from its ranks.[59]

Given these trade union attitudes and traditions combined with the employers' attachment to a neo-classical view of the labour market and the slow development of professional management in Britain, internal promotion systems long remained the preserve of the Civil Service plus the banks and financial organisations which were influenced by the public sector management pattern.

Above all, the British and American cases make it clear that there is no simple causal line from stages in the development of capitalism to changes in management structure and strategy. Recent labour process theorists, such as Braverman and Edwards, substitute for the broad processes of capitalism a single, overall trend, namely an imperative of control of the labour process without specifying the nature and basis of this imperative. But in practice and in history, social groups and factions, such as managers and trade unions, mediate any relationship between the development of capitalism and changes in work organisation and industrial relations. In this context it is only detailed studies of particular historical sequences, such as are pursued in the chapters of this book, that enable us to decide between theories of historical change.

Notes

1. R.M. Marsh and H. Mannari, *Modernization and the Japanese Factory* (1976), pp. 336-7; also R.E. Cole, *Work, Mobility and Participation: A comparative study of American and Japanese industry* (1979), pp. 30-1.
2. See A.D. Chandler, *Strategy and Structure: Chapters in the History of the American Industrial Enterprise* (1962); Chandler, *The Visible Hand: The Managerial Revolution in American Business* (1977); A.D. Chandler and H. Daems (eds.), *Managerial Hierarchies: Comparative Perspective on the Rise of the Modern Industrial Enterprise* (1980).
3. H. Braverman, *Labor and Monopoly Capital* (1974).
4. Ibid. p. 120.
5. R. Edwards, 'Social Relations of Production at the Point of Production',

Insurgent Sociologist (1978), p. 109; R. Edwards, *Contested Terrain* (1979).

6. E. Mandel, *Late Capitalism* (1975), pp. 268-9; Braverman (1974), pp. 213-23.
7. This table is based on the debates within the Japanese literature. See especially Kazuo Koike, *Shokuba no Rodo Kumiai to Sanka—Roshi Kankei no Nichibei Hikaku* [Labour Unions at the Workshop and Their Participation: A Comparison of Industrial Relations in Japan and the United States] (1977).
8. Building on the work of Kerr, Dunlop and Becker, P.B. Doeringer and M.J. Piore published their classic text *Internal Labor Markets and Manpower Analysis* in 1971. For a review of the extensive literature in the 1970s see R. Loveridge and A.L. Mok, *Theories of Labour Market Segmentation* (1979). For an attempt to reformulate the Japanese theories of employment relations in terms of Doeringer and Piore's ideas see M. Sumiya, *Rodo Keizai no Riron* (Theory of Labour Economy) (1976).
9. S. and B. Webb, *Industrial Democracy* (1898), pp. 489-91.
10. M.J. Piore, 'Economic Fluctuation, Job Security and Labor-Market Duality in Italy, France and the United States', *Politics and Society* (1980), p. 382.
11. V.P. Goldberg, '*A Relational Exchange Perspective on the Employment Relationship*'. SSRC Conference on the Economics of Work Organisation, March 1982, mimeo.
12. Ibid. p. 11.
13. J. Russell, 'The Coming of the Line: The Ford Highland Park Plant, 1910-14', *Radical America* (1978), p. 40; also see S. Meyer, 'Adapting the Immigrant to the Line: Americanization in the Ford factory, 1914-21', *Journal of Social History* (1980), p. 69.
14. Chandler (1977), pp. 6-7.
15. Loveridge and Mok (1979), pp. 123-6; also see F.C. Valkenburg and A.M.C. Vissiers, 'Segmentation of the Labour Market: The Theory of the Dual Labour Market', *The Netherlands Journal of Sociology* (1980).
16. A.L. Friedman, *Industry and Labour* (1977), p. 108.
17. S. and B. Webb (1898), chapters V and VI.
18. E.H. Phelps-Brown, *The Growth of British Industrial Relations* (1959), p. 124.
19. See Gospel in this volume; and also Zeitlin on employers' federations in British engineering.
20. H.R. Northrup, *Boulwarism* (1964).
21. This view is also put forward by M. Shalev, 'Industrial Relations Theory and the Comparative Study of Industrial Relations and Industrial Conflict', *British Journal of Industrial Relations* (1980).
22. My conceptualization of labour market contexts has been influenced by S.B. Levine and K. Taira 'Labour Markets, Trade Unions and Social Justice: Japanese Failures', *Japanese Economic Studies* (1977).
23. A.D. Chandler, 'The Railroads: Pioneers in Modern Corporate Management', *Business History Review* (1965).
24. Chandler and Daems (1980), pp. 5-6.
25. Daems seems to arrive at this conclusion too. See H. Daems, 'The Rise of the Modern Industrial Enterprise: A New Perspective' in Chandler and Daems (1980), p. 221 n. 3.
26. K. Yamamura, 'Zaibatsu Prewar and Zaibatsu Postwar', *Journal of Asian Studies* (1964); Yamamura, 'A Compromise with Culture: The Historical Evolution of the Managerial Structure of Large Japanese Firms' in H.F. Williamson (ed.), *Evolution of International Management Structures* (1975).
27. H.T. Patrick, 'Comment' in H.F. Williamson (1975), pp. 190-1.
28. P.L. Payne, 'British Entrepreneurship in the Nineteenth Century' (1974), p. 20.
29. M.A. Utton, 'Some Features of the Early Merger Movements in British Manufacturing Industry', *Business History* (1972), pp. 54-5; Payne (1974), p. 22.
30. Chandler and Daems (1980), p. 6. Though Chandler exaggerates somewhat by claiming that the British economy can be characterised as one of 'family capital-

ism' up to 1939. There were significant changes during the course of the 1930s.
31. See J. Foster, *Class Struggle and the Industrial Revolution* (1974).
32. See 'Comment' by G.D.H. Cole in E. Cadbury, 'Some Principles of Industrial Organization: The Case for and against Scientific Management', *Sociological Review* (1914), p. 120.
33. See C.R. Littler, *The Development of the Labour Process in Capitalist Societies* (1982).
34. Strictly speaking internal promotion systems etc. represent the bureaucratization of the *employment relationship*. Taylorite strategies already involved elements of bureaucratic control. See Littler (1982), pp. 58–9.
35. Lewchuk in this volume, p. 110 n. 94.
36. S. Ujihara, *Daikojo Rodosha no Seikaku* [The Characteristics of Workers at Large Factories] (1953); J.C. Abbegglen, *The Japanese Factory* (1958).
37. The assumption of historical continuity is itself problematic as cultural traditions have to be reproduced and mobilised.
38. See Okayama in this volume; also Sumiya (1976). This view of cultural non-continuity has been most forcefully argued by K. Taira, *Economic Development and the Labor Market in Japan* (1970).
39. H. Hazama, *Japanese Industrialization and Labor-Management Relations*, SSRC Conference on Business and Labour History, March 1981, mimeo, pp. 13–14; R. Dore, *British Factory – Japanese Factory* (1973), p. 395; T. Nakase, 'The Introduction of Scientific Management in Japan and Its Characteristics – Case Studies of Companies in the Sumitomo Zaibatsu' in K. Nakagawa, *Labor and Management* (1979), pp. 183–4.
40. This discussion of scientific management in Japan is based on: K. Okuda, 'Managerial Evolution in Japan I: 1911–25' and 'Management Evolution in Japan II: 1926–45', *Management Japan* (1971) and (1972) respectively; S.B. Levine and H. Kawada, *Human Resources in Japanese Industrial Development* (1980); R.E. Cole (1979), pp. 108–11; Nakase (1979), and Hazama (1981).
41. Littler (1982) p. 157.
42. Hazama (1981).
43. M. Sumiya, 'The Emergence of Modern Japan' in K. Okochi, B. Karsh and S.B. Levine (eds.), *Workers and Employers in Japan: The Japanese Employment Relations System* (1973), pp. 46–7.
44. D. Brody, 'The Rise and Decline of Welfare Capitalism' in J. Braeman *et al.* (eds.), *Change and Continuity in Twentieth-Century America: The 1920s* (1968); S. Brandes, *American Welfare Capitalism, 1880–1940* (1976); R. Ozanne, *A Century of Labor–Management Relations at McCormick and International Harvester* (1967); also see D. Nelson, *Managers and Workers: Origins of the New Factory System in the United States, 1880–1920* (1975), pp. 101–21.
45. Brandes (1976), p. 138.
46. Quoted in Brandes (1976), pp. 142–3.
47. For the continued use of factory dormitories and dormitory supervisors see Satoshi Kamata's account of Toyota, translated as *Japan in the Passing Lane* (1983).
48. Piore (1980), p. 400.
49. Ibid. p. 401.
50. J. Hirschmeier and T. Yui, *The Development of Japanese Business* (1981 edn), p. 88; D.S. Landes, 'Japan and Europe: Contrasts in Industrialization' in W.W. Lockwood, *The State and Economic Enterprise in Japan* (1965), pp. 172–5.
51. Landes (1965), p. 173; W. Fischer, 'Labor–Management and Industrial Relations in Germany, 1870–1930' in Nakagawa (1979), p. 103.
52. Fischer (1979), pp. 103–5.
53. Levine and Kawada (1980), p. 263
54. Homburg in this volume, p. 149.
55. We still lack a good history of Westinghouse Electric. In its early years the company was not paternalistic and lacked a welfare programme, and it became a strong

advocate of Taylorism, time study and systematic job analysis. In the early 1920s, Westinghouse established generous employee welfare schemes and a company union as an alternative to craft unions, but this was combined with continued development and application of Taylorite techniques. In the 1930s, Westinghouse delayed recognition or formal bargaining with the United Electrical Workers for as long as possible (1939 in fact) despite the Wagner Act. See Nelson (1975), p. 118; H. Passer, 'The Development of Large-Scale Organization: Electrical Manufacturing around 1900', *Journal of Economic History* (1952); J. Backman, *The Economies of the Electrical Machinery Industry* (1962); R. Schatz, 'The End of Corporate Liberalism: Class Struggle in the Electrical Manufacturing Industry, 1933–50' in *Radical America* (1975).

56. A.L. Stinchcombe, *Theoretical Methods in Social History* (1978), distinguishes between two forms of 'ideal' types: (a) the principle of cumulative causation ideal type versus (b) the virtual choice ideal type. Type (a) consists of a set of factors characterizing a social structure, 'which are simultaneously transformed by a causal process of a cumulative or self-reinforcing sort', whilst type (b) are typological constructions that are psychologically and socially real alternatives to the people in the historical situation *and, therefore, have more historical specificity*. Paternalism is a type (b) concept and for a period in the United States (1890–1920s) it was viewed by managers and employers as an alternative strategy to Taylorism. The latter embodied neo-classical assumptions about labour, i.e. that employment relations are commodity relations and are not durable so that there is a complete substitutability of workers. See R. Ozanne's comments on these perceived alternatives, 'United States Labor–Management Relations, 1860–1930' in Nakagawa (1979), p. 90; also D. Nelson and S. Campbell, 'Taylorism Versus Welfare Work in American Industry: H.L. Gantt and the Bancrofts', *Business History Review* (1972).

57. See *Financial Times*, 11 March 1982; R.T. Pascale and A.G. Athos, *The Art of Japanese Management: Applications for American Executives* (1981); W.G. Ouchi, *Theory Z: How American Business Can Meet the Japanese Challenge* (1981).

58. Webbs (1898), p. 493.

59. Ibid. p. 495.

Index